AUTOBIOGRAPHY

of

MICHAEL GEORGE MARKULIS

A Professional Police Officer,
Educator, Family Man

Autobiography of Michael George Markulis
A Professional Police Officer Educator Family Man

© 2021, Michael George Markulis

DEDICATION

Dedicated to my family; wife Alicia, daughter Elaine and son Mark, his wife Eva and my grandsons Michael, Matthew and granddaughter Madeline who made this journey of life with me; for without them there would be no story. To my son Mark who was instrumental in the completion of my autobiography by encouraging me to continue with it when I had given up on it on several occasions. A special thanks to Veronica Ruelas-Diaz, my friend and next door neighbor for all help in finalizing this book as required by the publishing company.

Top row: Michael M., Madeline, Matthew/
Bottom row: Elaine, Michael G., Mark, Eva/
Below: Alicia

CONTENTS

INTRODUCTION

M y wonderful life has stories of my personal life and my professional life. My personal life of growing up as an adolescent in the states of Utah, Pennsylvania and California. These stories include my education, employment as a teenager, my army service during the Korean War. My professional life as a police Officer with the Los Angeles Police Department, my advanced education, graduating from two colleges.

My professional life also includes teaching in the Los Angeles Community College District for thirty years as a part-time instructor. My professional life includes being employed by the University of Southern California as the Director of a prestigious law enforcement program, "The Delinquency Control Institute," under the School of Public Administration.

This journey of mine includes my retirement years, the loss of my beautiful wife Alicia in 2009 and the void that her loss has left in me and will continue for the rest of my life. We had a special relationship.

Included are my retirement years. My continued relationship with other retired Los Angeles police officers. Some noteworthy journeys, cruises of parts of God's beautiful earth.

FOREWORD

My life story as recorded in this book will take you on a sentimental journey experiencing a lifetime of joy, happiness, heartaches, hardships, and sadness. But most of it is a story of my love of life that My Dear Lord allowed me to experience.

I have been blessed in this life of mine with a mother and father who lived their own lives with many hardships, raising five boys through very difficult times during the Great depression years in our history. They were immigrants from Greece migrating to the United States in 1929 looking for and working for the American dream. Their American dream was Love of Family. My mother and father did not find material riches, as they were never rich nor poor. But they would never exchange their Spiritual Love and Love of Family for all the material riches in the world.

But through all their hardships, they had a fulfilling life of love and happiness, leaving this Earth to be with our Dear Lord. This Markulis legacy will live on forever. The Markulis legacy was told in my first book *Terpsihori*, my mother's name. My mother and father left their mark on every member of the Markulis family and will continue through all the ancestral siblings for generations to come.

I have been blessed with my own family. My wife Alicia, without her this journey could not have happened. She stayed by my side throughout my journey of life, helping me to succeed in all that I did and worked for. She bore us two wonderful children, a daughter and a son. Both were very successful in their own right.

My daughter, Elaine, worked in the Superior Court clerking for many judges. In fact, she was responsible for helping and training new judges to become knowledgeable on court operations and procedures.

My son, Mark, Sales Manager for Puritan Bakery, worked and established himself as an invaluable employee for Puritan Bakery. He began working at Puritan when he was sixteen years old. His Uncle John, half owner of the Bakery, saw a potential valuable employee in Mark.

He started him out as a yardman and elevated him to running their large Sales Department. His knowledge of bakery operations and working and maintaining a personal and professional relationship with his employees and customers has made him valuable to Puritan Bakery's multimillion-dollar operation. His tenure with Puritan is over forty-five years. I am extremely proud of both Elaine and Mark.

Thanks for the Memories

– *Michael George Markulis*

CHAPTER 1:

THE BEGINNING

Adventure, Wonderful Life: Legacy for My Family. This is my story.

I was encouraged to write this Legacy by my son, Mark Michael Markulis, as he believed I had a story to tell.

The story begins when I was born on October 18, 1931, to Terpsihori and George Markulis. I was born in a coal-mining shantytown of Mutual, Utah. My father was a coal miner who came to the United States in 1912 to work the coal mines of Utah. Through a contractual marriage arrangement between his family, Marcoulakis and my mother's family, the Galanis family, my father being in the United States and my mother living in Greece, was arranged. The marriage was decided upon and set in concrete. My father went back to Greece in 1929 where he met his wife to-be for the first time. After a short courtship, they were married on June 29, 1929, on the island of Crete.

The Galanis family was well off with servants to do all the chores. My mother was pretty spoiled as she did little if any chores at all. She didn't even know how to cook. She believed that she was marrying a rich Greek coal miner from America.

After a short honeymoon, they left Greece for her new land, the United States. Upon arriving they traveled by bus and train to Sunnyside, Utah. My mother was totally disillusioned upon seeing the Rocky Mountains and barren land that was to be her new home. She gave up her beautiful home and family in Greece to live in, what she believed, to be a godforsaken land. She would no longer be able to see the beautiful Aegean Sea and talk to her family. My mother had two sisters and a brother whom she loved very much, and not to be able to talk to them anymore was unimaginable.

Coal mining was a dangerous occupation, as the miners would work from sun-up to dusk and run the risk of getting black-lung disease, as well as getting hurt or killed in a mine disaster of some sort.

My brother John was born on March 29, 1930 in Sunnyside. I was born in October 1931. I had three other brothers, Nick born in 1933, Chuck born in 1937, and James born in 1947. Nick was also born in Utah. Chuck was born in Pennsylvania and James was born in California.

We grew up as kids during the Depression years moving from one coal mining town to another. My brother John and I, being only a year and a half apart in age, were inseparable. I would tag along with John wherever he went. We were mischievous kids getting in to all kinds of trouble. We had the Rocky Mountains in our backyard and were constantly playing in the mountains or in the river that flowed through our town of Helper.

In our childhood years and living in these small towns where there was a strong Greek influence, our parents spoke to us in Greek. We communicated in Greek and slowly started picking up English as we got older. We were more fluent in the Greek language. Of course, in our later years and after the death of our parents where there was no need to converse in Greek, we began to forget our Greek. I can still speak Greek if I have to and the language does seem to come back. In 2012, I took my family to Greece for two weeks and talking to the Greeks there, my Greek started coming back to me.

There were many times that we almost drove our mother to a nervous breakdown. John being the oldest got the blunt of our scolding's and whippings as my mother and father blamed him for us getting into trouble. There are many stories which can be told about those early years. I am talking about being four, five, six years old and older. With the Rocky Mountains in our backyard, a river running through our town, we always had things to do. In Pennsylvania, there was a large pond full of quicksand that we would find ourselves going to, playing or fishing there.

As a result of the Depression, our family moved several times in Utah and then to Pennsylvania where we lived for several years. After learning that the coal mines there were having a difficult time, we moved back to Utah where my dad bought his own coal mine.

In 1943, my father had to have eye surgery, as he had glaucoma in his right eye and it had to be surgically removed. My father had to go to California for the eye surgery. He left with my brother John for California and stayed with a Greek family whom my parents had known for many years.

Several months after the eye surgery, my father sent for the rest of the family to join him in San Pedro, California. My father was not only an excellent coal miner but he was also an outstanding cook. He got a job being the night cook of a café owned by the Greek family that he stayed with during the surgery. At first, we had a hard time adjusting to the new life in California, especially my brothers and I as we had left all of our friends in Utah and now starting in new schools.

It didn't take long to get re-adjusted and make new friends. My father purchased his first home in the Barton Hill area, which was in the lower economic area of San Pedro. It was the first and only time I had ever experienced discrimination because of being Greek. I was called Greaser, among other slanderous names.

The Barton Hill community was pretty much a culturally mixed area, as was the town of San Pedro. There was a strong influence of Mexican, Black, Italian, and Slavic races. There were some Greek families, but unlike the Greek influence in the towns where we grew up as kids in Utah.

My brother John went to a different grammar school from the rest of us as he continued to use the address of the Greek family where he and my father stayed for the eye surgery. John attended Cabrillo Avenue Elementary School and the rest of us attended Barton Hill Elementary School, which was only a block from our home.

For the first time, John and I were not together and soon we had different friends. I was twelve years old and John was now thirteen. It was strange not having him around during the day and we seemed to now drift apart because of this separation. We all excelled in school. We were all very athletic and got involved in sporting activities in San Pedro.

The Barton Hill Elementary School had a large playground that stayed open until 9:00 p.m. on weekdays and Saturdays. The playground was heaven-sent for us as we had some place to go after school and take part in all the activities. As the Rocky Mountains of Utah was our playground, the Barton Hill school playground substituted for those mountains. We spent many hours on this playground.

The playground director organized the Barton Hill Athletic Club, also known as the Barton Hill Cougars. I along with brothers Nick and Chuck became members as did Jimmy later on. The Director formed leagues and we played each other and even played other athletic teams in San Pedro and surrounding cities.

Over the years, Barton Hill Cougars produced some great athletes, excelling in high school and college sports.

I played baseball, basketball, and football for the Barton Hill Cougars. My best sport was baseball. When I got to San Pedro High School, I made the Junior Varsity as a tenth grader and Varsity my junior and senior years. I also played two years of Varsity Football.

My brother John was an outstanding football player. He broke his back his first year. The doctor told him that he would never be able to play football again. He went out for the Varsity team his junior and senior years, making first string right guard. John made First String All League those two years.

Brothers Nick and Chuck played football in high school also. Both made All League with Chuck making All City first string. Nick and Chuck both got football scholarships. Nick to the University of Oregon and Chuck to the University of Washington. Chuck had to attend Everett Junior College in Everett Washington. He played football there making "All American" on the Junior College level.

While going to school, I had several jobs. The first was a paper route delivering the *San Pedro News Pilot*. The second job I had was at Bernard's Dress Shop in San Pedro as a stock boy. I was fourteen years old and earned ten dollars a week working an hour and a half after school and all day on Saturday. Brother John had the job at the dress shop before I did. He quit to take a job at Todd Naval Shipyard in San Pedro. The owner sold the dress shop and I was laid off. The bookkeeper at the shop told me that she was taking unemployment out of my check and told me to go the Unemployment Office. I did as she suggested and found out that I qualified for unemployment. I received fifteen dollars a week now, making five dollars more than when I was working.

After several months, I also began to work at DiCarlo's Bakery earning one dollar an hour. DiCarlo's bakery was a Union Shop so those of us going to school worked as Scabs. It was a good job for a fifteen-year-old. I would clean bread pans, dump flour into the flour bins, and sweep and clean up. When the Union representative would come into the bakery, we would go hide in the warehouse so we would not be seen. I worked ten, twenty, thirty hours a week while going to school. After school on weekdays and all day on Saturdays and Sundays. I was making pretty good money for being just fifteen. I believe this was around 1946. The war had just ended. The money that John and I made was given to our parents to help make ends meet. We also kept some spending money.

CHAPTER 2:

CLOSE FRIENDS AND SCHOOL YEARS

O ne of my close and good friends was Robert Sanchez who lived in the same block as I did but on the opposite street. I lived on Oliver Street and he lived on O'Farrell Street. An alley separated our homes. I could walk out through a rear gate of my home, cross the alley, and Robert's house was there. My other close friend was Robert Wynn. He lived across the street from Robert on O'Farrell Street. Our families became very close.

Robert had three sisters, Lucia, Julia, and Alicia. They were all older than Robert with Alicia being the youngest of the girls. He also had a younger brother, Armando.

Both the Roberts and I were in the same classroom at Barton Hill Elementary School. We were only a year apart in age. Robert Wynn had two older sisters and an older brother. The one sister Katherine was closest to our age, but a year older. We were all very good friends. I had other friends from school and the playground at Barton Hill.

I remember meeting Alicia for the first time after we moved in our new home on Oliver Street. There was a small market a block away and I was on my way there to buy a few items that my mother needed. I walked through the gate of my backyard, across the alley and along a small path that was adjacent to the Sanchez house. This was several days after we moved in to our home. Keep in mind I was twelve years old. I remember seeing this pretty young girl sitting on the front stairs of her home brushing her long beautiful black hair. It was in the morning and the sun was warm and bright and sunlight was reflecting off her hair. I looked over at her and saw how pretty she was. When she looked over at me, she smiled, and what a beautiful smile she had. I smiled back. I later learned that she was thirteen years old

Later on, when I met her brother Robert and we became best friends, I always found an excuse to go visit Robert at his home so I could see and talk to Alicia. Little did I know then, in 1943, that eleven years later in 1954, Alicia and I would be married.

As I am writing this and reminiscing about that time, I get blurry-eyed, as it is now 2021 and I lost that beautiful girl in 2009 after fifty-five years of marriage. I will get to that part of my story a little later, but I felt that I had to mention that fact of my life here.

When I started Barton Hill Elementary School, I was supposed to be put in the sixth grade. But due to a mix-up in my age, I was put back in the A-5. I lost a half semester of school. My brother John and I were in the same grade through our school years in Utah. However, because of his age he was accelerated a semester and was put in the A-6. Our parents did not look into our grade changes, as they were not familiar with how the system worked.

It was later on when I was in Junior High School that I was summoned to the school registrar's office and was asked if I wanted to be accelerated one semester because of my age, and was also getting good grades. I told the registrar, that I did not want to be accelerated because I had too many friends in my present class and that I wanted to stay in the same class. I was told I could. That was the reason I graduated from high school at the age of nineteen.

**My Sixth Grade Teacher: Mrs. Juliet Moore*

I enjoyed my school years. Elementary school was wonderful, as I had several good teachers. My sixth-grade teacher was Mrs. Juliet Moore. She was an excellent teacher who took an active interest in all her students. Even after leaving Barton Hill School, she remained in contact with her students, mentoring those who needed it. Even after I got married, Alicia and I remained good friends with her, visiting her and taking her on outings occasionally.

Jumping way ahead here, only because I am talking about my sixth-grade teacher, Mrs. Juliet Moore. When I was on the police department working Community Relations in the Harbor, I was contacted by a woman's group of which Mrs. Moore was a member. They had selected her as the "Woman of The Year" and were in the planning stages of the dinner where they were going to honor her. Since I was a former student of hers, I was asked to be one of the speakers and to be on the committee planning her dinner. I accepted and helped out with the program.

When I left Barton Hill Elementary School going to junior high school, Mrs. Moore wrote a letter to me talking about some of my shortcomings and to leave them at Barton Hill. To me it was a very powerful letter wishing me the very best in my future endeavors. As part of my speech at the dinner I talked about the letter and that I kept it all these years. I read the letter as part of my presentation. In fact, it was a very touching moment for all who were present. Just think about this, a student that Mrs. Moore taught some thirty years hence kept a letter that she had written him wishing him well and was read by him at her Woman of the Year Dinner. There were many tears shed at that moment, for everyone now knew that this very precious lady deserved the honor bestowed upon her that evening.

My Junior High School Years

I also enjoyed my junior high school years at Richard Henry Dana Junior High School. Now, my brother John was also at the same junior high school but a year ahead of me. This school was a little over a mile away from our home in Barton Hill and we walked to school every day. A bunch of us would usually meet in the morning and walk to school together. A little later, when we were able to afford a bicycle, we would ride our bikes to school.

On one morning, I was giving a ride to one of my friends by letting him sit on my handlebars, which we did occasionally. On this morning going down a steep street, I had to apply my brake and my friend fell off the bike headfirst. He was bruised up pretty bad, but nothing was broken. Needless to say, that was the last time I ever gave a ride to someone riding on my handlebars.

In junior high school, I was a good student. Almost got a gold seal on my diploma for a high- grade point average. What stopped the gold seal was a grade of "C" in my Latin class. I thought I was getting a "B" but it did not work out.

I held many school student body offices, which included being elected Student Body President. I was also awarded the "American Legion Award," the highest award that was given to a student at that time. My brother John had also received the award a year before I received it. All throughout my junior high school years, I worked after school, first selling the *Saturday Evening Post* magazine, and later delivering the *San Pedro News Pilot* newspaper.

I also remained active at the playground playing whatever sport was in season. The Barton Hill Cougars developed outstanding athletes. Our biggest rivalry was the San Pedro Boys Club that was located on the other side of the town. The Boys Club had a strong reputation of being the very best in sports. We all went to the same junior high school. We would always argue as to who had the better teams and players, especially when it came to Tackle Football. Those of us on both sides agreed to play a football game to see who would claim the title of being the best.

The San Pedro Boys Club had new uniforms and those of us from Barton Hill had old used uniforms that were donated to us by the Navy on Terminal Island. We had to paint our helmets so they would all be uniform in color. We painted them blue with a gold stripe down the center.

We selected a day that the game would be played after school at Daniels Field, which was the San Pedro Boys Club home field. All the students at our junior high school and many of the students from San Pedro High School were anxious to see this game that was to determine which team was the best. The Barton Hill Playground Director and coach could not make this game because of another commitment and could not get out of it.

My brother John who was an outstanding football player at San Pedro High School agreed to coach our team for that game.

The game was played with hundreds of students in the stands to watch this historic event. The Barton Hill Cougars, after a hard clean, game beat the San Pedro Boys Club by a score of 6-0. The feud was settled and the Barton Hill Cougars were written up in the local newspaper as being the best boys' football team in San Pedro.

The boys from the Boys Club wanted a rematch. The next year a game was scheduled and played with the Barton Hill Cougars winning again.

Many of the boys from both teams who went on to high school became top-notch football players. Many went on to college and performed well.

Members of the Barton Hill Cougars dominated the teams at San Pedro High School. The varsity baseball team at the high school had seven of the nine first stringers on the team.

This fact in itself brought a lot of good publicity and notoriety to the Barton Hill area that had a stigma attached to it because of being the lower economic area of San Pedro. It also had a stigma that all the troublemakers and tough kids came from that area. Many of the kids from Barton Hill excelled later in life, becoming professional businessmen and women, teachers, police officers, firefighters and CEOs of large companies. Many went off to the service during WWII and Korea where lives were lost.

My High School Years

After graduating from junior high school and going on to the next level of my education, I went on to San Pedro High School. I was also now working at DiCarlo's Bakery helping out my Mom and Dad with expenses. I had an Academic Major, as I wanted to go on to college after I graduated. I found myself studying and doing most of my homework in a Study-Hall class, as I was playing sports, be it baseball or football and working at DiCarlo's after school. I worked from 4:00 p.m. to 10:00 p.m. When I got home, I would try to do some of my homework and still try to get a good night's sleep. I was getting Bs and Cs instead of the As that I was getting in junior high school. It's funny thinking back at all the things we were doing and still able to have a normal life. As a kid growing up, we were very fortunate.

I was also popular in high school as I held many student body offices. I was elected as the Boys League President and President of the Knights, which was one the most prestigious honor groups in high school. I lettered three years in baseball and made the varsity football team two years. I ran for Student Body President but lost out to one of my classmates, a fellow Barton Hill Cougar.

While in high school, I never attended many of the after-school functions, due to working at the bakery. I went on very few dates. I still had a crush on Alicia and was able to see her now and then and took her to a movie once and a while. Alicia graduated from high school in the summer of 1948. I only got to see her for one semester when I went to high school. When Alicia was a senior, I was a freshman. I didn't realize then how much in love I was with her. But I was.

In the Barton Hill Area, there was one movie theater, the Barton Hill Theater. I with my brothers and friends would go to this theater once in a while. There were also four other theaters in San Pedro, the Warner Brothers, the Cabrillo, the Strand, and the Globe.

My brother John while in high school was not only an outstanding football player and excellent student but he also formed a group called the "Football Quartet." They would lip sync songs that recording artiste Spike Jones recorded. This was a wonderful entertaining group as they were more than funny, they were hilarious. They entered many talent contests and always took first place. They performed their act at the Warner Brothers and Cabrillo theaters in San Pedro. They were all football players in high school.

I mentioned that we were five brothers, John, Mike, Nick, Chuck, and Jimmy. We all played sports at San Pedro High School. We all lettered. John was a great football player. He broke his back playing Bee football. Doctors told him he would never be able to play football again. That was his first year in high school. The following year John went out for varsity football and made first string right guard. He made All Marine League. He did it again in his senior year and made All Marine again. He would have made All City, but it was rumored that he had more penalty yards against him than any other linemen in the city.

I played baseball three years in high school and also played varsity football two years. My brother Nick played football three years in high school making All Marine. Brother Chuck played football three years making All Marine and also All City. Chuck also made Junior College All American at Everett Junior College in Everett Washington. Brother Jimmy also played varsity football for three years at San Pedro High School.

San Pedro High School Athletic Hall of Fame

The reason I mention our high school athletic achievements here is that some sixty years later on November 19, 2016, the Markulis Brothers were inducted into the San Pedro High School Athletic Hall of Fame as "Siblings Inductees." That was an honor that made us all proud. My mother, father, John, and Chuck were smiling from Heaven on this occasion.

Brother John was also mechanically inclined and would work on cars of friends using our garage to do the work. I remember him buying an old 1930s vintage Buick. He rebuilt the engine and we would ride it to school. Some of the time we would have to push it to get it started. There were several times that we would push him almost to school before the car started. Good times.

John also bought an old Lincoln Zephyr. It had a twelve-cylinder motor in it. John pulled the motor out and put in an eight-cylinder Ford Motor. It was a cool-looking streamlined car. He was the envy of many kids, including me. I remember one time when I took it without his knowledge. Our Barton Hill Cougar Basketball team had a game in Wilmington and we had no way of getting there. So I took John's car without his consent, and I had no drivers' license. I was just learning to drive. I took our team to Wilmington and we played our game, then I took everyone home. I thought I drove very well up until the time I got to our house and drove the car up the driveway where it was originally parked.

I had a little trouble as the car jerked up the driveway. John was now home and he came out of the house yelling at me. He was mad and I thought he was going to hit me. But he didn't. I knew from then on not to touch his car without his permission.

I enjoyed my school years and I was sad that they did come to an end. They were memorable years. I graduated from high school in January of 1951. My graduation day was one that I will never forget. We never had any organized graduation party or dance. There were a few of us that knew of several parties being thrown by some of our classmates and we decided to go to one of them. The party we went to was at a girl's house located on 19th Street near Patton in San Pedro. It was a nice large home with a large basement.

I had just gotten to the party and a friend of mine bet me twenty dollars. I couldn't drink a water glass full of whiskey straight. I was not a drinker of alcohol of any sort. I never drank, period. But the twenty dollars sounded good and I thought I could do that easy. I took him up on that bet and drank that glass of whiskey right down. He then told me that he would double the twenty dollars if I drank another glass. I felt pretty good and thought that was an easy bet. I took him up on it and drank another glass of whiskey straight down. After a few minutes, it was like someone had hit me with a baseball bat. I found myself in the backyard of this house puking my guts out. One of my close friends who was there helped me as I was throwing up. I totally ruined my graduation evening. If I had not immediately begun to puke, I later learned, I could have died from acute alcohol poisoning. This was a night I will never forget. The kicker is that I never collected the money.

Probably as a result of that night, I could never stand, even to this day, the smell of whiskey. I remained a non-drinker and never had a desire to consume alcohol of any sort. Oh, on an occasion I might have a small glass of champagne at a wedding reception or on a special occasion, but that's it. I do not like beer, wine, or hard liquor of any kind.

My mom Tepsihori, with John and Mike

Alicia age 19

Members of Knights, flag raising

San Pedro High School Letterman

Football coach John Santchi and players. Mike No42

1950 San Pedro High School Baseball Team; 9 players Barton Hill
Cougars. Drawing by Walter Hendrickson team member.

HALL OF FAME SIBLING INDUCTEES

Markulis Brothers

The story of the five Markulis brothers who played sports for San Pedro High began in Crete, where an arranged marriage united their mother, Terpsihori, and George John Marcoulakis in 1929.

The last name went through a number of changes before it finally became Markulis and the family found itself in San Pedro. Their story is recounted in the book A Greek Woman, an American Immigrant by Michael George Markulis, a tribute to a mother who battled hard times while raising five boys, a father who taught his sons the meaning of hard work, and the town that was blessed to be called their home.

The Markulis brothers all attended Dana Junior High before going to San Pedro High.

John (S'49)—The only brother to attend Cabrillo Avenue Elementary (the others all went to Barton Hill). He played one year of Bee football at San Pedro before breaking his spine. Doctors told him he would never play football again, but he not only played varsity football as a junior, as a senior, the 5-8, 178-pound guard made first team All-Marine League. He was told that he might have made All-City except for the fact that he totaled more penalty yards than any other lineman in the city. Off the field, Markulis was president of the Lettermen's Club and a Knight. John died in 2014.

Mike (W'51)—He played two years of varsity baseball and two years of varsity football, which included the 1950 Eastern-Marine League title. He was student body president at Dana and, like John before him, received the American Legion Award upon graduation. At San Pedro, Mike was president of the Knights and Boys League president.

Nick (W'53)—He played varsity football for two years, earning second team All-Marine League honors as a 6-foot, 175-pound end his senior season. He received a scholarship to Oregon, where he lettered from 1954-56.

Chuck (S'56)—He played varsity football for two years, making first team All-Marine League in his senior season as a 5-8, 160-pound fullback and adding third team All-City honors. Heavily recruited, he chose Washington, which sent him to Everett Junior College to make up some grades. While there, he made JC All-American. Chuck died in 2008.

Jimmy (W'66)—Continuing the family tradition, Jimmy was a two-year letterman in varsity football. He also was Varsity Club president. Upon graduating, he went to work for DiCarlo's Bakery, where he figured out that he wanted to have a career as a businessman. He later worked for Puritan Bakery and also had some side businesses in San Pedro.

CHAPTER 3:

KOREAN WAR

The Korean War had started in June of 1950 and many of us knew that we would be going into the service. There were a few of us who talked about enlisting in the United States Air Force. One day three of us went down to the Main Post Office in San Pedro. We were told that all enlistments were frozen for the Air Force and the Navy, as there were too many enlistments in those branches of the service, and not enough for the Army. We were dead-set on the Air Force so we put our names on the waiting list. I was number 42 on the waiting list.

There were many seniors in our class that enlisted in the Marine Corp Reserve. Not long after they enlisted their unit was activated.

Alicia's brother Robert was one of them. He stayed in the Marine Corp Reserve and attained the rank of Master Sergeant. He retired from the Marine Corp Reserve. The family was very proud of Robert for his achievements in the Reserves.

Now if you remember I mentioned that I was nineteen when I graduated. Well, in February I got my notice from the Draft Board telling me that I had to appear at a location in Los Angeles to take my Physical for the Draft. I did and I was classified as 1A, fit for the draft.

I continued working at DiCarlo's Bakery making fairly good wages. Alicia and I were seeing each other quite often now and my love for her was out of sight. I was madly in love with her and she loved me also. We both knew that I was going to go into the Service, but did not know when.

My brother John, in the meantime, had gotten married. He was married at nineteen to Anita McGuiness who at that time was sixteen. John had gotten drafted into the Army and was sent to Camp Roberts in northern California for his basic training. John and Anita now had a baby girl, Lorraine.

My brother John was concerned that his wife was not getting her allotment checks. He petitioned the Army for a hardship discharge due to his marriage and baby. The Army granted his discharge.

Draft Notice and Basic Training

I was sitting at home one day and the telephone rang. I answered it and it was the Air Force Recruiting Sergeant. He told me that my number had come up and if I was still interested in the Air Force to come down to the Post Office. I told him that I would be right down. As I was walking out the front door, I met the mailman. He handed me this official looking letter. I opened it and it said, "From the President of the United States to Michael George Markulis, you are hereby given notice that you have been inducted into the United States Army." You are to report to your Local Draft Board to be transported to Fort Ord Army Base in California.

I took the letter and showed it to the Recruiting Sergeant and he told me that he could do nothing for me and that I was now Army.

My three friends, whom I originally went with down to the Air Force Recruiting Office, did not get draft notices. I guess that was because I was already nineteen and they were still eighteen years old. They did get to join the Air Force.

I had to report to the Draft Board in Long Beach along with everyone else that got drafted. They loaded us on a bus and took us to Fort Ord located near Monterey, California.

Once we arrived, we immediately knew that we were in the Army. Several solders in fatigue uniforms met us and started barking out orders at us. We were immediately put in squads and platoons. They let us know from the beginning that we were the lowest of the lowest human beings that walked this Earth. From that moment on, we were disciplined to a rigorous army life. We marched to our barracks and assigned our bunks.

We each were given a footlocker and bedding. We were lectured as to what was going to happen during the next three months while in basic training. We were told that after we finish our training we would be shipped out to Korea. We were also told that it depended on us individually on how seriously we took to our training if we wanted to survive the war. They got our attention, real quick.

After a thorough brainwashing session, they marched us to the mess hall to get dinner.

We returned to our barracks and were shown how to make up our bunks. The sheets and blankets had to be put on a certain way. The blankets were supposed to be so tight that when a coin was flipped on the bunk that the coin would have to bounce. After a little practice my bunk was perfect. That was a long day and we finally got to hit the sack, as our next day was going to start early in the morning.

It was hard falling asleep that first night, as everything was being played back in my mind as to what we had gone through and what was in store for me, for all of us, as we went through this training. Also, what was going to happen to all of us when we finished our training and sent overseas to Korea? I have to admit I was not scarred, but I was worried and apprehensive about what was going to happen to all of us.

The next morning, we were awakened at 5:00 a.m. We had to shower, shave, and fall out in formation. We were still in our civilian clothes as our fatigues and uniforms were going to be issued to us after breakfast. We were marched to the mess hall. I have to admit that I did not mind Army food. There was plenty to eat and it was nourishing. We were told that we had to eat everything that was put on our trays. We were also told that we would have to pull KP (kitchen police) duty, which was the term used when you were assigned to the mess hall to wash the trays, peel potatoes, and clean all the cooking equipment. We also learned that as a matter of discipline, if you screwed up you could be punished by pulling KP duty, among other types of discipline duty that they would find for you.

After breakfast the whole company had to fall out in formation and our Company Commander, a Captain, addressed all of us to tell us what to expect and that we would be held accountable for our actions and that we better take this training seriously, as our lives would depend on it.

No Combat Boots My Size in Stock

We were then marched to the quartermaster warehouse where we were issued our fatigues, uniforms, and boots. I was issued everything except my boots. They did not have a size 12D boot in stock. I was told that I would have to wait. When they came in, I would be notified to go pick them up. For several weeks I had only my civilian shoes to wear and that was when we had some rigorous training, which included a lot of running and forced marches.

After several weeks I was still without my combat boots. My civilian shoes were now beginning to fall apart. One day we had to stand inspection. I was standing at attention and the First Sergeant walked up to me and checked me up and down. He looked down at my civilian shoes and he started yelling at me and asking me what I was trying to prove wearing those shoes. I immediately responded I was never issued my combat boots because they ran out of my size. That I had checked with the quartermaster personnel and they told me they still had not received them. He asked me if I was doing all my training in those civilian shoes. I responded in the affirmative. He wanted me to report to his office after the inspection.

After inspection, I reported to him and he immediately took me to the quartermaster warehouse. He immediately started jumping on the personnel there and told them they better find me a pair of boots, like now! It didn't take them long to came back with a pair of 12D boots. I thanked the Sergeant and we returned to our barracks. I started shining those boots and there wasn't another pair that shinned like mine. Was I proud to have those boots! The guys in my platoon got a real big kick out of that incident and never let me live it down. There were several soldiers in my platoon from San Pedro. One was Jesse Martinez and the other was Jesse Soto. They would tell my boots story over and over and laugh about it.

We were issued our M1 rifles and taught how to break the weapon down, clean it, and then put it back together again. You were also timed on how fast you could do this process. Your rifle had to be clean, as it was inspected by the cadre each and every day. When in platoon formation, the First Sergeant called for an inspection, he personally walked by each squad and inspected each rifle. If it was not clean you would suffer some sort of disciplinary punishment. We were taught that you treat your rifle as if were a family member. Your life would depend on the operation of your rifle. We learned well.

Basic Training was three months long. It was very rigorous physical training. We double-timed everywhere we went, forced marches, physical exercises until we were exhausted. We shot our rifles on the firing range until we all became proficient with the M1 rifle. We also fired bazookas, 50-caliber machine guns and taught on how to throw hand grenades. We also became pretty proficient with the 45-caliber pistol, which was the side arm that we would have to carry. Our Company was ready for combat as the Army made sure they trained us well. During our training we were asked what we would like to do in the Army. They gave us three choices. They were trying to convince me in going to Cooks School because I worked in a bakery. I told them absolutely not! My three choices were 1. Airborne, 2 Airborne, 3. Airborne. I really wanted to go to Paratroopers Training. I soon found out that those in our Company that enlisted for the Airborne were the ones that would be sent to Fort Benning, Georgia, for training. The rest of us would be sent overseas as infantry soldiers.

Greek Orthodox Easter

One side note of interest is that I was the only Greek in the Company. Our Company Commander summoned me to his office. The Captain asked me if I was Greek Orthodox. I told him that I was. He asked me if I would like to go on leave for the Greek Easter Holiday. Of course, I told him yes. I would get to go home during that weekend and see my family and, of course, Alicia.

Our whole Company was restricted to the base with no leaves until we hit a certain week of our training, which meant that I was the only one getting a pass. After leaving his office, I immediately went down to the main drag of Fort Ord to go to the Greyhound bus station to find out what time the busses were leaving. I did a stupid thing. I went down to the main drag in my fatigues. You did not want to get caught there, after 5:00 p.m. when retreat was played in your fatigues. Well, I did, and an MP (Military Police) unit immediately pulled up and took me into custody. They transported me to the MP station and wrote me up. A report would be sent to my Captain and I would be given the proper disciplinary action as he sought fit.

When I returned to my Company, I requested to see the Captain. I told him about the incident and if my pass was cancelled. He told me not to worry about it and that I could still go on leave. Well, I did and got to go home for that weekend. It was nice seeing my mom and dad and brothers. I think the best part of the leave was getting to see Alicia. I didn't realize how much I missed her until I saw her on that leave.

Now the rest of this story…

Several weeks later we had gone on a forced march. When we returned to our Company, we were all in formation and at that   time we had gotten a new Commanding Officer, as our previous Captain had been transferred. We were all standing at attention when our new Commanding Officer addressed us. This was the first weekend that our Company would get to go on a weekend leave. Our new captain, called out, "Private Markulis front and center." I doubled time up to where the captain was and snapped to attention and responded "Private Markulis, Sir." He hesitated for a minute, staring at me and then in a loud voice yelled out, "This was the weekend that you were all going to go out on pass, but because this man who got picked up by the MPs on date, etc., you are all restricted to the base." He was restricting the whole Company because of my incident. He then dismissed the Company.

We all went to our barracks. I really felt like hell because everyone was looking forward to this weekend to go home. I don't have to tell you how mad all these guys were. In fact, a bunch of guys came down to my barracks, came in, and wanted to see Markulis. I stepped forward and said I was Markulis. They told me that they were going to "kick the shit out of me." I told them just a second and I walked over to my bunk and got my bayonet. With the bayonet in the scabbard, I walked back to where they were standing and I told them that I may be going to the hospital, but some of them were going with me. At this time, my friend Jesse Martinez stepped forward and said in order to get to Markulis that they would have to go through our whole platoon as they all stepped forward. Thank God for Jesse and my friends because we had a standoff with nothing happening and they left our barracks.

I felt terrible for some time because of that incident. The next day I had to report to the CO and I tried to explain the incident about getting caught in the main drag of Fort Ord in my fatigues after 5:00 p.m. He couldn't care less about what I had to say and he restricted me to the Company for several weeks and during my off time, I had to pull KP and had to do other work around the Company as punishment.

Periodically, we had to pull guard duty in our class A uniforms. My turn had come up to pull the duty. There were about twelve of us and we had to report to the sergeant for our assignments. Before he assigned us, he wanted to inspect us. We all stood at attention and he inspected each one of us. He checked us from head to foot and also inspected our rifles. After the inspection and before being assigned, he would select the sharpest soldier and would relieve him from pulling guard duty. I got picked and got to return to my barracks. When I returned, my platoon sergeant questioned me as to why I was not on guard duty. I told him about getting selected as the sharpest in the squad. His immediate response was, "great," change into your fatigues, and join us in a GI party, which meant scrubbing the floors in the barracks.

I could go on and on about my basic training. I did get to go home a couple more times on pass and visit with the folks and Alicia.

Our basic training did come to an end and our Company was ordered to report to Pittsburg, California, which was near San Francisco, where we would get shipped out to Korea.

We all got a week's furlough before having to report to Pittsburg, California.

That was a whole week at home to see my family, Alicia, and friends. It went by very fast. I did get to see Alicia almost every day of that week. She was working at JJ Newberry's Five and Ten Cent Store on Pacific Ave. and 9th street in San Pedro. I would go over her house after she got home and visit.

I also would go down to my father's café in the evening and wash dishes for him. It was tough thinking about going overseas and not seeing my family for a while. Most of my close friends were in the military, Army, Navy, Marines, or the Air Force.

CHAPTER 4:

SHIPPING OUT TO KOREA

There were five of us that were going to meet at the Union Train Station in Los Angeles. Three of us were from San Pedro and the other two from the Gardena area. Jesse Soto, Jesse Martinez, and myself were from San Pedro, and Bob Masakawa and Tommy Minosoto were from Gardena. Tommy bought our tickets for us and we met at the train station. Alicia and both Jesses' girlfriends rode up with us. It was really tough saying goodbye to Alicia. I knew that I was madly in love with her and she with me. We promised to write to each other. She told me to be safe and that she would pray for all of us.

Tommy got the tickets for us up to Monterey, California. He thought he would save us a few dollars by using the bus tickets the Army gave us from Monterey to Pittsburg. That turned out to be a total disaster. We all got off in Monterey, but our checked-in duffle bags did not. We were told that they would be in on the next train the following day. What that meant was, that if we waited twenty-four hours for the next train that we would be AWOL (Absent Without Leave). I called the Debarkation Section where we were supposed to check in before midnight. I explained to the Sergeant what our problem was. I gave him our names and asked if we should report without our duffle bags. He told me no, that we were going to need them and for us to wait for them.

We slept that night in the train station while we waited for the train with our bags. The train arrived and our duffle bags were taken off. Now, our problem was getting on a Greyhound bus going to Pittsburg. The next big problem we ran into was the day was Saturday and there were many soldiers from Fort Ord and Camp Roberts going home on leave for the weekend and it was tough getting seats on a bus. We had to split up and take what seats were available to get to our destination.

We finally got there but we were twenty-four hours AWOL. They knew what our predicament was so they let us slide without any kind of punishment.

During that twenty-four-hour period, our entire Company from Fort Ord had already been put on board a troop ship and shipped out to Korea. That was a bummer for us. Our whole Company already shipped out and we were left behind. We were told it would be a week before we got shipped out. I called home and talked to my mother and told her about our situation. Of course, I also called Alicia and told her. She told me that maybe that was a good thing.

About the third day we were there I was summoned to the Commanding Officer's office. When I got to his office, I was told to go in. I walked in his office saluted and there before my eyes were my mother and brother Jimmy. The CO asked me if I knew the woman in his office. I responded, "Yes, sir, she is my mother and the little boy was my kid brother." I think Jimmy was four years old. The CO told me that she was there trying to talk him out of sending me to Korea. The CO and I kept telling my mother that it was not up to him. He was very kind to her as we walked out of his office. She and Jimmy went back to San Pedro. I will never forget that moment, as it showed how much my mother loved me and did not want me to go to war in Korea.

Now this is where this story gets a little hairy and maybe in a good way, for me and my four buddies. Our whole Company got to Korea and sent up on the frontlines. Later, we heard that most of our Company from Fort Ord was killed or wounded. I guess the five of us lucked out except for Jesse Martinez. He was sent to the 25th Division and was wounded.

8049 Army Unit 8th Army Pusan Korea

I was the first to get my orders and I was assigned to the 8th Army, 8049 Army Unit in Pusan, Korea. I gave my new location address to the other four and told them to make sure they drop me a line and let me know where they got assigned. It just happened that Jesse Soto was sent to medics' school, and Bob Masakawa and Tommy Minosoto were sent to interpreters' school since they were both fluent in the Japanese language. Jesse Martinez was assigned to the 25th Division on the frontlines.

The next day I found myself with many other soldiers on a train going south to Japan to one of the ports. From there I was to board another ship to Korea. I finally arrived to the 8049th Army Unit in Pusan and learned it was a Supply (quartermaster division). I was disappointed because I was trained as an infantry soldier and wanted to get assigned to one of the combat divisions on the front lines. The war was still going on very strong.

I did get to meet some great guys who were assigned there and we became good friends. I remained in contact with them after the war. Some of the soldiers assigned there had been on the frontlines, wounded, and then reassigned to our unit.

One soldier who I got to know fairly well had been wounded twice and each time sent back up to his combat division. After the second time he was wounded, they reassigned him to our unit permanently. This poor guy and another soldier were killed right before my eyes several months later.

It was raining and I was looking out of a window on the second floor of this warehouse where I had been assigned. I was looking down and we had several hundred North Korean prisoners of war (POWs) lifting a huge conveyer to put it in position where a huge crane would pick it up and place it in position. The POWs set the conveyer down and ordered to move away from it. Then two of our soldiers each took one end of the conveyer and the crane operator set the crane down to pick it up. As he did, the two soldiers each grabbed an end to guide the conveyer where it was going to be placed.

They were standing in water and mud. The crane operator hooked on to the conveyer, with the two soldiers to guide it, and he lifted it up. And as he was maneuvering it into place, the top of the crane hit a high-power electric line and as I was watching, huge electric sparks caused me to jump back in the warehouse. I did see the two soldiers get knocked down, both electrocuted. The two soldiers were not moving.

I ran down to where they were and pulled them out from under the conveyer. The first one was dead. The second one that I had gotten to know pretty well appeared to be alive. I immediately started performing CPR on him until the ambulance arrived. I rode in the ambulance with him to the 21st Evacuation Hospital, giving him CPR all the way.

When we got there, the medics took over. I was told that he died before he got to the hospital. This is the soldier who had been wounded twice on the frontlines but ended up getting killed moving a conveyer behind the frontlines. Our whole Company grieved the deaths of these two soldiers. One was from Compton, California, and I do not remember where the other one was from.

Interesting to note that since the crane was on big rubber tires the crane operator did not even get singed.

I seemed to have gotten carried away and lost my train of thought, so back to arriving to the 8049th Army Unit. We received our duffle bags and were assigned to our quarters. They were large tents, with wood floors. The latrines were separated from the live-in tents. Each tent had several stoves for heating the tents in the winter time. We got to meet with the Commanding Officer of the division and given our assignments. We were responsible for the security of all the supplies. Many of the supplies were expensive items, which were sent to different post exchanges (PXs) throughout South Korea. Our job was primarily security for all the supplies under our control. Korean civilians did the actual labor work.

It was here that I purchased my first good camera. It was an Argus C-3. A beautiful camera with which I took hundreds of pictures. Most of them on color slides.

I became very good friends with many of the soldiers assigned to the Unit. Three especially. They were Russ Morrison from Santa Barbara, Frank Mena from East Los Angeles, and Angelo (Fernie) Nunez also from

Los Angeles. We were assigned to the same tent quarters along with about twenty other soldiers. Around six months later, the engineers built quantum huts to replace the tents.

In Korea the winters were pretty cold. I thought of our combat troops on the frontlines and what they had to endure during those winter months. Up on the frontlines the temperatures could get to 30 degrees to below zero. Before I arrived in Korea, the 1st Marine Division suffered severe casualties when the Chinese entered the war and thousands of the Chinese soldiers over ran the marines at the Chosen Reservoir. Thousands of our troops were killed and several thousand others wounded.

Jesse Martinez Wounded and Transfer Request

I had been to the unit about two weeks when I got a letter from Jesse Martinez that said, "I hope you did better than I did. I was assigned to the 25th combat division and my first day there we were to assault this hill. I got shot through the arm and am now at the 21 Evac. Hospital in Pusan." He was the first one that I heard from.

I went to see our Commanding Officer to get his permission to check out a jeep so that I could go see Jesse. He gave his permission and as I was leaving our Company, the First Sergeant stopped me and asked me where I was going. I told him to the 21st Evac. Hospital to see my friend. He asked me to take his buddy back to the 23rd Evac. Hospital that was on the other end of Pusan. I did and then went to see Jesse.

We had a great visit. I learned that his wound was a flesh wound with no bones broken. He told me that as soon as he heals, that he will be going back up to his division on the frontlines. He advised me to stay where I am and not even try to get sent up to the frontlines. Jesse told me where Jesse Soto, Tommy, and Bob were assigned.

It was about a month later and I knew Jesse was going to be sent back up on the frontlines. I wanted to see him before he left. I went back to the CO to get his permission to check out a jeep. He refused my request saying that the last time he granted me a jeep, he saw me "tomcatting around" in it.

I asked him to explain what he meant and he said that about an hour after he granted me the jeep, he saw me drive by the Company. I explained that I was asked by the First Sgt. to take his friend back to the 23rd Evac. Hospital, which was on the other side of Pusan.

He refused my request. I then told him I wanted a transfer out of this Company. His comment was, you transfer out and you know it will be up on the frontlines. I told him that is where I wanted to go in the first place and that I was trained as an infantry soldier. He told me my transfer had been granted and to go see the First Sergeant.

When I went to see the First Sgt., and explained to him what happened he felt bad that he put me in this situation. He said that he would put my transfer through.

Several months had gone by and I never heard anything about the transfer. I went to see the First Sgt. and he told me that he did not know why my transfer had not gone through and that he would check up on it.

I was now in Korea for thirteen months and I had been promoted to PFC and then to Corporal. The First Sergeant called me to his office and told me that my transfer request is going through. I asked him if he could pull it and he said that he would. If the transfer had gone through after a few months there I would have gladly taken it. But, after being in my Company for thirteen months with only five more months to go before I got sent home, I told the First Sgt. that my luck I would get up to the frontlines and I would get killed or wounded. I only had a few months to go before being sent home. He agreed. If I would have been sent up when I first requested the transfer, I would have been home by now. Frontline troops only had to spend nine months on the line.

Even though we were not on the frontlines, we always had to be alert for anything that could happen. For example, on one occasion I was assigned to ride shotgun on one of our boxcars for security reasons, as we were sending supplies up to the frontlines. I had been on that train for about a half an hour when this jeep pulls up and orders me to get off as I was to go back to our unit. Another soldier took my place. I later learned that the train had been sabotaged with explosives as it was traveling to the north. Never heard or knew what happened to the soldier that took my place.

On one other occasion, a Korean civilian was standing on top of one of the boxcars directing the engineer into our depot so it could be loaded with supplies. He was not paying attention to his surrounding and he got caught around his neck area with a high voltage wire and was electrocuted on top of the boxcar.

A couple more incidents and then I will move on. I remember this one time when I was on security patrol and I observed this Korean worker at the top of the conveyer belt stealing some items. I jumped up on the conveyer belt and rode it up to where this activity was taking place. As I went to step off the belt on to the deck, my boot got stuck between the belt and the roller as it was passing through. Immediately, I felt extreme pain and yelled out, "Stop the conveyer belt!" The conveyer was stopped and I pulled my boot out. I took off my boot and saw that my toes were bloody. I was lucky that none of my toes were broken. I just laid around the barrack for a few days then went back on duty. That was the only wound I received while on duty in Korea and it did not even warrant a Purple Heart. Just kidding. SMILE.

Arrest of Korean Burglar

On one other occasion, I was patrolling in a jeep around the perimeter of our compound when I saw this Korean civilian breaking into a warehouse next to our compound. The warehouse belongs to the Korean Army. I took this person into custody and took him to our security section. After explaining what had taken place, the sergeant called the Korean Military Police. Two MPs showed up and we explained the situation to them. They took this man into custody, but, before they left, in front of us, they had the man get on his knees and place his hands on the floor with fingers spread out. With the butt of a rifle the one MP smashed this man's hands and then took him away. We were told that this was the way they handled thieves who would steal from their army facilities.

Opening up New Depots, Seoul and Inchon

During my eighteen months in South Korea, we opened up several other depots. We opened up one in Seoul and another in Inchon. While we were in Inchon, we could see the flashes at night of the artillery fire on the frontlines. We could see the fighter jets flying to the north on their missions and then returning again.

One day when we had a day off, we (Russ Morrison, Fernie Nunez, Frankie Mena and myself) got the bright idea that since we were so close to the frontlines, we might as well take a ride and see what was going on. All we had was our 45s in our holsters and in a Jeep truck we took off for the frontlines. When we got to a certain point, there was an outpost with our troops in it. They stopped us and we had to identify ourselves and explain why we were there. They politely told us to get "your asses out of here" and head back to where we were stationed.

Probably a good thing. I guess, someone was watching over us—at least me anyway. We did get to see the devastation of the war with buildings and bridges destroyed; much of the destruction of the war up to that time was very visible. Destroyed tanks were left sitting exactly where they felt their demise. War is ugly for both sides involved in the conflict. I vividly remember the homeless and orphaned children as a result of the war. I took pictures and kept one picture of a little orphaned child about three years old, dirty and asleep leaning against a shack, where I could see it every day, to remind me of what those poor South Koreans went through.

United Nations Cemetery, Tanggot, Korea

One thing about the Korean War, it was truly a United Nations War with many countries involved in the conflict. The United States had the most troops committed to the war. Many countries suffered casualties. The United Nations Military Cemetery located in Tanggok, Korea, reflected those losses with the many gravesites for each country. These words are inscribed there: "Here lie the heroic dead of many nations who gave their lives in the cause of freedom and world peace." Internments were begun on January 18, 1951. This cemetery of seventy-three acres was officially dedicated to the United Nations on April 6, 1951.

Twenty-one nations are represented there.

Each grave is appropriately marked according to religious preference and the name of the deceased. Complete and accurate files are maintained of all internments and disinterment's.

The war lasted from 1950 to 1953. The United States committed 5,720,000 troops. During that time, we had 54,246 servicemen die in action. We had 103,384 wounded, 8,177 MIAs (missing in action), and 7,140 taken as POWs (prisoners of war). Total casualties were 172,847. This war was known as a "Police Action" and the "Forgotten War." But, to the Korean Veterans, they knew different and felt their commitment was to secure freedom for the Korean people and for the continued freedom for the citizens of the United States and all the other countries which had troops committed to it.

Meeting Greek Soldiers from Greece

I had to make a run to downtown Pusan to pick up confidential information for our Company. On the way I saw four soldiers wearing Greek shoulder patches. I stopped the jeep and asked them if I could give them a ride. They got in the jeep and I started talking to them in Greek. They were amazed and thrilled that here is this American soldier talking to them in Greek. I explained to them that I was a Greek American and that my parents were both born and raised in Greece.

We got to know each other pretty well, even though today as I am writing this, I cannot remember their names. They served a year on the frontlines and they were now being rotated back to Greece. As we were talking, I mentioned to them that my mother Terpsihori Markulis was in Greece visiting her family. I told them that she was in Piraeus, the seaport of Athens. They told me that was the port where they were going. They wanted my mother's family name and when they got back, they would try to see if they could locate her. I gave them what information I had on the Galanis family.

It was about a month or so later that I received a letter from Alicia, telling me that those Greek soldiers found my mother and brother Jimmy in Piraeus and they told her that I was all right and not in harm's way. The more I think about this, the harder it is for me to understand how something like this could happen. Unbelievable! I guess I do have a story to tell with things like this happening in my life.

Alicia and I wrote to each other almost every day. The letters I received from her kept my spirits up and I looked forward to every one of her letters. In my letters to her, I would place a stick of gum with little love notes written on them. She saved all those letters and gum. After I got home, I asked her about the letters and she told me that she burned them after I got home. Gum and all. She told me those were her letters and only for her eyes to see and when I got home and she knew that I was no longer in harm's way, she burned them. I saved all of her letters and after that brief discussion about burning the letters, I did the same thing. After all they were only for my eyes to see and read.

In one letter I received in July 1952, Alicia broke the news to me that her father had passed away. I felt bad for her and all the Sanchez family, as I knew how much they all loved him. I had made a desk name plate for him to put on his desk and I was going to mail it to him. The name plate was black with Mother of Pearl sea shells that spelt out his name, Amado Sanchez. After I got home and a few years later, I gave it to my nephew, Nick Sanchez, as he was the only male left on the Sanchez side of the family.

South Korea was a beautiful country, even with all the devastation brought upon it because of the war. On occasion, the four of us, Russ, Fernie, Frank, and I, would go sight-seeing by driving through some of the areas around Pusan. One area was Taegu, where there was an abundance of rice paddy fields; the colors of the rice paddy planted in the valleys and mountainsides were beautiful. The colors of the green rice paddy with the surrounding trees and brush were beautiful, especially with the clear blue skies and scattered white clouds. If I could paint, this area would be the perfect place to spend many days taking in all this beautiful scenery. The war had not left its mark on this land or to the people who lived here. We took many pictures of this area.

Saber Tooth Deer

On one occasion, a couple of us went in the mountains near Taegu. Two of the guys took shotguns in hopes of getting some pheasant. I took my camera and went with them. They did pretty well and did get a few pheasants. One of the guys talked me into taking the shotgun and to try my luck. I did and as we were walking up this hillside, I saw a deer take off about twenty-five yards from where I was standing. I fired several rounds at the deer. I thought I had missed it. But as we were walking further up the hill, we found it in the brush. We studied the deer and found it to have two saber teeth. One was broken from the shot to the head but the other was intact.

We later found out that saber tooth deer were common in Korea. They did not grow as large as other reindeer. The Koreans we talked to told us that the meat was very tasty and good eating. We found a Korean boy who carried the deer down on an "A" frame to our jeep. When we got back to our Company, I took some pictures of it and with a pair of pliers I borrowed from the motor pool, I pulled out the saber tooth that was not broken.

I gave the deer to the Korean boy who carried it down for us and he took it home to his family.

Now for the end of this story, when I got home from the war and after Alicia and I were married, I had given this saber tooth to her and told her the story. For some reason, she thought I had said a saber tooth tiger. She took the tooth to a jeweler and had it made into a pendant that I could wear around my neck. She even told the story to some of her friends that I shot a saber tooth tiger in Korea. I made sure she understood that it was not a tiger but a deer. She meant well, but now did not appreciate the story as much as when she had believed it to be a tiger. Many years later after she had passed, I gave the pendant to my son, Mark, who still has it in his possession.

My eighteen months in Korea came to a close and I was getting ready to rotate home. The war was still going on, but Eisenhower had now been elected president. He made a special trip to Korea to negotiate a United Nations truce between the North and South Koreans. It looked like the war would soon come to an end.

My eighteen months went by pretty fast. I never did get to the front-lines, something that I regretted, as I wanted to see combat. It was just not to be. Even though I did not get to the frontlines, the assignments I had helped in the war effort. Some of the duties I held at the 8049 Amy Unit were security of our supplies, responsible for all courier and mail that came to our Company, and as a Corporal I was assigned the responsibility to operate the NCO (Non-Commission Officers' Mess) for our Company. I lost many of my friends from basic training on the frontlines. I also made many friends at our Company.

I wondered if my mother talking to the Commanding Officer at the debarkation center before I got shipped out had anything to do with my being stationed behind the frontlines. I get a strong feeling that her showing up in Pittsburg, California, from San Pedro did influence the Commanding Officer to pull some strings keeping me behind the frontlines. I will never know, but her prayers worked for her.

I did stay physically fit while I was there. I worked out with makeshift weights and participated in the sporting activities we had at the base. I was amazed how I looked physically as I was now 198 pounds. When I went in the Army, I was about 164 pounds. Gained a lot of muscle mass and my speed and coordination picked up considerably compared to when I was in high school playing baseball and football. I could run and throw a jump pass almost fifty yards to completion. I excelled in volleyball matches that we had on base.

One day, one of our soldiers came up to me, after one of our flag football games and asked me if I planned on going to college after I got discharged. I told him that I was planning on it, and that I wanted to go into police or probation work. He told me that if I wanted to go to California University at Berkley, where they had excellent law enforcement classes, he may be able to help get me in. I thanked him for the offer. He thought I had great potential as a football player. That was really nice to hear after my two years of high school varsity football sitting mostly on the bench.

Court Martial of Commanding Officer

The Lieutenant Colonel that refused me the jeep to go see Jesse Martinez got into a little trouble while he was there. I just have to tell this story.

This Lt. Col. was involved in selling merchandise on the black market in Pusan. When I first got there to the Company, there was this beautiful 1950 brand new red Ford sedan parked in our compound. Everyone said that it belonged to the Lt. Col. Well and he sold it on the black market along with hundreds of dollars of merchandise he had ordered from major department stores in the States.

We all knew something was wrong because he had been relieved of his command and placed under house arrest pending his hearings. This was during the time that I would go to the Main Army Headquarters where I would pick up all the security correspondence.

On this one occasion, I picked up this package that was marked "Confidential Court Martial Information." My curiosity got the best of me and I peeked, "OLAH," it was the Court Martial of the Lieutenant Colonel. I laughed but at the same time I felt sorry for this dumb jerk. His court martial read, "Dishonorable Discharge from the U.S. Army. Loss of pay and benefits." I think he lost everything.

Black marketing was a big thing in Korea. Whether it was the American dollar or merchandise. When I carried my Argus C-3 camera, I would have Koreans running up to me wanting to buy it from me. We had to be careful with the items we carried.

My eighteen months in Korea were all behind the frontlines; I spent my time working my assigned duties. We, who were stationed in this army facility, could not complain about our duty and service. We had nice barracks, warm cooked meals every day, and we even had a houseboy who cleaned our facilities and saw that our uniforms (fatigues and underclothes) were washed and ironed. There were so many of us that they would take the laundry home and their mothers or other family members would wash them. The houseboys would even shine our boots. Of course, our houseboys received good salaries for doing these chores. Our houseboy's name was Kim. Well, almost every boy in Korea was named Kim. I always wondered what had become of him and the all the other houseboys. Probably millionaires and owners of mega electronic companies or Korean automotive companies like Kia. They all had an excellent work ethic.

When we were there for nine months, the army sent us to Japan for what they called R&R (rest and recuperation). The Army would fly us to one of the locations where there were Army facilities. We did not have to do anything but relax. I was sent to Osaka, Japan. A beautiful city. Took many pictures with my Argus C 3 camera. I also saved some money for this trip and got to buy a few souvenirs. I bought Alicia a few things. I bought her some oriental silk pajamas. I also bought her a beautiful jade and pearl ring. She loved the ring and wore it for many years.

If you were in Korea for eighteen for months, you actually got two R&Rs. The second one I got to pick, and I picked Tokyo. I was looking forward to that trip. The Army was paying me a little over ten dollars a month as a salary. I forgot what the actual salary was, but Army pay was not very much. When I got promoted to PFC and then to Corporal that meant a few more dollars for me.

My turn had come up for my R&R. I was somewhat excited because I would get to see Tokyo. However, I received a letter from my brother Nick asking me if I had any extra money saved, that he needed some help. He said that he got a scholarship from the University of Oregon and he needed some money to get started there. I was sending an allotment check for fifty dollars every month to my mother to help her with the household expenses. I was also taking out a fifty-dollar savings bond each month for me when I got back home. That was the reason I was not getting much cash for my expenses in Korea. But I did not need much money because everything was provided for me. What money I did get, I was able to save to buy my camera and for the R&R trips. Well, I felt guilty about going to Japan when my brother Nick needed some help. I went and bought him a Parker pen and pencil set from the post exchange. I sent it to him along with the money I had saved for R&R as a high school graduation present.

The saving bonds I sent home each month paid for my and Alicia's wedding and helped with our honeymoon trip to Mexico City. I will talk about this later.

US Army March 1951

1951 Fort ORD Basic Training

Class A Uniform Fort ORD

Korea Bound from Fort ORD

Frank Mena, Russ Morrison 8049 Army Unit Pusan Korea

50 years later Army buddies; Mike Markulis, Fernando
Nunez, Frank Mena, Russell Morrison

8049 Army Unit Pusan Korea

Mike Markulis and Jesse Martinez

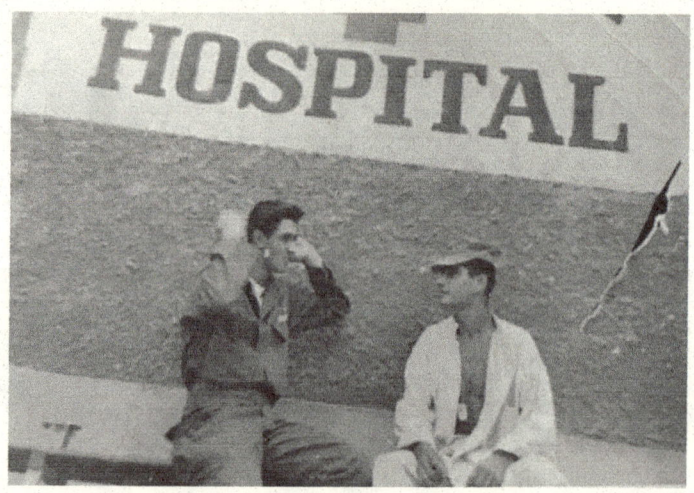

Jesse Martinez in 21 Evac Hospital Pusan Korea

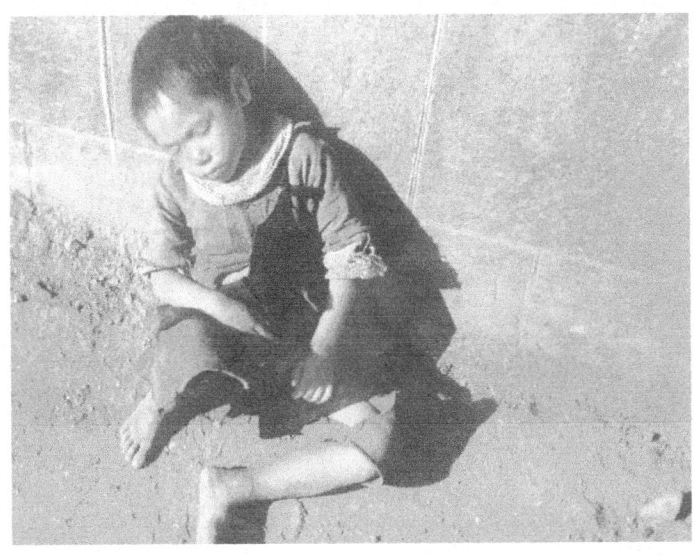

3 year old war orphan, taken to orphanage

Orphanage Pusan Korea, Mike Markulis

Greek Soldiers rotating back to Greece after 1 year at the front lines.

Collage South Korea

CHAPTER 5:

RETURNING TO THE STATES

Around the end of January 1953, I received my orders to go back to the States to get discharged. I was excited, as this meant another journey to take, now in civilian life. The time had come for me to leave.

I was happy and at the same time somewhat sad, as I spent eighteen months in Korea, made a lot of friends, and saw the tragedies of what war does to a people and their country. The casualties of this war were tremendous, both for our troops as well as the troops of all the countries involved in this conflict. My thoughts also brought the reality of what our country, United States of America, would look like if war actually struck directly on our soil. God forbid, for we have to do everything in our power to prevent this from ever happening to our country.

I finally received my orders on February 19, 1953, that I was returning to the States via Sasebo, Japan. Thanks to my wife Alicia, saving all those documents for me, I found them. When I read the orders, I noticed that Fernando Nunez was on the same orders also returning to the States. For some reason I thought that he had left a couple of months before me. I was wrong.

I now found myself on a troop ship with about 3,000 other servicemen. On our way back to the States. We were to enter into the same port that we left from in Pittsburg, California. I remember the wonderful feeling that we all got when we cruised under the Golden Gate Bridge. When we entered the port, there was a small military band playing welcoming us home. We were a little disappointed in that we expected to see a contingent of families there. I guess we just were not important anymore. This was only a "Police Action" and later labeled "The Forgotten War." But those of us who were there knew better. This was a terrible war with many casualties.

We were all processed out of the Regular Army and assigned to the Army Reserve for a period of five years. I received my orders dated April 6, 1953 assigning me to Fort Ord, California.

I also received my Separation Papers DD 214, stating that I was honorably separated from active duty. The document contained other important information such as my serial number, my total time in Korea, and decorations received. I received the Korea Service Medal with four bronze stars and the United Nations Ribbon. Each Bronze Star indicated that I was in Korea during four major campaigns. Later, the Country of South Korea honored us with their "Korean War Service Medal."

My close friends, Russ Morrison and Frank Mena, had already been sent home, as they were there a couple of months before I got there. I kept in touch with them. Russ Morrison passed away in the early 2000s. I still keep in touch with Fernando Nunez who lives in Whittier, California, and Frank Mena now living in the state of Washington.

I was formally released from the Army on March 24, 1954. Again, it was a good feeling and at the same time a sad moment too. I think, even to this day, that if I could have enlisted in the U.S. Air Force, I might have stayed in and made it a career.

Home, Alicia, Dad's Restaurant

It was nice coming home. The family was happy to see me and glad that I was out of the Army. It was late in the evening when I got home via the Greyhound bus. Many hugs and kisses were exchanged with the family. I couldn't get over how big brother Jimmy had grown. He was now six years old. My mother and father were elated that their son was now home.

My father now owned his own café on the waterfront in San Pedro. He would open in the afternoon and serve lunch, dinner, and early breakfast. He would close around six in the morning. He worked it by himself as cook, server, all-around maintenance man, and dish washer. Occasionally one of his sons, John, Nick, or myself, would go down in the evening and help him. The waterfront was pretty tough in those days, with a lot of fights and drunks on the street. My dad was always afraid for us and after a certain hour he would send us home.

He was an outstanding cook. His café, George's Café, was widely known by seamen, longshoremen, servicemen, and many of the residents of San Pedro. He was best known for his chili beans, fish, and steaks. Foreign seamen when they docked in San Pedro would go to his café to eat. My father never turned anyone away if they were destitute and could not afford to pay for a meal. He would always serve them. My dad was well liked by all. Occasionally, a person would order a big meal and then complain after they ate it that it was not any good and would refuse to pay him.

My father was a very strong man even in his sixties and older, and would not take any guff from these types of people and they knew he meant business so in most of those cases they would end up paying. If they became physical, he kept a small baseball bat behind the counter near the register and would use it if he had to.

I remember on one occasion when I went to the café to help him, there was this man who started to give my dad a hard time. My dad told him to leave the café. This guy had been drinking and was somewhat intoxicated. I went over to help my dad and told the man to leave or I would call the police. He left and then about ten minutes later he came back in. This time he was holding a broken whiskey bottle in his hand and started threatening my dad. I immediately went to my father's aid. I jumped on top of the counter and stomped on this man's hand, which was holding the bottle. He let go of it. I went over the counter and grabbed the man from the back of his collar and the seat of his pants and ran him out the door and threw him down on the sidewalk. He slid into a light pole and hit his head. He got up dazed and walked away.

My father was extremely mad at me for doing that. He told me he handles those kinds of problems daily. He told me that I could no longer go down to the café and help him. He said that he did not want me to get hurt.

That was the last time that I ever helped him at his café. I would go visit with him and he always fed me, of course.

A side note on this is that the San Pedro waterfront had a notorious reputation for being one of the roughest waterfronts in the world. The street one block west of where my dad's café was mentioned in the Guinness Book of Records as one of the roughest streets in the world during World War II. The street experienced one murder almost each day.

My father was well liked. There was a bus stop right on the corner where his last café was located. Friends, when they were waiting for the bus, would stop in to tell him hello. My dad would always serve them something to eat even if it was only an ice cream cone. This one friend would always comment on how generous he was. She even told me that she would sometimes go out of her way to go see him because she knew that she would at least get a free ice cream cone.

My father's last restaurant, which was located on the corner of Sixth Street and Harbor Blvd. in San Pedro's waterfront, was taken over by the City of Los Angeles as they tore down that whole section of San Pedro for urban development.

There are a couple other items I wish to talk about this section of San Pedro and will be mentioned later on, after I became a Los Angeles Police Officer assigned to Harbor Division in San Pedro.

I really got sidetracked after my discharge from the Army. There are many things that took place after I came home.

Courting Alicia

My first morning back, I went over to Alicia's house to see her. It was early about eight in the morning and when I was walking up the walkway to her home, the door opened and out came a friend named Cruz Lucero followed by Alicia and her sisters Julia and Lucia. He obviously spent the night at the Sanchez residence.

I shook Cruz's hand and we talked briefly. Cruz had been home from Korea several months now and was assigned the 2nd Division on the front lines. After a brief conversation with Cruz, Alicia and her sisters finally acknowledged me. I got this funny feeling. I guess I was a little jealous that Cruz was there and I knew that the Sanchez girls liked him an awful lot.

Cruz's family and the Sanchez family were old acquaintances. Anyway, Alicia and her sisters were glad to see me and that I was now home and out of the Army. I stayed there for a little while talking to them while Alicia was getting ready to go to work. She was working at J.J. Newberry's Store in San Pedro. I walked her to the bus stop, which was right on the corner by her home.

I would always tease Alicia about that morning, in that Cruz seemed more important to her than I did. After all, I was only gone out of her life for two years. I always did believe or think that she had a crush on him and he on her.

My brother John came over and we reminisced about old times. I had no civilian clothes, so John and I went to downtown San Pedro and bought a few clothes along with a pair of sharp blue suede shoes. Those shoes were really sharp. When I got mustered out of the Army, they gave me a total of three hundred dollars severance pay. So, I had money to buy the clothes. Keep in mind this was in 1953 and three hundred dollars was a lot of money. My brother Nick was living in Oregon attending the University of Oregon. Brother Chuck was a senior in high school. Jimmy was a cute little boy. He was six years old and a mischievous little kid. He reminded me of John and me when we were his age. My mother had spoiled him rotten. He was a good kid, but spoiled. I remember my mother always worrying about him, as he gave her a lot to worry about. Just like John and I did when we were his age.

There were times when Jimmy never told our mother that he was going somewhere, which would cause our mother to worry about him. I remember one day that Jim had left the house not telling anyone where he was going and no one saw him for several hours. We would all be out looking for him, but could not find him or find someone who may have seen him. My mother called the police and two officers arrived at the house. My mother in her broken English was telling them about her missing son. The officers took his description and went out looking for him. After about forty-five minutes, they returned to the house and had Jimmy with them. I forget where they found him, but my mother was happy that they found him and brought him home. I thought John and I were the only ones that drove my mother crazy, but now Jimmy was doing it all over again. We still believe that Jimmy was her favorite.

A little sidenote about Brother Jim. Our mother wanted a girl so bad that when he was born, she tried to make him a little girl. Jim had curly hair and our mother would not cut it. It was getting pretty long. One day John took Jimmy to the barber shop and told the barber to give him a boy's haircut. The barber resisted because he knew that our mother would get mad. John told the barber to put all of his cut hair in a bag. He then took Jimmy home, dropped him off, and gave him the paper bag and told him to go in the house and give the paper bag to his mother. When she saw Jimmy, she got mad. It was a good thing John didn't stay.

My brother John took me to DiCarlo's Bakery and I talked to my old boss, Lawrence DiCarlo, about going back to work. He did not hesitate to tell me I could have my old job back. They now had new bread-wrapping machines and that I would have to be trained on how to operate them. I told Lawrence that I appreciated him giving me my job back, but I told him that I was not planning to stay at the bakery because I had wanted a position with the Los Angeles Police Department. He appreciated that I was honest with him and gave me a job on the bread-wrapping machine. I would take the wrapped bread off the conveyer and box it up for delivery.

John helped me shop around for a car. We found this cool 1949 Oldsmobile 88 two-door coupe. I bought it with a small down payment. I was now in my glory, as I had new clothes and a car all my own. I took good care of that car. It was originally gray in color, with a cream-colored top. I painted it a pretty blue with a cream top. It really was a neat car. I now had my first car. I could take Alicia out on dates and rides. I also drove my mom and dad to places where they needed to go.

John was married and he did not have the time that I did to take the folks places. I always took my dad to do his shopping at the market for items he needed for the restaurant. Of course, I no longer had to take the bus or walk to go to work.

The months seemed to go by pretty fast now. Alicia and I began to see each other quite often. She worked during the day and I worked at DiCarlo's in the evening. I would pick her up during her lunch break and we would go to Point Fermin Park or Royal Palms beach while she ate her lunch. I would always stop and pick up a desert that we would share. She seemed prettier every time I would see her. I was so very much in love with her and she with me. I had asked her to marry me and she said that she would. I was one happy individual.

We began to talk about what kind of wedding we wanted. I suggested that we marry in the Greek Orthodox Church. Alicia and I talked to her mother and sisters about the wedding and they were all very happy for us. We agreed on getting married in the Greek Orthodox Church. We talked to my mother and she was also very happy for us. On the other hand, my father was totally against the marriage. He wanted me to marry a Greek girl. He was very unhappy that I was marrying Alicia. He liked her, but did not want me to marry her. My dad and I had many discussions about this. He liked the idea of getting married in the Greek Church, but Alicia was not Greek. He did have a hard time with it.

As time went by, my father learned to love Alicia as if she was his own daughter. I will go into this a little later.

I was still working at the bakery and earning about sixty dollars a week and Alicia was working at J.J. Newberry's earning a decent salary, also considering it was 1953. Alicia would always give her mother her paycheck, but would keep some spending money. Alicia's mother, Felicitas, was a widow, drawing her husband's small Army pension.

I forgot to mention that Alicia's father Amado was a very sick man. He had a bad heart condition and was in the Veterans' Hospital in Long Beach, California, off and on. I would often go with Alicia to visit him. We would take the bus or sometimes, Robert Wynn would drive us in a car that Alicia and her sisters bought for their brother Robert. While I was in Korea, Mr. Sanchez passed away. I remember when I got the news, I felt bad for the Sanchez family, as they were all were very close.

Lucy, Julia, and Alicia along with Robert would help their mother with the household expenses. Alicia's family was a beautiful family, well liked, and admired by many, many people. They would never hesitate to reach out and help someone in need. They lived in a small house with only a kitchen, living room, and a bathroom. Yet that family of seven lived comfortably in that little house. This was truly a happy family. I learned to love all of them, as they immediately made me feel as I belonged to the family.

I enrolled in Los Angeles Harbor Junior College majoring in Police Science and Administration. I was taking a full load and working after classes at the bakery. I was attending college under the G.I. Bill, as the government paid for my tuition and even helped out with my books. I did well, maintaining a 3.0 grade point average.

CHAPTER 6:

APPLYING FOR
THE LOS ANGELES
POLICE DEPARTMENT

I applied for employment with the Los Angeles Police Department. I took the written test and passed it. I then went for my job interview and also passed that with a high enough score. The next phase was the physical agility. I was still in pretty good physical condition and also passed that phase. Now came the last step and that was the medical examination. When I got to a certain phase of the medical examination, I was eliminated from the process for something the doctor found. They would not tell me why I flunked out, other than I would be receiving a letter explaining why I was not accepted.

After several weeks, I did receive the letter and the reason I was not accepted. The reason was that, "You have a deviated septum therefore not eligible to be a Los Angeles Police Officer." I did not know what a deviated septum was, so I looked it up in the encyclopedia. What I read was that a "septum is the partition which separates the right and left part of the heart." I thought to myself I was recently discharged from the Army and had a rigorous examination and I was never told that I had any kind of a heart condition.

I called my doctor and made an appointment with him. I went in to see him, showed him the letter, and the first thing he did was look up the nostrils of my nose. He then looked at me and told me that I had a bad deviated septum and went on to tell me the septum is the partition that goes down the center of my nose. He asked me if I had played football. I told him that I had and he explained that he sees many of these with football players. When I played high school football, the helmets did not have face guards.

The doctor went on to tell me that if I wanted to fix that problem, he would send me to an eye, ear, nose specialist. I told him that I did and then I could appeal my medical and be re-examined.

Nose Operation

My doctor made an appointment with the specialist. I went in to see him and after an examination, he scheduled a date for the surgery. I took a week off from work to have the operation and to recuperate.

The operation was performed at the old San Pedro Hospital. I was totally awake when the doctor operated. He numbed my nose and then started cutting and chipping away. I heard every crunch that was taking place. After a period of time, the doctor started stuffing gauze up into my nostrils. There were yards of gauze stuffed up my nose.

I spent two days in the hospital to make sure that I would not hemorrhage. Both of my eyes turned black and blue. I was released, went home, and took it easy for several days. A week after the surgery, I went back to the doctor and he took all the gauze out of my nose. I was off work for two weeks, as I had to be careful that I would not hemorrhage. I did not see Alicia during that period. I would talk to her on the phone. She was amazing throughout this ordeal, as she supported me joining the police department. We were still making plans for the wedding.

My two weeks were up and I went back to work at the bakery. It was a Sunday afternoon and I was working on what was called the round table conveyer packaging French rolls. While I was working, I felt a blood drop from my nose. Then, my nose started hemorrhaging. I used the apron I was wearing to hold it up to my nose to try to stop the bleeding. I told the foreman what was going on and that I had to go to the emergency hospital to try and stop the bleeding. One of my employee friend's drove me.

When we got to the emergency hospital, I explained to the nurse on duty about the nose operation and who the doctor was. The nurse immediately tried to contact the doctor, but he was out of town. She did talk to the doctor who was his partner and taking his calls. He advised the nurse that he would meet me at his office and that he would take care of the problem.

I went to his office and he examined me and immediately started stuffing the gauze back into my nose. The bleeding stopped and I had to go home and lay down for a few hours. I had to stay home another week. My nose finally healed and I went back to work.

CHAPTER 7:

WEDDING PLANS

Alicia and I selected the wedding announcements and they were beautiful and unique. We selected the date of June 20, a Sunday. Since we were paying for the wedding, we selected the Homer Toberman Settlement Hall located in the Barton Hill Area for the reception. Alicia and her sisters knew the director of the hall and she let us rent it at a very reasonable price. Also, she liked us a lot, as we were both members of the Hall as kids. Alicia learned a lot of crafts there and I belonged to the Wood Craft Rangers there also. We both went to outings and camping with Toberman.

Alicia's friends from Sana Rosa, California, owned a restaurant and did most of the cooking and serving. Alicia's family bought the food. It was a simple menu, with turkey, mashed potatoes, gravy, vegetables, and a salad. As simple as it was the people loved it. Alicia's family also bought the wedding cake.

We continued to plan for our wedding. We had made appointments with Father Billiris, the priest at the Long Beach Greek Orthodox Church. He immediately took a liking to Alicia and me. He counseled us on marriage and the responsibilities of marriage and what the ceremony would involve. Father Billiris was a wonderful priest.

A little side note here. This Greek Church was newly built and Father Billiris was assigned to the church. This had to be in 1947. The very first baptism in this church was my brother Jimmy.

In the Greek Church, priests can get married. Father Billiris was married with children.

In the meantime, I was filing an appeal for the police department. I was going through the appeal process and that was taking some time. I was still working at the bakery and had gotten several raises and promotions. I was still determined to become a Los Angeles Police Officer and going to college. I did graduate from Harbor College with an Associate of Science Degree in Police Science.

Graduating from Harbor Junior College was a wonderful feeling. My mother and father were extremely proud of me, as was Alicia. My next step was to enroll at the California State University of Long Beach. The college had an excellent Police Science and Administration of Justice Program.

I am getting a little ahead of myself. I have to get back to one of the most important parts of my life and that was marrying my beautiful Alicia. Alicia and I spent many hours talking about our wedding plans. She and her sisters went to Downtown Los Angeles at a bridal shop, where Alicia selected and was fitted for her wedding dress. Her sister Lucia who was to be her maid of honor and sister Julia, her bridesmaid, were also fitted into their dresses. Alicia's wedding dress was gorgeous as were Lucia and Julia's dresses.

I wanted my brother John to be my best man, but learned from Father Billiris that he could not because he had been married in the Catholic Church. The best man had to be of the Greek Orthodox Religion. John was raised, as we all were, Greek Orthodox, but the marriage in the Catholic Church prevented him from being my best man. So, my brother Nick was my best man and my best friend Robert Wynn was an usher.

After several sessions with Father Billiris, we picked the date for the wedding. The date of June 20, 1954, a Sunday, and also Father's Day was the day we would be getting married.

There was a lot of excitement about our wedding as we got down to making the arrangements for the wedding and the reception to follow. We wanted our wedding to be small with family and close friends.

The next-door neighbors to Alicia were an elderly couple, who took a liking to the Sanchez family. This couple asked if they could be their grandparents. Lucy went and talked to her mother and father and told them what Mr. and Mrs. Jackson had told her. They both said, "Of course." They became very close friends. Alicia's father, later on, knowing he was a sick man, told the girls that if he should pass away, when they got married, he wanted Mr. Jackson to walk them down the aisle in his place. Considering the Sanchez family's affection for Charles and Mary Jackson, they felt that it would be an honor to have them as their grandparents and to call them Grandma and Grandpa Jackson.

On June 20, 1954, our wedding date, Mr. Charles Jackson (Grandpa Jackson) walked Alicia down the aisle for Amado Sanchez. Alicia's father had passed away two years previously. Alicia's father's wish was fulfilled.

I believe that our wedding was the only one that ever had a wedding reception at Toberman. It was a plain-looking facility with a kitchen, but Alicia, her sisters, and friends who came down from Santa Rosa helped decorate the hall.

Alicia's friends from Santa Rosa, the Peterson family, did most of the cooking and serving. They owned a family restaurant in Santa Rosa and were experts at catering. They were a wonderful family and close friends. They made everything look easy and we were praised many years later as to what a lovely wedding and reception we had. And, it was on a low-income budget.

The wedding party looked wonderful in their attire. Alicia made a beautiful bride and her sisters were also very pretty. The men folk looked great also, even if I do say so myself.

Our wedding budget pretty much took up all of our savings. Included in our budget was a honeymoon to Mexico City and surrounding areas. We rented a very small two-room apartment in San Pedro that was recommended to Alicia by one of her co-workers at Newberry's. It had a living room, a kitchen, and a bathroom, much like the little house that Alicia grew up in. It was located at 631 W. 3rd Street in San Pedro.

A nice starter for us. We had given three months' advance on the rent so we wouldn't have to worry about that. As I said, money was going to be tight after we got back from our honeymoon. Alicia's family bought the turkeys for the reception and the wedding cake. What we also did was make three payments in advance on the 1949 Oldsmobile.

We also knew that I would have one paycheck at DiCarlo's when we got back from our honeymoon so we would have money to start our new life with. All the money I had saved in saving bonds while in Korea, and money saved after I got home plus Alicia's savings were spent on our wedding. And, believe me it was not a lot of money according to the present-day (2021) standards.

I had a good job. Alicia was working and she had received a promotion as the supervisor of the Newberry's Stock Department. She was an outstanding employee and thought of very highly by all her co-workers and friends.

Honeymoon, Mexico City

Our honeymoon was beautiful. Alicia had uncles, aunts and cousins living in Mexico City that we wanted to visit. She also had a grandmother (abuelita) on her father's side living in the city of Puebla that she had never met. I promised her that we would go to Puebla so that she could meet her grandmother.

I don't remember all the particulars on how we made our plans for our honeymoon, except that the arrangements were made through a Mexican travel agency. Our arrangements were that after our wedding, we would drive from San Pedro to Tijuana, Mexico, where we would catch our flight via Mexicana Airlines to Mexico City.

The travel agency made all the reservations for the airlines and hotel accommodations.

After the wedding and reception, I went to my home, changed clothes, and picked up my luggage. My mother and father hugged me and told me to have a good life and to be careful. I went on to Alicia's home and picked up Alicia. She changed into a pretty two-piece suit and her brothers Robert and Armando put her luggage in the car. Hugs and kisses were exchanged and I promised her family that I would take good care of their daughter and sister. A very tearful send-off. They were good, happy tears as the Sanchez family has been a close-knit family.

This was now late in the afternoon. Our wedding was at 3:00 p.m. with the reception immediately after and saying our goodbyes, as it was now early evening.

Alicia's Wedding Bouquet

Alicia did not throw her wedding bouquet, as she wanted to take it to her father's gravesite and leave it for him. She was very close to her father and missed him very much. She had told me that was what she wanted to do with her bouquet. Of course, I told her that it was a wonderful thought. So, we went to Green Hills Cemetery and after meditating awhile left her bouquet with her dad. I know that her father knew she was there. A few more tears were shed, as she so wanted her father to walk her down the aisle.

Well, we were married and madly in love with each other. Hard to believe that we were married. I guess it was meant to be after I saw this beautiful thirteen-year-old girl smile at this twelve-year-old eleven years ago in 1943, that now in 1954 we would be husband and wife. A beautiful love story, if I do say so myself. If you are wondering if we experienced each other sexually in those eleven years, the answer is no. I loved Alicia too much and respected her and she felt the same with me that our relationship never went to that extent. So now the world knows!

Greek Orthodox Wedding

However, we were now husband and wife and Alicia would always tell me that during the wedding ceremony she never did say, "I Do." I would tell her that after the two-hour ordeal she went through during the wedding ceremony she was too exhausted to say "I Do." We would always chuckle when we would think of getting married in the Greek Orthodox Church.

The wedding ceremony was a traditional, Greek Orthodox wedding. The service is abundant with symbols that reflect marriage: love, mutual respect, equality, and sacrifice. The ceremony consists of two distinct parts, the Betrothal and the Sacrament of Marriage. Everything has a special meaning and significance, including petitions, the crowning, readings from the Bible, the offering of the common cup, the circling of the ceremonial table, and the benediction. At the conclusion of the prayers, the priest joins hands of the bride and groom. The hands are kept joined until the end of the service to symbolize the union and the oneness of the couple. The ceremony is performed in the Greek language and followed with an English interpretation. The ceremony did last for almost two hours. Alicia did not realize that the wedding would be that long.

However, on with the story. We did stop on the way down to Tijuana at a motel near San Diego as we were both pretty tired. And yes, the marriage was consummated. NO DETAILS.

Tijuana Mexico and Flight to Mexico City

In the morning, we went the rest of the way to Tijuana to catch our flight to Mexico City. We only had one little problem and that was we had to store the car somewhere. After making some inquiries, we found a place that assured us the car would be taken care of and stored in their underground facility for the two weeks we would be gone. Alicia's beauty and her beautiful smile worked miracles for us. Oh yes, the fact that she was Mexican and spoke fluent Spanish helped us a lot also.

We took a taxi to the airport and had no difficulty catching our flight. This was also a very interesting part of our journey. Alicia had never flown before and the airplane we were making our trip on was a four-engine plane and the trip to Mexico City was going to take approximately five hours. They did have a few jet planes at that time, but not in Mexico that I recall. The plane was clean and the airline staff (pilot and stewardess) were very courteous and polite. We made ourselves comfortable and I knew Alicia was a little apprehensive and nervous about flying. I tried to assure her that flying in an airplane was a piece of cake and that she would enjoy the flight.

Well, we were okay for an hour or so in our flight, but then we hit a lot of turbulence. The stewardess told us to keep buckled up because of the turbulence. Now Alicia was scared and to be honest I even got a little nervous when we hit turbulence for several hours before we settled down. I really felt bad for Alicia, as she was really frightened. She told me that once we get back home that she never wanted to fly again. The flight back to Tijuana was just as bad and that reaffirmed her feeling about not wanting to fly again.

A little antidote here regarding flying. Several years into our marriage, I took Alicia to the movies to see a double feature. One movie was *The Poseidon Adventure* and the second movie was *Airport*. *The Poseidon Adventure* was about this large cruise ship that turns upside down in the ocean and only a few survive. *Airport* was a large passenger plane that crashes and sank to the bottom of the ocean. Most survived in this movie. From that moment on Alicia never wanted to fly again or ever go on a cruise.

Mexico City and Rio Hotel

Well, we finally landed in Mexico City, and took a taxi to the Rio Hotel. A very nice hotel. Probably, according to the hotel rating system, a four- or five-star hotel. The travel agent booked us into a very nice suite. We finally got to relax. That flight was an ordeal. We stayed in the hotel the rest of the day and had dinner in the hotel restaurant. A little story goes here regarding the restaurant.

A beautiful restaurant and the food was excellent. One thing we learned was that they served very few Mexican dishes. They served more American dishes. Alicia did all the ordering as she spoke to the waiter in Spanish. After we were there for several days, whether it was breakfast or dinner we seemed to get the same waiter. He seemed to be rude with me, but not with Alicia. Alicia got irritated at his behavior and asked him what his problem was.

He told Alicia, "What is the matter with your husband, why do you have to do all the ordering?" Alicia responded he is not Mexican, he is Greek, and does not speak Spanish. The waiter immediately apologized to Alicia and me for his rude behavior. He left and a few minutes later the restaurant manager came over to our table and started talking to me in Greek. I conversed with him for a little while and now, we were really in as far as this restaurant was concerned. He was born in Greece and wanted to go to the United States.

However, when he arrived in Mexico, he fell in love with the country and decided to make it his home. When we were not on the road, site-seeing or visiting relatives, we would dine at this restaurant.

Our honeymoon was fantastic. We got to visit Alicia's uncles and aunts along with many of her cousins. They were very gracious hosts and wonderful people. Alicia's aunt fixed dinner for us on a couple occasions. Their home was a modest, beautiful home in Mexico City. They wanted us to stay with them, but we told them that we were staying at the Rio Hotel and we were fine. We also were visiting the sites in and around Mexico City.

Tours of Mexico City and Surrounding Area

Several of the places we wanted to see was the pyramids, Xochimilco, the Floating Gardens, the glass factory, the market place where the Indians would come to do their shopping and the art museum, the Capitol, and some of the unique historic churches.

We hired a guide arranged for us through the hotel. A very nice gentleman in his fifties. This was his trade and for a nice fee he was ours as long as we were going to be there. The first tour we took was the Capitol, the National Palace and the surrounding area, which included some beautiful historic buildings, and the art museum.

In the National Palace we got to see some famous paintings by Diego Rivera, a noted Mexican painter. His paintings did reflect his philosophical beliefs. He was a noted Communist. He had married a well-known woman, Frida Kahlo, also an artist. There was a movie made about her and her turbulent life with Diego Rivera. Our guide did an excellent job, as he was well educated and informed on the history of Mexico.

On another day, our guide drove us to the Teotihuacan, where the famous pyramids are located. Teotihuacan is located in the Valley of Mexico thirty miles northeast of Mexico City. The ride to the pyramids was interesting, as we got to see some of the exotic cactus plants on the way. The guide explained that some of the cactus plants were used to make a beverage called pulque and also for making twine and rope.

We arrived at the location of the pyramids and saw many pyramids in what they called "The Avenue of the Dead." On the one end was the Pyramid of the Moon and on the other end was the Pyramid of the Sun. The Pyramid of the Sun was the largest and highest of the pyramids. In fact, we were told that the Pyramid of the Sun is the world's third largest pyramid. It stood two hundred thirty feet high.

The weather was overcast with the possibility of some rain. Alicia and I decided to walk up to the top of the Pyramid of the Sun. I can't remember how long it took us, as it was a fairly steep climb. We took our time and made it to the top. Alicia was in her glory, as she did not think she would be able to climb it. She looked so beautiful standing on the very top of this pyramid. The wind picked up and it even started to rain. I took some pictures from the top of the pyramid of the surrounding area. Yes, I did take a few pictures of us on the top of the pyramid. That was one of the highlights of our honeymoon. We were very careful climbing down, as there was nothing to hold on to.

Our guide was waiting for us then drove us to a large cave. In the cave was a large restaurant where we ate. The restaurant décor was very unique, as it reflected the pyramids, exotic cactus plants, and flowers. The food was excellent. Alicia and I both had a Mexican dinner. This was a magnificent day that neither one of us would ever forget.

The weather in that part of Mexico was odd, but according to our guide was different, in that the day would be beautiful with blue skies, sunny, and maybe a few scattered clouds. But in the late afternoon, there would be a cloudburst, with rain anywhere from a heavy drizzle to a heavy rain. It would rain for about an hour or two. The sun would come out again and the rest of the day would be beautiful. The rain would make everything sparkle, the air clear, and the streets clean. Alicia and I both enjoyed the short rainfall almost every day.

The next day, Alicia and I went to the famous Bull Fighting Arena in Mexico City. Bullfighting is the country's national sport. The stadium was packed and you could hear mariachi music as the people were getting excited anticipating the bullfighting. We got to watch several bull fights and the art that goes into the fighting of the bulls. To be honest, it is a brutal sport, as you know the bull is going to die. But the people enjoyed it.

After being in the arena for about an hour or so, again at this hour in the afternoon, it began to rain. The rain was very heavy and Alicia and I did not have any rain gear. We decided to leave and went to Alicia's Tio Lalo's house. We visited with her Uncle Lalo and Alicia's Aunt (Tia) Chavela. We also had a chance to meet some of her cousins, as they came over to see us.

For the first time, Alicia met her Uncles Maximo and Pio and their wives. The entire family was very charming. We had a wonderful visit. And yes, her Aunt Chavela made us a delicious dinner. We stayed until late evening, then took a taxi back to the hotel.

The next day we were up early, had breakfast at the hotel, and then met our guide in the lobby. This was the day we had planned to go to Xochimilco to see the Floating Gardens.

It was a nice ride out to the gardens, as the day was beautiful. The Floating Gardens was a unique experience, as you see all these beautifully decorated boats with flowers. It was almost like looking at the Rose Bowl Parade in Pasadena, California, except the floats were all in the water. Each boat had a distinctive look, all decorated with flowers with a different woman's name on an arch over the top of the boat.

We got to go in a boat with the name of "Alicia.". Now this was really cool. The beauty of the Floating Gardens is a photographer's paradise. Everyone with cameras was taking many pictures. One of my favorites, even to this day, was a mother with her little girl, around five or six years old, rowing in a decorated canoe. This picture could be entered in photo contest and it would be a winner. You just couldn't take a bad picture here.

We had a late lunch, early dinner at one of the restaurants nearby. This day was also a day to remember. We have not had a bad day on our honeymoon. Alicia and I were extremely happy.

In our two weeks in Mexico City, we had the opportunity to visit the University of Mexico. At that time, it was recently built with a magnificent Aztec décor. A few years later when Mexico hosted the Olympics, this university was the main venue.

We also got to visit a glass factory where they manufactured beautiful glass sculptures, that is, vases, bottles, dishes, and many other ceramic items. It was an interesting process to watch the workers handle the molten glass and the glass blowers as they shaped beautiful vases.

Another interesting venue was the market place where the Indians would come down to do their shopping. Hundreds of Indians in their traditional cultural colorful attire bargaining for food items, materials, and many other kinds of objects. The festivities were very colorful and there was music being played wherever you went. Alicia and I thoroughly enjoyed watching these beautiful people in their traditional customs as they bartered for their wares.

Alicia's Grandmother and City of Puebla

The last place, and one of the most important parts of our honeymoon, was to visit the city of Puebla. This was the village where Alicia's father was born and raised by his mother, Alicia's grandmother Lucia Ortega whom she never met.

We took a bus from Mexico City to Puebla. The bus was an antiquated bus with many passengers. Alicia enjoyed talking to some of the passengers and they with her. When they learned that we were from the United States and Alicia was going to meet her grandmother for the first time in Puebla, more of the passengers got involved in the conversation.

The ride to Puebla took us several hours. We got to see hundreds of old churches while we were in route. We were able to go into a few of the churches on several of the stops we made. The few we went into were not in use any longer as churches. They were historical and with a tour you could go in and appreciate these old churches, as each one had a unique history. I took some great pictures inside and outside several of these churches.

When we arrived in Puebla, we made some inquiries as to where we could stay. We were directed to a quaint and charming hotel. We got settled in and then we left looking for the address of Alicia's grandmothers house.

We found it, and for the first time Alicia got to meet her grandmother. It was a beautiful moment with hugs and tears. I don't think I have ever seen Alicia as happy as she was at that moment.

Her grandmother was very short. If I were to guess her height, I would say 4'5" at the most. Alicia at 5'4" stood at least a foot taller than her. I, at 6'1", looked like a giant next to her. Her grandmother was definitely a full-blooded Aztec Indian. She was very sweet and seemed very happy to meet Alicia. They talked for several hours and then we took her to dinner at a very quaint, little café. This was a very emotional time for both of them. Alicia just could not get enough of her. Alicia's father had passed two years before, and her grandmother had many questions to ask about her son (Amado). It was evening now and we left her, but told her we would see her the next day.

Alicia and I went back to the hotel. The city of Puebla was very small with an atmosphere of Old Mexico and cobblestone roads. A beautiful community.

Mariachis for Alicia

Back at the hotel, Alicia went upstairs to our room. I stayed down in the lobby for a while and with my broken Spanish and the clerk's broken English we were able to communicate. I asked the clerk if I could hire a few musicians to play some songs for Alicia. Our room had a balcony that overlooked the street below. I was able to come in contact with a small mariachi group who would play a few songs, as I wanted to serenade Alicia in this most beautiful atmosphere of Puebla.

I gave the group ten dollars to play a few songs. Alicia and I were in our room talking about the day and her grandmother. At a certain given time, the mariachi group began to play. Alicia commented on how nice and beautiful the music was and wondered where it was coming from. I then told her to step out on the balcony and look down on the sidewalk. She did and she gave me one of her beautiful smiles and said, "You didn't!" She gave me a big hug and thanked me for that moment.

The irony of this was that I thought I paid them for a few songs, but they played almost through the whole night. This put the icing on our honeymoon. Alicia could not get over that day and evening.

The next day we went back to visit Alicia's grandmother. She took us to meet Alicia's other aunts who lived close by. We got to meet Alicia's Tia Hortencia and Tia Maria. These aunts were her father Amado's half-sisters. I couldn't get over the close resemblance of Alicia and her Aunt Maria. Alicia had heard from her mom and dad that she looked like her Aunt Maria. And it was true. Their home was a very pretty small hacienda type with many chickens running through the house and veranda. They made us very comfortable and wanted us to stay for dinner. We did. Tia Hortencia had a wonderful personality and smiled and laughed a lot. She and Tia Maria loved Alicia tremendously and even took a liking to me. I took many pictures, as these moments were very precious to us. It was sad that we had to leave the next morning to go back to Mexico City, as it was getting close for us to leave for home. We said our goodbyes, and yes, emotional Alicia shed more tears. She mentioned to me that she probably would never see them again.

The next morning, we took a bus back to Mexico City. The long ride back was very relaxing and very emotional for Alicia. Her thoughts were with her grandmother and her aunts. Those moments of joy and sadness cannot be described as my beautiful wife finally met her grandmother and Aunts.

This honeymoon surpassed my expectations of the beginning of a new life with my beautiful wife. We will always remember each and every moment we spent on our honeymoon. But the biggest joy and thrill were those moments in Puebla and meeting Alicia's grandmother. Several years later, her grandmother passed away. No one from the family could go to the funeral. Alicia said over and over she would always treasure that moment in time that she spent with her grandmother.

Leaving Mexico City for Home

Well, it was time for us to leave for home, as our honeymoon was coming to closure. The next morning, we were to leave for the airport to catch our plane for Tijuana. We packed the night before so as to not to waste any time. Alicia's uncles, Lalo, Pio, Maximo, and their wives and even some of the cousins met us at the airport, as they wanted to say goodbye. I forgot to mention that Lalo,

Pio, and Maximo were also half-brothers to Alicia's father. This was also a very emotional time for Alicia. Her aunts brought some snacks for us to eat on the plane. A very nice gesture on their part. We said our goodbyes and boarded the plane. We could see the family waving to us as the plane was taking off. Again, Alicia shed a few tears.

The flight to Tijuana was okay for several hours, but then we hit turbulence. Alicia reiterated what she had said on the flight to Mexico City—that she would never fly again.

We arrived in Tijuana and took a taxi to the garage where we had our car stored. The car was in perfect condition, as they took good care of it while we were gone. On top of the storage fee for two weeks, I gave them a nice tip for taking good care of our car. They had even washed it before they turned it over to us. We left Tijuana and drove back across the border. We were on our way home. We stopped in San Juan Capistrano to get a bite to eat, then drove the rest of the way home.

We finally arrived to our little apartment and relaxed. We had unpacking to do and sort out souvenirs that we brought home for the family. We called our families to let them know we were back and that we would see them the next day.

Our wedding and honeymoon were behind us, but one thing for sure, those wonderful moments would never fade from our memories.

Wedding reception starting from left to right; Robert Wynn, Julia
Sanchez, Alicia and Mike Markulis, Lucia Sanchez, Nick Markulis

Wedding June 20,1954, Mike and Alicia

Sisters – Lucia, Alicia, Julia Sanchez

Alicia thanking guests for coming to the wedding

Mr. and Mrs. Jackson, Alicia's neighbors.
Mr. Jackson walked Alicia down the aisle for her father.

Wedding; arriving to reception Tobberman Hall

Greeting arriving guests

Wedding Collage
June 20,1954

Honey moon, Alicia meets her grandmother
for the first time in Puebla, Mexico.

Honey moon visited Xochimilco, Mexico
the floating gardens mother and daughter.

Alicia's grandmother along side with Alicia's father

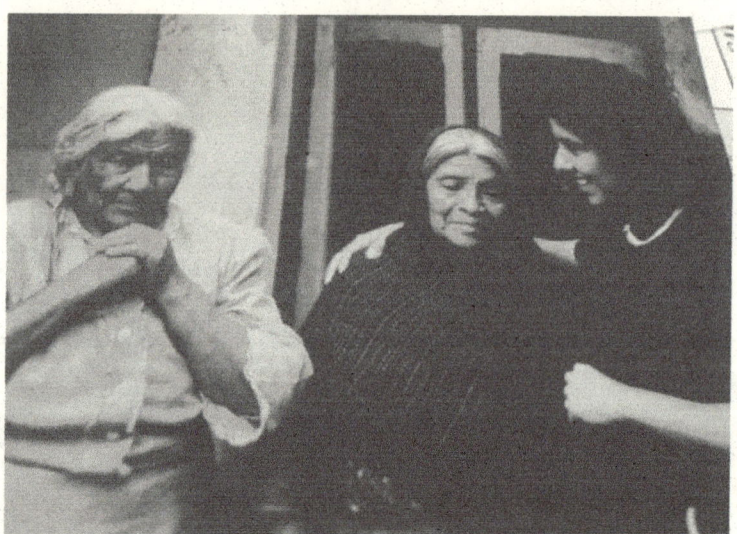

Alicia's Aunts, Uncles and Cousins in Mexico City and Puebla

Left side pictures–Marriage June 20, 1954,
Right side pictures–50 years later.

CHAPTER 8:

LIFE AFTER MARRIAGE AND HONEYMOON

Alicia and I began to build on our lives and the future. We both went back to work and began saving some money to buy our first home. Alicia did very well at J.J. Newberry's and me at DiCarlo's Bakery. Our life together was like a fairytale and writing this story has brought back memories that I wish every married couple could have experienced.

First Vacation

Alicia and I were now married a little over a year and we talked about taking a trip on our two-week vacation from work. We talked about a camping trip stopping at some of the National Parks and even driving up to Eugene, Oregon, where my brother Nick was going to school. We got the necessary maps from the Auto Club and planned out our trip. We thought we would rent the camping equipment we would need from the Union War Surplus Store in San Pedro. We rented a tent, sleeping bags, and a portable butane gas stove. We bought an assortment of supplies that we felt we would need. I bought a car-rack to put on the roof of the car so that we could tie down the tent and sleeping bags. We loaded everything else in the trunk of the car. We planned our trip to stop at Sequoia National Park, Yosemite Park, and even go to Crater Lake in Oregon. I even bought a window air cooler for the car as we knew we would be driving in a lot of warm weather. Our 1949 Oldsmobile did not have air conditioning. Alicia and I talked about asking her little brother Armando if he would like to go with us. We asked Alicia's mother and she thought that if he wanted to go with us, she would let him. Armando said yes.

We got to Sequoia, our first stop, and found a nice campsite to pitch our tent. The only tent I ever set up was a small one-man pup-tent in the army. We had instructions that told us step by step on how to pitch this six-by-eight-foot tent. Other campers were watching us and were actually laughing at Armando and me trying to set up the tent. We were a hysterical sight as we set up this lopsided tent. Finally, a man who was watching came over and asked us if he could give us a hand. Thanks to this nice gentleman, we got it right and learned what we were doing wrong. We got better as we went along on our trip.

In Yosemite, after we got our tent up and settled in, we barbequed some hamburgers. The national parks were absolutely beautiful. The sequoia trees and pine trees were enormous in height and width. One tree in Sequoia was so large that it was hollowed out at the base so a car could drive through it. These were magnificent wonders of the world. Evenings were hard to describe. The smell of the pine trees and the clear dark skies gave us a view of millions of stars with the ability to see shooting stars. God's work was truly reflected through the beauty of His creations. Only God could have created such spectacular beauty. This experience brought us closer to God as we saw his creations in its natural habitat.

After enjoying the beauty of the forest, we got into our sleeping bags to get some sleep. Armando and I both heard loud noises outside our tent and we looked out to see what it was. Well, a big, I mean, huge brown bear had gotten our ice chest and was trying to open it. About this time, Alicia woke up and told us that she had to go to the restroom. Armando and I both told her "NO, YOU DON'T!" She kept telling us that she had to go to the restroom. We opened the tent and she saw the bear and panicked. We told her to be quiet and that the bear would go away. About this time, a lady from the next campsite came out with a lantern and shooed the bear away. We thanked her and told her she was one brave lady to do what she did. She told us that she was used to this and told us not to leave our ice chest where the bears can get it, as the bears can smell the butter, eggs, and bacon. Alicia did get to go to the restroom as Armando and I both walked her to it.

In the morning, we looked at our ice chest. Other than a few scratch marks on it, it was not damaged at all. The bear knew exactly what he was doing. I took the ice chest and washed it well so that we could use it again. Next time we learned to put the ice chest up in a tree where a bear could not reach it. We also learned a good lesson and that was to never put your ice chest in your tent because bears had a strong sense of smell.

The three of us were having a spectacular time. We were enjoying our wonderful adventure. Alicia and I were glad that we brought Armando with us, as he was having a good time.

Our drive to Oregon looked like it was going to be a long ride. By looking at the map, I saw a road that was a lot shorter than the main highway and decided to take it. What a mistake that was! The road was on the map, but a great portion of it was not paved. It was forests, brush, and a very narrow road. It seemed like forever to get through this road and back on to a main highway. The car was filthy and needed a good washing.

We got the car washed and we spent the night in a motel. Finally a little comfort. The next morning, we pushed on to Crater Lake, Oregon. This was another spectacular park. The reason it is called Crater Lake is that the crater was formed after a volcano erupted many years. The inside of the crater is now a lake.

It was a steep climb to the bottom of the crater where the lake was. We rented a small rowboat and went out on the lake and enjoyed the crystal-clear water. We camped here for a few days and enjoyed the surrounding beauty of this national park.

The last leg of our trip was to drive to Eugene, Oregon, where the University of Oregon is located. We wanted to see the university that brother Nick was attending. Eugene was a pretty town, definitely a university town. Nick was not there at this time,

We stayed at another motel and then began the long drive back home. In fact, on the way back, we stayed at several motels and lived it up. No camping on the way back. I don't remember how long it took us to drive back, but we took our time and enjoyed the coastal scenery. We took many pictures on this trip. Alicia and I enjoyed this very first vacation of our marriage. In fact, when we got back, Alicia went to the doctor for a check-up and she learned that she was pregnant. That may have explained her wanting to go to the restroom the night bear invaded our camp. WOW! We were going to have our first baby. More on this later.

Appeal Of Medical Examination for LAPD

Now getting back to reality. My dream and goal to become a Los Angeles Police Officer weighed heavy on my mind. So much was going on that I didn't pursue that dream as fast as I wanted to. I was going to California State University Long Beach working on my Bachelor's degree, and working at the bakery full-time. I procrastinated on my medical appeal and Alicia told me several times that if I wanted to be a police officer that I should not let any more time to go by. She was right. I made the necessary inquiries and my appeal went through. I was summoned to take another medical examination to see if I was qualified to be a Los Angeles Police Officer.

The doctor who examined me the first time examined me again. He looked up my nostrils and said, "Anybody who would go through that kind of surgery and wants this job that bad, I am surely not going to hold you back." He passed me and now the department had to do a background investigation to see if there was anything in my background that would prevent me from being a police officer. I passed with flying colors and was notified that I would start the Los Angeles Police Academy on February 1, 1956. Alicia and I were both elated that my goal and dream was going to be a reality. Alicia told me that she would help me every step of the way.

I gave notice to my boss Lawrence DiCarlo that I was accepted to become a police officer and that I would be leaving the bakery. He told me that he was very proud of me and that I was an outstanding employee. He also told me that if I ever wanted my job back he would give it to me. He was very gracious. His father Pietro DiCarlo saw me and told me that I should not leave the bakery because they spent a lot of money training me. I told Mr.

DiCarlo that the only way that I would stay was if he would give me a bread route. He told me that was not possible. I told Mr. DiCarlo that my mind was made up and that I wanted to pursue my dream.

Building our Home

Alicia and I saved up enough money to put a down payment on a home. On our days off, we began driving around San Pedro and looking at the newspaper ads on homes. We just could not find anything we liked or could afford. They were building new homes out in the South Shore area in San Pedro and we went out and looked at them. The prices began at $15,500 up to $19,500. I remember telling Alicia, "Who can afford those prices?" Those same houses today, 2021, are being sold from $800,000 to over $1 million. Alicia suggested that we borrow what we needed to put down on one of those homes. After discussing that idea, we came to a conclusion that it was not a good way to start off with a huge debt.

Alicia's brother Robert purchased a house and the lot next to their mother's home. We were talking one day about Alicia and me looking for a home. He suggested that we buy the lot between his house and his mother's home and use the lot for collateral to build a home on it. He said he would sell it to us for what he paid for it. Alicia and I talked about it and thought that would be great. We bought the lot from Robert for $1,500. We found a local contractor and looked through many floor plans of homes that he had built. We found one that we liked and with a few modifications would be perfect for us. We agreed and the contractor, Mr. Julian Hernandez, began construction. The home was to have three bedrooms and one-and-a-half baths.

Now here is another interesting part to this story. I had quit my job at the bakery and was about to start the Los Angeles Police Academy. My beautiful, excited wife had just learned that she was pregnant. She was to quit her job. We had made an agreement that once we started having children, she would no longer work. Her sole job was to be there for our children. Alicia thought that after the kids were in school maybe she could work during those hours while our kids were in school. That was going to be a while, so we left it there.

Our house was to be completed by April or May of 1956. I was worried that if I got dropped out of the Academy, what would happen to our new home and our new baby on the way. I knew that I had to graduate. Alicia was due in the month of April. You can see the dilemma we were in.

Sworn in to LAPD

Well, I was sworn in as police officer on February 1, 1956. We had to buy our uniforms, Sam Browne belt, shoes, revolver, etc. The only items the city provided us with were our badge, cap piece, and four brass buttons that went on our uniform. The initial cost was a little over $300. We were fortunate that we still had some money in our savings to pay for the items. Some of the recruits in my class had to borrow money through the police credit union to pay for their equipment.

This training was very vigorous. It was almost like going through army basic training. We had to fall out for inspection every morning. Our khaki uniforms had to be clean, spotless, and neatly pressed, and our belts and shoes had to be polished.

Our classroom instruction covered every aspect of police work, including criminal law and evidence. I was fortunate that I had taken those courses in college so I was a little ahead of some of the other recruits in our class. I studied hard and was able to keep up with the vigorous academy program.

In the evenings when I got home, Alicia would wash, dry and iron my khakis. She would shine my badge and leather every night. All I had to do in the evenings was study. Alicia was a jewel, as she made me shine in the academy.

The only area with some difficulty was on the firing range. I was able to qualify with no problem, but the shooting cadre wanted us all to qualify for medals such as Marksman, Sharpshooter or Expert. With each category you earned extra money on your paycheck at the end of the month. It was two, four, or six dollars more. Well, my whole class qualified for money except me.

The cadre wanted everyone in the class to qualify for one of the medals before graduation. On one of the days close to graduation, the cadre sergeant pulled me out of class and took me up the shooting range. He stood behind me and coached every shot. Well, with his help I qualified for Marksman and earned two dollars a month more on my check. Now our whole class would be wearing a shooting medal on their uniform on the day of graduation.

Alicia and Birth of Our First Baby

Alicia was now at full-term in her pregnancy and due to have the baby any day. This was the month of April. We were still living in the small apartment, as the house was not finished. Alicia's water broke and I took her to the hospital. She was in hard labor. This was in the evening of April 22. I stayed with her but I had to leave because I could not take any days off while in the Academy.

I talked to everyone I could, but they would not let me go. In fact, on the evening of April 23, we had to stay late, as we had a night shoot. We had to qualify on this night shoot or we would not be able to graduate. The cadre told me they would put me up on the first relay and that I could leave immediately afterwards. They did try to work with me to get me out of there. After I shot the relay, I left and took off for the hospital in San Pedro.

I remember the Harbor Freeway was under construction and not completed all the way. I had to drive on Figueroa Street until I got to the finished part of the freeway. I was driving exceedingly fast to get to the hospital. I was lucky that I did not get stopped for speeding. I did get to the hospital and got there several hours before Alicia gave birth to our beautiful baby girl. This was on April 23. She was absolutely beautiful as was Alicia. My poor wife labored for over thirty-six hours before she gave birth. We were now a family of three.

We had already decided on a name. If we had a girl, she would be named Elaine. In fact, she was to take my first name as her middle name. This is an old Greek custom. Alicia did not particularly like that part.

The next day, a hospital staff member went to Alicia's room and asked her if she had selected a name for the baby. Alicia stated that we had and told her the name will be Elaine Markulis. The staff member filled out the necessary information for the birth certificate. When I went to visit her that evening, she told me about the birth certificate. When I asked her if she included my first name for her middle name, she said no. Well, the birth certificate information had been submitted to be recorded. I had to go to the County Registrar's Office to make a formal request to add Michael as her middle name on the birth certificate. It was changed to read, "Elaine Michael Markulis." Alicia went along with the change.

Years later when Elaine was a little girl and Alicia would call her, she would call her only by her first name, Elaine. When Elaine would ignore her and not answer, then Alicia would yell out "Elaine Michael!" Elaine knew that her mother was getting a little upset with her and would immediately respond. Alicia and Elaine both liked her middle name being Michael.

Alicia and I loved our baby girl to no end. She was a beautiful baby girl with big brown eyes and dark brown hair. When she was born, she weighed seven pounds and eleven ounces. Everyone who saw her said that they had never seen a more beautiful baby. I took many pictures as Alicia and I could not get enough of her. We always took her with us whenever we went out. There was only one occasion that we got a babysitter to stay with Elaine when she a little over a year old. I wanted a night out with just the two of us. Alicia did not want to leave Elaine with anyone. Well, this one time, I talked her into going to a movie this one evening. Alicia called this young teenage girl who lived down the street from us and asked her if she would baby-sit Elaine for a few hours. She said she would.

Alicia and I were going to make it a nice evening by taking in a movie and getting a bite to eat afterwards. We went to the Warner Brothers Theater in San Pedro. I remember us sitting next to each other, holding hands, watching the movie. We were not in the theater very long when I heard Alicia crying. I asked her if she was all right. She said yes, but was still in tears. I knew that she missed her baby girl and did not like leaving her with anyone else. I asked Alicia if she wanted to leave and she told me yes, if I didn't mind. I told her we would go.

The moment we got home, Alicia picked up Elaine and held her tight. She loved, we both loved, our baby girl so very much. That was the one and only time that we left Elaine with a babysitter. Whenever we went out, Elaine went with us. I would not do that to Alicia again. It was too painful, emotionally, for her to leave her little girl with anyone.

Even after our son Mark was born, we never went anywhere without them. The irony of this was we had Alicia's mom living next door to us on one side, and her brother Robert and his wife living on the other side of us. My mother and father were on the next block behind us. We had plenty of relatives that we could have left them with, but we took them with us whenever we went out. On my days off, we would often go for a nice ride and enjoyed taking our children with us.

It was getting close to graduation at the police academy. The date for graduation was to be on May 4. With Alicia having given birth just ten days before, having labored so long and having developed a few minor complications, she was prevented from going to the graduation. We both felt badly, as we really wanted to be there together. This graduation meant so much to the both of us.

One good thing was that our new home would be finished and we would soon be able to move in. Alicia was still staying with her mother while she was healing.

LAPD Graduation

Graduation day was now upon us. My mother, father, Alicia's mother, and my brother-in-law Robert and his wife came to the graduation. Again, I felt bad that Alicia was not able to attend. The graduation went very well, as Chief William H. Parker presented the certificates of graduation.

The highlight of the graduation was the presentation of a plaque to the number one graduate of the class. Low and behold, my name was called out. This was a shock, as we had many sharp officers in our class of thirty-four. I walked up on the stage and Chief Parker congratulated me and presented me with the plaque.

I was happy and at the same time sad, for this was a moment that Alicia should have been here. After all, it was only through her hard work helping me during those three months of training, taking care of my uniforms, shining my leather, and polishing my badge every night that gave me the time to study and excel in the academic portion of the training. The plaque really belonged to her.

My parents and Alicia's mom and brother were also very happy for me. When we got home, I presented the plaque to Alicia and thanked her for all her hard work that made this possible. The class had a graduation party at the academy that evening. I was not going to go, but Alicia wanted me to go and encouraged me to go. Alicia asked her sister Lucia if she would go with me. Lucy said that she would. We went to the party and it turned out real nice.

CHAPTER 9:

FIRST ASSIGNMENT– CENTRAL JAIL DIVISION

We had been given our assignments. We were given three choices where we could go. 1. Patrol 2. Parking and Intersection Control, or 3. Jail Division. I think we all put in for a Patrol Division. My first assignment was Central Jail Division. That is where I would be during my probation period. We were all on probation for a year. If we did not perform up to the department standards we could be terminated. It was a good beginning, as I had the opportunity to see the kinds of people I would be coming in contact with when I did go to a patrol division.

I stayed with the Los Angeles Police Department for almost thirty-seven years before I retired. I went to the department when I was twenty-four years old and retired when I was sixty-one years old.

I loved police work and enjoyed going to work every day. I never had a bad assignment while on the department. I am not going to go into any lengthy dissertation about all that I did on the police department, as that would be a book in itself. However, I will give a few brief highlights of some of the incidents worth mentioning as I am going along.

In my thirty-seven years in the department, I worked Jail Davison, 77th Street Division (Patrol), Harbor Division Patrol and Vice, Georgia Street Juvenile Headquarters, Juvenile Patrol, 77th Street Division Juvenile, Watts Juvenile located in 77th Street Division, Juvenile Narcotics Unit out of Georgia Street Juvenile Headquarter, Administrative Narcotics Division out of Parker Center, Training Division out of the Police Academy, Hollenbeck Patrol

Division in East Los Angeles, Accident Investigation Division out of Parker Center, South Traffic Division South Bureau, Harbor Detective Division, Gang Activities Section, Officer-in-Charge, out of Detective Support Division, Parker Center, Harbor Detective Division as Commanding Officer, and my last assignment was South Bureau Homicide Unit as the Commanding Officer.

Our new home was finished and Alicia and I went out and bought new furniture. We were very practical because we had a lot to buy. We bought a Gaffers and Sattler gas stove. It was a beautiful stove, and believe it or not, it is the same stove which is in our home now in 2021. That is sixty-five years later. Alicia always polished that stove and it is a collector's item today. We also bought furniture for the rest of the house. Elaine had her own bedroom with all her furniture. My parents had a sofa they were going to get rid of and we took it, had it reupholstered and put it in the spare bedroom. It was actually like a den for us.

The house was comfortable and we loved it—it was ours. I wanted to finance it through the California Veterans Administration, as the interest rates and payments would be lower. We learned that Cal. Vet. would not finance a house while it was under construction. With the help of our contractor, Mr. Hernandez, we financed it through the bank. We had a first of seventy-five dollars and a second of twenty-five dollars a month. That was a lot of money in 1956.

I reapplied for a Cal. Vet. loan, now that the house was completed and we had moved into it. It was approved and changed our payments to sixty-five dollars a month with no second. We financed the house for 25 years.

Alicia and I were very happy, as our life was like a fairytale story come true. A good job, a beautiful home and a beautiful baby girl.

Elaine's Baptism

We baptized Elaine in the Greek Orthodox Church that Alicia and I were married in, six months after she was born. Alicia and I picked Tony Stavros to be her godfather. I knew the Stavros family very well and Tony and Alicia were in the same class in high school.

Tony would talk to me often about Alicia, telling me she was a beautiful girl. If I didn't know better, I would think he had a crush on her in high school. Well, a year or so later Tony was killed in an elevator accident in Torrance, California. Tony worked for the Otis Elevator Company. We took his death very hard. He left a young wife and two small children, one a newborn little girl. We continued a wonderful friend ship with his wife Helen.

I had to landscape the yard and found that the dirt around the house was adobe so we had to haul in top soil in order to plant a lawn and flowers. It took a while, but we managed and over a period of time we not only had a beautiful home but also a beautiful yard. Our parents were extremely proud and happy for us.

I was assigned the morning watch at Central Jail Division, which meant that I started work at midnight and got off at 8:30 a.m. I would catch the Barton Hill Bus, which stopped at the corner from our house and it would take me to the Pacific Electric Union Station in San Pedro. I would then ride the P.E. car to downtown Los Angeles. I would walk about five blocks to the Police Administration Building also known as Parker Center where the jail was located.

On the Pacific Electric Street Car, I would not have to pay anything, as they let police officers ride at no charge. The conductors always felt safe knowing that they had a police officer on board. It was good for them and me also, as I did not have to drive my car to work.

I worked different details in the jail. I would book arrestees, search them, or kept watch over all the inmates. Most of the arrestees that would be brought in would be for drunk, driving under the influence, and other types of misdemeanor violations.

This was a very mundane assignment and once in a while you would encounter a combative drunk that did not want to go to jail. This is where your academy training came into play where you tried to talk the arrestee into settling down. If that did not work, and the arrestee was belligerent and combative, I would apply the department approved "choke hold" rendering the person unconscious for a few minutes, place him in a drunk tank until he began to sober up and then process him. The choke hold was removed as one of the department's restraints in the mid-1960s.

On one occasion, a man arrested for being drunk, who happened to be a repeater, was known to all the officers and they knew him to be combative when he was processed. The officers would wait until he settled down before they would bring him out to be processed. On this occasion he started a fight in the drunk tank with another arrestee. I had to go in and break up the fight. This individual had to be almost seven feet tall and strong. I tried to break up the fight and I was having a hard time. I reached up and applied the choke hold, rendering him unconscious, and tried to let him down easy on the floor. In doing so I strained my back. That was the first time I ever hurt my back. I was miserable for several days and I continued to work but just worked booking arrestees. I did not have to have any physical contact with them.

Transfer to 77th Division

I worked the jail a year. I then got transferred to 77th Street Division located in South Central Area of Los Angeles, working patrol. I started out on the Day Watch and was assigned a partner who also lived in San Pedro. We would ride together to work, changing off, as to who would drive, every other day.

Now that I was working patrol and assigned to the Watts District, which had one of the highest crime areas in the City of Los Angeles. Alicia started worrying about me when I left for work. She would always kiss me goodbye and tell me, "Please be careful and don't take any chances." Of course, I would tell her not to worry and that I would see her after work.

My partners and I made many arrests. In one incident, my partner and I got a "415 domestic violence call.. As we pulled up in front of the house, we could hear yelling, and what sounded like glass or dishes breaking coming from inside towards the back of the house. As we approached and said "Police Officers" and opened the back door, this man lunged at me and was very combative. I tried restraining him by putting the choke hold on him, but as I tried to get my arm around his neck, he bit my forearm and I couldn't get my arm out of his mouth. I yelled out to my partner that he was biting me and my partner assisted me and we finally subdued and handcuffed him. We arrested him for assaulting a police officer, which was a felony violation. My forearm was bleeding from the bite. He bit me so hard that the bite went through my uniform sleeve and into the flesh of my arm. I had to go to go to Georgia Street Receiving Hospital and get treated. The doctor had to stitch my arm and give be a tetanus shot.

When I appeared in court on this case and testified about the incident, the female judge asked to see the wound on my arm. I took off my jacket and rolled up my sleeve and showed her the bite mark, which was ugly as it was healing. She looked at me and said, "Officer, did he do that to you?" I replied, "Yes, ma'am." She then looked at the defendant and found him guilty as charged. She ordered him to come back on another date for sentencing, and told him to bring his toothbrush because he was going to do some time. Justice was served.

A Deadly Encounter

One more interesting item before I leave 77th Street Division. My partner and I were working the day watch, when we received a radio call ADW IN PROGRESS CODE 3 (Assault with Deadly Weapon in Progress). We rolled on the call Code 3 (Red Lights and Siren). We arrived in time to prevent serious injury to a victim by an assailant who was threatening him with a large knife. We took the suspect into custody and recovered the knife. The moment we took him into custody, another young male adult came at us and he had a large butcher knife in his hand, threatening to use it on us if we did not let his brother go. I told my partner to take the suspect we had in custody to the patrol car, and I would try to handle the brother with the butcher knife.

I kept asking the suspect to drop the knife and he just shifted it from one hand to the other advancing towards me in a threatening manner. After several times of asking him to drop the knife, and before I even realized it, my six-inch revolver was out of my clam shell holster and my gun was pointed at the suspect's face, telling him to drop the knife or that I would kill him. He immediately dropped the knife and turned and ran into one of the projects. I picked up the knife. I holstered my gun and took chase after him. I remember a large, heavy-set woman getting in front of the doorway entrance trying to stop me from entering. I pushed her out of the way and went in, found the suspect arrested, handcuffed him and took him out of the unit and walked him to our patrol car. My partner was putting out a broadcast that "Officers Needs Help Call." We cancelled the call and proceeded to take the suspects to the station.

My partner, a seasoned old-timer, was mad as hell at me. I asked him what was wrong. He proceeded to take off his Sam Browne belt, lifted his shirt up, and showed me several scars on his body. He told me, "See these scars. This is what happened to me when I tried that dumb foolish act that you did." I asked him what he thought I should have done. His immediate response was that I should have shot that SOB. I told him, but I didn't have to and it all worked out. My partner (Harry) lectured me the rest of the day. Basically, that if I wanted to survive this job, I should be more careful and not take any chances like I did. It was at this moment that Alicia's words came to mind as I left for work each day. She would tell me as she kissed me, "Please be careful and don't take any chances." I always promised her that I would be okay and not to worry. I do not believe I ever told her about that incident.

By the way, my Sergeant called me to the side and told me that what I did was the right thing, not shooting the suspect. I got a nice pat on the back from him.

Transfer to Harbor Division

A year had gone by and the transfer I had put in for Harbor Patrol came through. It was approved and now I would be working out of San Pedro. This is my city and an area that I thought I knew. Harbor Division took in addition to San Pedro, Wilmington and the Harbor City Strip area. My first assignment was the car working the Harbor City Strip area. I had a seasoned good partner.

I also worked one of the Wilmington Cars as well one of the San Pedro Cars. The very first radio call I received working San Pedro, I never heard of the street and I had to look it up in my street guide. That was embarrassing to me, as I grew up in San Pedro and thought I knew the town and would not have any problems finding streets or locations. Was I wrong!

I loved police work because I found we were doing a lot of good in the community, arresting bad guys and helping victims of crimes. My name and my partner's names were coming out in the local paper on the many arrests we were making. Alicia, unknown to me at the time, was keeping a scrapbook of all the articles that came out in the paper. Alicia was very proud of her police officer husband.

On one occasion, I was loaned to work the Harbor Vice Squad. They wanted a young-looking officer to try to arrest prostitutes working out of some of the bars on Beacon Street. I was advised on what to do and how to operate prostitutes. The main element was to get a monetary offer. The two vice officers I was assigned to drove about a block away from one of the bars and let me out.

I walked into the bar and sat on one of the stools at the bar. I noticed that there were around five to six prostitutes at the end of the bar. The moment they saw me they all got up and walked out. I guess they made me for an undercover vice cop.

I sat at the bar and ordered a beer. I did not drink any kind of alcoholic drinks so this was all new to me. An old friend from high school, whom I had not seen in years, walked in and sat down next to me. We started talking about what we were doing in our lives. I told him that I had just gotten out of the army, been to Korea and back, and now working at DiCarlo's Bakery where he knew I had worked at one time. One of the prostitutes walked back into the bar and was listening to our conversation.

She then came and sat next to me and asked me if I was looking for a good time. I told her maybe, and she told me for so much money she would show me a good time. I had the offering I needed to make the arrest. We walked out of the bar and she was going to take me to her room, when I gave the signal for the two vice officers I was working with. They drove to where we were. I identified myself as a police officer and placed her under arrest.

The senior vice officer then tells me, "Is that the best you can do, Markulis? She is one of our informants." We let her go. That was the only time that I operated a prostitute.

During that week that I was loaned to the vice squad I did assist in some gambling arrests. I liked working vice and I made it known to the Vice Sergeant.

My week loan to the vice squad was up and now I was back in patrol. The job was never boring. There was always something going on. Whether it was writing tickets for traffic violations, patrolling some of the hot spot crime areas or making arrests, we were always busy.

One more incident working Harbor Patrol, then I will move on. One night my partner and I working when one of the San Pedro cars drove by a location where there was a big celebration party. A fight had broken out on the sidewalk and my partner parked the car and we approached the group to break up the fight. The next thing we knew, we were the target and objects of this major 415 (disturbance). I put out an "officer needs help" call, major 415 at this location. When an "officer needs help" request goes out over the air, all units respond Code 3 red lights and sirens. Only one unit is actually assigned the Code 3 call to respond with red lights and siren. But that is not the case when an "officer needs help: call goes out. All units that hear this call roll Code 3.

My partner and I were being assaulted and our patrol car was being destroyed. One suspect tried to run my partner down with his car. I ran over to the car and pulled the driver out, and handcuffed him to the door of the police car. We could hear the sirens and how beautiful that sounded, as the patrol and motor officers started pulling in. The officers made many arrests that evening. Our police car could not be driven and had to go through major repairs.

The *San Pedro News Pilot* as well as other papers ran a big story on that incident. Alicia was near tears when she read the article. She was constantly worried about me when I went to work. By the way, that article also went in her scrapbook.

There is a sad sidenote that I should mention here. My partner was a veteran officer, well liked and hard worker. He evidently was having some domestic problems at home and committed suicide. I felt bad as did all the officers and families that knew him. His death left a void in our division.

Assigned to Harbor Vice Squad

After a year working patrol, Sergeant Roger Mairs, the Sergeant of the Harbor Vice Unit, asked me to work the vice squad. I had a taste of working vice when I was loaned to the vice squad for one week. I accepted the assignment. I found working vice to be a very interesting assignment. I found that to be a good policy. This is an assignment where you would have to drink alcohol if you went into a bar to operate it.

The department had a policy, that you could only work for whatever illegal activity that was taking place, serving alcohol to a person who was intoxicated, serving alcohol after hours or when the bar was closed, operating prostitutes, illegal bookmaking activity and any gambling activity that was taking place.

The department put a limit on this assignment so that the officer would not become corrupt. There are many temptations that could corrupt an officer if he did not have good morals. Eighteen months on this assignment was just right.

A few interesting incidents and arrests in which I was involved included working bookmakers. I found working bookmakers to be a challenge. On one occasion I was checking out a bookmaking complaint at a café on south Gaffey Street in San Pedro. I went in several times to check it out and found that the owner of the café was taking bets from customers and then going outside to a phone booth where he would call the bets in to his phone spot.

The following day I went in dressed in my army fatigues, as Fort Macarthur was not too far from this café. I sat down at the counter and ordered breakfast. I saw him take several bets from a couple of customers. I told him that I bet the horses and I would like to place a bet. He hesitated for a moment then handed me a scratch sheet (a sheet with all the horse races and parks where they were racing).

I looked it over and picked a horse and gave him two dollars to win. He then said why not take another horse that was from the same stable as the horse that I had picked. My odds would be better if I did that and if either horse came in, I would collect on both horses. I told him no, just the horse I picked. I waited for him to go out to the phone booth to call the bets in. Just before he started to call the bet in, I approached him and told him that I changed my mind and gave him two more dollars to place it on the horse that he gave me. He took that bet also. I watched him dial the number and memorized it.

I left the café and met my partner who was parked down the street. I told him that I got a couple of bets in. He wanted to arrest him then. I told him no and to write this number down before I forget it. He did, and then I told him that was his phone spot and how I was able to get it.

We went back to our office and told our Sergeant what we had. We immediately ran the phone number through our Organized Crime Division. Now we had the location where that number is registered to. Our plan now was to make arrests at both locations.

We had one unit go to the location where the phone was registered at, and one of the officers would attempt to stiff a bet in via the telephone. My partner and I went to the café and arrested the bookmaker. Both operations were successful, as we now closed down a phone spot and made arrests at both locations.

I enjoyed working bookmakers. I made several other arrests using the same tactics as the other incident by getting the phone numbers and arresting the bookies and closing down the phone spots.

Bookmaking was a big problem not only in the Harbor Area but also every division in the city of Los Angeles. There was organized crime elements involved with this crime.

Receiving a Class A Commendation

On one occasion, my partner and I were in Wilmington checking out some bookmaking activity when we drove by Banning High School and saw that there was a football game going on. My partner had gone to Banning High School. We stopped to watch the game for a few minutes through the fence.

All of a sudden, a fight broke out with some other people watching the game through the fence. We were not going to get involved, as we were in civilian clothes dressed like longshore men. One individual pulled a handgun out and started firing it at people. My partner and I now had to take some action to stop this suspect.

There were too many people and we could not use our revolvers. We went after this suspect. A car pulled up and the suspect jumped in the back seat. My partner and I were trying to pull the suspect out of the car as it was moving. Suspects in the car grabbed on to the arm of my partner as the vehicle started picking up speed. We were both getting dragged, I fell down on the pavement and my partner was being dragged. I took out my revolver and aimed at the back window of the car. I fired one round. My shot hit the axel of the car, ricocheted into the left rear tire and made it go flat. The suspects let my partner go and he fell to the pavement.

A Motor Officer drove by at this moment and I yelled out to him to stop that car and that one of the suspects had a gun. He stopped them at gun point, and took the suspects into custody.

I ran over to my partner and saw that he was injured pretty bad. An ambulance transported both of us to the emergency room at San Pedro Hospital. I was treated for abrasions on my knee and forearm and released. My partner was admitted for observation, as he had many abrasions and was hurt badly. He was released a couple days later. He had no broken bones.

Sergeant Mairs notified my partner's wife of the incident and that her husband was in the hospital. One of the vice officers went to her home and drove her to the hospital. Sergeant Mairs wanted to go with me to tell my wife of the incident. He went with me to the house and explained to Alicia about the incident and what a brave thing her husband and his partner did under the circumstances. Alicia was grateful for Sergeant Mairs coming to the house and telling her. She was very nervous and afraid that I could have gotten hurt a lot worse.

The investigation revealed that the gun was a pellet gun and that several of the people who had been shot received no serious injury.

The principal of Banning High School called the Captain at Harbor Station and commended my partner and me for taking the action that we did. He stated that we averted a major incident that could have gotten much worse. Our Vice Sergeant wrote a commendation on us. The Department classified it as a Class A Commendation. This was the highest Commendation for bravery the department gave out at that time.

Birth of Son Mark

My eighteen months working vice came up pretty fast and I was due to leave. However, during my tenure on the vice squad my beautiful wife became pregnant and on November 2, 1959 she gave birth to a healthy baby boy. We named him Mark Michael. He was a big baby over nine pounds and gave his mother a hard time at birth. Alicia had hard labor for many hours and the doctor decided to take the baby by Caesarian.

The doctor always remembered my first words when I saw my son for the first time, "Wow! Look at those shoulders, a football player for sure." The doctor laughed and was proud of Alicia and me for being good and proud parents. He remained our family doctor and a good friend until he passed away. I first started going to him after Alicia and I were married. He had been Alicia's and her family's doctor for years before I met him. This great doctor and friend was Doctor Bernard J. Korn. A marvelous individual.

We had now lived in our new home for three years. A beautiful home it was. Elaine and Mark had their own bedrooms and we had a bath and a half. All my spare time was used working around the house. Top soil had to be brought in, and I planted a beautiful lawn and many beautiful flowers. Alicia wanted daisies on the side of the house where our side porch is. I built a planter and planted many different colored pansies and marigolds. Alicia and I were very happy, as we felt very blessed. Later on, I took out the planter and laid bricks to cover that entire area. It turned out to be a nice patio and we used the area for barbequing.

There was no walkway on the side of the garage and we wanted one so that we could access the garage from the back if we wanted to. We had no fence in the rear of the backyard to keep anyone from coming in the yard, as the rear of the house had an alley that ran east to west.

I had never built a fence nor did any type of cement work before. It's funny, I could envision in my mind what I wanted, talked it over with Alicia then proceeded to lay the cement for the walkway and build a six foot red-wood fence and angled it so that I would have easy access driving the car and parking it in the garage.

A side note to this story is, Alicia's mother, Felicitas, would come over. Remember she lived right next door, and she would watch me and talk to me. On several of the occasions, she would help me mix the concrete for the footing of the fence and the walkway. She was an amazing mother-in-law and I loved her as if she was my own mother.

Alicia and I were still madly in love with each other and we leaned on each other, working together to get things done. Our life felt like a fairytale love story in the making.

Alicia handled the budget and did a marvelous job of paying our mortgage and bills. She was able to save money each month where we had an emergency fund if we needed it. Dave Ramsey, the famous financial adviser, could have taken a course from Alicia on finances.

The years began to slip by on us. Alicia and I were very blessed with our new home and our two little ones, a boy for me and a girl for Alicia.

Now the year is 1960, and I was still working the vice squad in the Harbor Division. My brother Chuck was no going to college in the state of Washington. He was going on a football scholarship and playing football for Everett Junior College, making up grades to attend the University of Washington. He was an outstanding football player at San Pedro High School, making first string All City Full Back. He made All American Community College level playing for Everett College.

Brother Chuck's Automobile Accident

He gave up college to go into the music business and was very successful doing that. Chuck along with several of his friends had gotten involved in promoting rock and roll music. They formed a group called The Shades and were singing. Chuck sang baritone in the group. None of us in the family knew that Chuck had a singing voice. They discovered a young singer named Ron Holden and had him record several songs, one being *Love You So*, which became a big hit.

On this one day he was home and he needed to go to Hollywood to one of the studios, regarding a recording they were promoting. Chuck borrowed my car to make that trip. Well, he decided to take a cruise down Sixth Street in San Pedro. He ran into a trailer being towed by a car. The trailer had a new boat on it and the family was taking it down to the ocean to launch it for the first time. Chuck, rear-ending the trailer, did a lot of damage to the boat and the car that was towing it.

My beautiful 1949 Oldsmobile, my first car was totaled. Fortunately, Chuck and his friend were not injured. There were no injuries to the persons in the other car. Chuck called me and told me what happened. I immediately went to the location of the accident. I knew the officer handling the accident and he told me Chuck was at fault.

I kept the car in my garage for several months and ended up giving it to a person who worked at DiCarlo's Bakery.

I then bought a new 1959 Renault Dauphine compact car. We liked it and it worked out well for us. The only drawback was when I did a lot of freeway driving it was too much for it, as I blew two motors. It just was not made for constant driving of over 60 mph. I finally bought a 1963 Chevrolet Impala Station Wagon.

Transfer to Juvenile Division

The year was 1960, and I had applied for a transfer to Juvenile Division. I was interviewed by the Captain, Jim Glavas. He just happened to be Greek. We hit it off pretty good. And yes, I did get the transfer. This was one of the best assignments that I had to date. I loved working Juvenile. I was assigned to Georgia Street Juvenile working the night Juvenile Car. We worked different divisions in the city. We patrolled what we considered Juvenile "Hot Spots." These were locations where runaway juveniles would frequent, mostly in the Hollywood Division. We would also look for other juvenile violations, like truancy, narcotic, and alcohol violations. We would check bus stations and the Union train station for runaways and missing juveniles. It was amazing how many young kids were living on the streets that were runaways.

One really good thing that we had in Juvenile was women partners. In Patrol at that time no women were assigned to work a patrol car. They were only assigned to work Juvenile, the desk at a division, or the jail. Women did not start working Patrol until much later, as the department policy was that they were not field-certified.

The department, some years later, had special courses in the Academy to field certify police women to work patrol cars. This is a story in itself, about police women and their struggles in the department to be equal with the male officers. It did happen and we have women not only working patrol and detectives but also riding motorcycles.

At one time, the LAPD badge read Policeman or Policewoman. The badge was changed to read Police Officer to accommodate both male and female officers.

Women made many strides over the years. At one time they could not be promoted or advanced over the rank of Sergeant. Now as I am writing this in 2021, the department has many women of all ranks, including an Assistant Chief of Police. Someday we will see a female Chief of Police on the LAPD. Many women who retired from LAPD became Chiefs of Police in other Police Departments throughout the United States. Some of the best detectives I had working for me were women.

Georgia Street Juvenile was the Headquarters for Juvenile Division. The Captain assigned me to work 77th Street Division, Juvenile Section. Juvenile was part of the Detective Division. I was assigned to work the night watch J-Car. Two of the officers lived in San Pedro. When we were assigned to work together, we rode to work together. We were able to save on gas and car expenses. All were great partners. The ones from San Pedro were Fred Carrozo and Dominic Carr. My other partners were Cecil Larson and Al Shear. All are deceased as I write this. They were great police officers and well respected.

I had worked 77th Division in Patrol and I knew many of the patrol officers. Working the J-Car in 77th Division was a little different from Georgia Street. We did some follow-up work for our day-time Juvenile Detectives. We also rolled on calls that we were assigned and on all "hot-shot calls (Code 3 and Code 2 calls)." We also backed up patrol units when they needed some assistance. Work in 77th St. Div. was plentiful, as it was one of the highest crime areas in the city.

Robbery Suspect and Altercation

On one incident Cecil Larson and I were working together and we were going to Newton Division on a follow-up investigation for one of our day-watch detectives. A hot-shot call came out for 211 (robbery)—Shots Fired in Progress—at a market on south Central Street in Newton Division. We were only a few blocks away from the location so we rolled on the call.

A plain-clothes detective was putting a store employee in his vehicle and motioned for us to follow him. We followed him several blocks south of the market. We could see the store employee pointing to an individual standing on the corner. The detective parked and we parked right behind him. We all got out of our vehicles and the detective ran up to the suspect who was watching the commotion going on at the market that he robbed. The detective had his revolver out as did Cecil and I.

The detective put his gun in the back of the suspect and the suspect dropped a paper bag which contained the money that he robbed from the market. The bag had many coins in it along with paper currency. The bag broke and the money fell out of the bag. My partner and I covered the suspect as the detective shook him down for a weapon.

The detective did not have his handcuffs with him so I gave him mine to handcuff the suspect. A patrol unit had pulled up and the detective put the suspect in the back seat of the patrol car. After interviewing several witnesses, we asked the detective if he needed us anymore. He thanked us for backing him up and said that he did not need us anymore. I told one of the patrol officers I needed to take the suspect out of the patrol car so that I may retrieve my handcuffs and for him to put his handcuffs on the suspect.

I opened the back door to the patrol car and asked the suspect to get out. He told me, "No," and then said "You m----- f------- cop take me out if you can." I reached in to take him out and with his hands, handcuffed behind him. He turned on his side and pointed a six-inch revolver at me. I yelled out, "He has a gun," and I grabbed the revolver by the cylinder and pushed the gun inside toward him. My partner now reached over me and also grabbed on to the gun. We still couldn't wrench it out of his hand. A uniform Sergeant ran around the other side of the patrol car, opened the door and with a "Newton Sap," and started striking the suspect on the head with it. The suspect released the gun.

I was mad and yelled at the detective that he missed the gun when he shook him down. He told me that he had no gun when he shook him down. Someone in the crowd pointed to a woman and said he saw her hand the suspect the gun through the open window. She immediately started to run. She was apprehended and transported to Newton Station. The woman turned out to be the wife of the suspect. She denied giving her husband the gun and the witness who saw that incident was no longer around and could not be found. The suspect stated that he had the gun on him all the time and that the detective missed it when he shook him down.

Since the witness who saw the wife giving the suspect the gun could not be found and the suspect admitted to having the gun on him all the time, the wife was released.

After all the reports were completed, my partner and I drove ourselves to Receiving Hospital where we were treated for abrasions to our hands, which resulted from the front and rear sights of the gun as they were very sharp.

That was another story I never told Alicia, as I did not want her worrying about me when I went to work.

As I mentioned earlier, the 77th Division was a very active division. We very seldom had a quiet night. As busy as it was, I enjoyed working the division. A variety of crimes and police work. An excellent training ground for police officers.

One thing that I want to mention and it is a humorous note of an incident that occurred. I received a notice that I was to go to In-Service-Training School for two weeks at the Police Academy. We could wear our regular civies, except for the day we had to stand inspection in full uniform and be inspected by the Captain of the Training Division. I was in a dilemma, as my uniform was old. I was going to have buy a new one.

One of my partners, Cecil Larson, told me his uniform was new and that I could borrow it. We wore the same size. My other partner, Al Shear, shined his badge to perfection. He said he would loan me his badge and brass.

Well, to make this story short, on the last day of In-Service Training we all fell out in our uniforms to be inspected. The Captain inspected each of us from head to foot, and inspected our revolvers. I was selected as the sharpest looking officer of the class. I felt good, thanks to my partners. When I told Alicia about it, she smiled and gave me a hug, saying, "That's my guy, did it again."

When I got back to work, I told my partners and they were all happy for me. I thanked them, for without their help it would not have happened. About a week later, Sergeant Rudy Deleon, from Georgia Street Juvenile, came down to our unit. He was one of our night Supervisors and came down periodically to check up on us.

On that night he was to present me with a commendation that the Training Division Captain wrote, commending me for being the sharpest officer in that In-Service-Class. He made the announcement to our night unit. He walked up to me to present me with the commendation, stopped, looked at me then tore the commendation in three parts. He presented me with one part, Cecil Larson one part, and Al Shear the third part. He said, "I understand you all had something to do with this to make it happen, I believe you should share this with Markulis." We all clapped and had a good laugh. Sergeant Deleon then proceeded to give me the original one intact.

Racial Integration of the Department

Another important note to comment on was during that time in the early 1960s and prior, when the Los Angeles Police Department was a segregated department. Black officers were only allowed to work with Black officers and White officers worked with White officers. Chief of Police William H. Parker integrated the department for the first time. I was assigned 77th Street Juvenile Unit and we had only White officers in the unit. Our counterparts, Watts Juvenile Unit, still a part of 77th Street Division, were all black officers.

The Sergeant in charge of our unit had to make a decision and pick one officer from the unit and assign him to Watts Juvenile. The Sergeant assigned Watts Juvenile had to do the same. My Sergeant called me into his office and informed me that he picked me to work Watts Juvenile. An officer from Watts Juvenile would now be working the 77th Street Juvenile Unit. We all knew each other, liked each other, and never had any problems working in the manner as it was originally set up. The decision was made. The officer from the Watts Unit that took my place was Officer William Clay. We all knew Clay and knew he would work out well. I knew the officers that I was going to be working with and they were all great guys.

Officer Clay was an intelligent, sharp individual. He was going to law school, as he wanted to be an attorney. Clay did finish law school, became a lawyer, and practiced law after he retired. He was later appointed to the Superior Court as a Judge and sat as a Judge in Juvenile Court. This was a great success story for an LAPD Officer that fulfilled his dream.

I enjoyed my tenure both at 77th Street Juvenile Unit and the Watts Juvenile Unit. All the officers I worked with were great officers and wonderful human beings.

Transfer to Juvenile Narcotic Unit

One day while at work, I got a call from the Officer-in-Charge of the Juvenile Narcotic Unit out of Georgia Street Juvenile Headquarters. He told me that I was highly recommended to him and they were looking for an officer to work the Juvenile Narcotic Unit, and wanted to know if I was interested. I told him yes, that I was interested and would like to work that unit very much. I went to the Juvenile Narcotics Unit and was interviewed by Sergeant Gene Zappey. He told me that I was accepted and I would be notified when to start after he talked with the Commanding Officer of the Division.

It was an honor to be selected to work this critical assignment. It would be a great change, as it was a day assignment with very few weekends to work. When I told Alicia about the transfer, she was elated, especially when I told her that it was a day-watch assignment with most weekends off.

On my first day at the Juvenile Narcotic, I was assigned my new partner. A very professional and seasoned officer by the name of Allan Schlocker. He and I hit it off pretty good. We got to be good friends as well. After a period of time, Alicia and I were invited to his home for a couple of BBQs. We got to meet his wife and children.

Working Juvenile Narcotics, we had city-wide jurisdiction where we handled any juvenile who was arrested for a narcotic or drug charge. We also had the responsibility to handle all adults who furnished or sold drugs to juveniles. We also had a program where we would obtain young-looking police officers, just graduating from the Police Academy and place them as a student in one of the high schools that had a big problem. His job was to mingle with the students and buy dope from students who were selling narcotics in and around the school. The unit was very successful and had a good reputation with the department.

I became very knowledgeable about narcotics and drugs and qualified as an expert in this field whenever I went to court to testify. It was a lot of work, but very satisfying. The big problems among juveniles were drugs like amphetamines, barbiturates, marijuana, and heroin. While I was working Juvenile Narcotics, the new drug LSD (Lysergic Acid Diethylamide) was becoming rampant in Los Angeles and the country. I did a lot of research on this new drug, as it was becoming very popular. I became intrigued about how LSD could take hold and become a popular drug to abuse.

I also had the opportunity to work with some outstanding officers while working Juvenile Narcotics. Two were from San Pedro. We would share rides to work. Both were much senior to me, but we worked well together. One officer, Robert Vernon (Bob), and I became very good friends. He was a devout Christian. Bob was not only an outstanding officer but he was also a wonderful human being with high morals, which I believe was as a result of being a devout Christian. His father was a retired LAPD officer. So being a cop was in his blood.

Bob and I worked well together. Our families got together several times at Bob's house which was located above the Rose Bowl Stadium. We visited Bob and his family on a 4th of July and watched the fireworks from his backyard. My son and daughter still talk about that experience.

Bob and I made many arrests, both juvenile and adult for furnishing drugs to minors. We handled and set up narcotic buys using juveniles to buy drugs from adults who had sold them drugs in the past. We had to be careful in this type of operation. We needed not only the parents' approval but also the court's approval to run this kind of operation. We were very successful without any minor ever getting hurt. The penalties were very severe for adults who sold illicit drugs to minors. Bob and I enjoyed working together.

We had a way of passing our idle time while patrolling some of our narcotic hangouts and hotspots. As an example, Bob or I would take a situation that we observed and make up a fictitious narcotic story out of it. For example, there would be a little old lady watering her lawn and I would tell Bob that she really was a dope dealer and using the watering of her lawn as a front. On one occasion, we saw two young males walking towards us. Bob said jokingly that those males were holding drugs and then we both laughed. But as they got closer, I could see a reflection coming from one of the hands of one of the suspects. I told Bob, I think you are right and I mentioned the reflection. One of the means that suspects used to carry drugs was to wrap them in tin foil. Bob pulled the car in front of them and they both took off running. I chased one suspect and Bob the other. The one I was chasing threw the tin foil packet in the air. I caught it and continued after the suspect. I caught him in the middle of an intersection. He became combative. I immediately took him down to the ground and gave him a knee drop to the stomach to restrain him. He defecated (pooped) in his pants. Bob lost his suspect. When we examined the tin foil packet, it contained amphetamines and barbiturates. The suspect was placed under arrest.

The suspect had to be cleaned up before placing him in our vehicle. Bob told me that I had to clean him up. My reaction to Bob was, I caught him, you clean him. Then we both laughed at the situation. We both took him to the restroom of the service station located on the corner. While cleaning up the suspect, we found more drugs in his shorts. This suspect was over eighteen years old. He was booked for possession of drugs. A side note to this story: Bob gave many speeches at many of the Christian events that he would go to. He would always tell this story about his experience working Juvenile Narcotics. He would refer to me as "Big Mike." For a laugh, he would make a comment about hearing the statement about "kicking the shit" out of someone, but this was the first time that he knew the statement to be true.

My partner and I were making many arrests on both juveniles and adults who furnished drugs or narcotics to juveniles.

In June 1992, Bob, retired from the Police Department with the rank of Assistant Chief of Police.

The Sergeant's Examination was coming up and I wanted to promote. I knew I would have to study a lot.

Top right corner; Chief of Police Parker presenting me
a plaque for graduating number 1 in the class.

MIKE G. MARKULIS
Honor Police Guard

Markulis Gets Police Award

Mike G. Markulis of San Pedro has been presented with the Los Angeles Police Revolver and Athletic Club achievement award as the top graduate of the city Police Academy's recent graduating class.

Markulis, 25, a graduate of San Pedro High School, has been assigned as a police officer at the main jail in Los Angeles City Hall.

He is the son of Mr. and Mrs. George Markulis of 671 Oliver St. Markulis and his wife, Alice, live at 639 W. O'Farrel St.

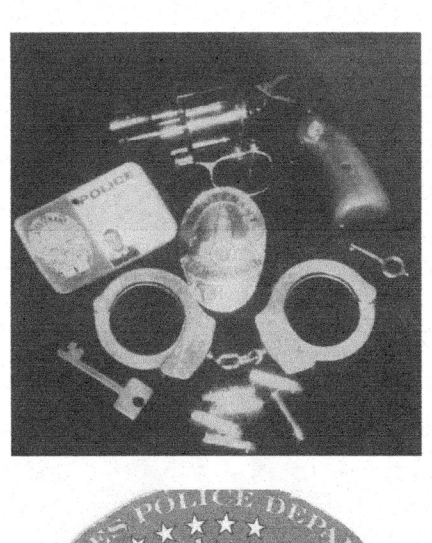

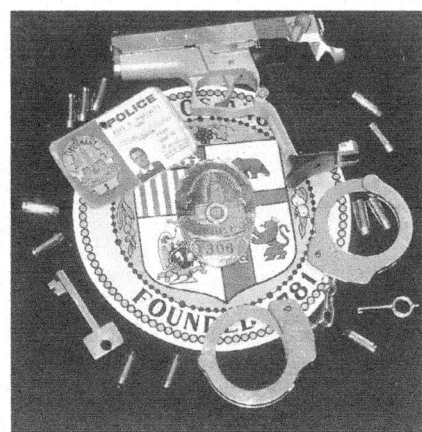

The LAPD Class of 2-1-56 celebrated their 62nd Class Reunion at the Glendale Elks Lodge on Sunday, June 24, 2018.

Standing left to right:
Ed Meckle #7612, Dick Matheny #7611, Ernie Glover #7604, Frank Clatanoff #7595, Mort Shea #7620, Mike Markulas #7610

CHAPTER 10:

GRADUATING FROM THE UNIVERSITY OF CALIFORNIA, LONG BEACH

In 1962 I had graduated and received my Bachelor of Science degree in Police Science and Administration from University of California, Long Beach, and knew that this would be a big plus on the oral interview. But I also knew that I would have to pass the written part of the exam to get the interview. It seemed as if everything was going in my favor of my career.

That was a proud moment, as it took me nine years to complete my education from when I first started college. I had to go to college part-time, taking fewer units because of my work schedule. I was determined to do this and again with Alicia's help we did it. At the graduation, my Alicia, our daughter Elaine, my mother, father attended. We took pictures and then went out and had a late lunch.

I studied many hard hours and took the Sergeant's Examination, which was my first time taking this exam. I got a high enough written score to qualify for the oral interview. I passed the oral and was placed high enough on the Sergeant's list to make Sergeant.

LAPD Sergeant Oral Interview

While preparing for the oral, I talked to several Sergeants for advice on what I might expect. Sergeant Deleon probably gave me the best advice. He told me that if I was asked any questions about the Police Science Program at

Long Beach State to choose my words carefully. One of the inspectors was an instructor at one of the universities and personally knew the Chairman of the Police Science and Administration program at Long Beach State. I immediately knew what he was referring to and it had to do with his affiliation with the ACLU (American Civil Liberties Union).

My interview was interesting, as the Board consisted of three inspectors. Well, when I was asked about Long Beach State College's Police Science program, I immediately knew what they were looking for. My answer was very positive towards the program and the professors and instructors. I did mention that one of the professors was a member of the ACLU and that it was obvious during his lectures he had a strong leaning in that direction. I also mentioned if a student was not aware of that fact, he or she could easily be swayed to that type of philosophy. Needless to say, I received a very high grade for my oral presentation and got placed high enough on the Sergeant's List to get promoted in 1962.

I happened to bump into one of the Juvenile Officers at Georgia Street Juvenile and knew that he had also gotten a Sergeant's Oral. I asked him if he had taken his oral yet and he stated that he did. I then asked him if they asked him any questions regarding Long Beach State's Police Science Program. He told me that he spoke very highly of the one professor who was a member of the ACLU. I told him what had happened to me and how I answered that question. Well, I received a higher score on my Oral than he did. I was promoted to Sergeant on that list and he had to wait several years to take the next Sergeant's Test.

This officer was one of the sharpest officers on our department. Long story short, every exam after that one, he always placed on the very top of every promotional list. He retired from the Department as an Assistant Chief of Police. He could have easily been the Chief of Police.

Alicia and all of my family were extremely proud of me for getting promoted to Sergeant. I was extremely proud of my accomplishments and myself thus far in my career.

When I got promoted to Sergeant, I was going to get transferred to a patrol division assignment. It so happened that my partner, Al Schlocker, was already a Sergeant and he decided to transfer to a patrol division to get the supervisory experience he would need to promote to Lieutenant. With Al doing that, a Sergeant's vacancy opened up in Juvenile Narcotics and I did not have to transfer out. I replaced Al's position and we got a new officer in the unit to fill my vacancy. I was teamed up with the new officer who transferred in. His name was Gilbert Dominguez. A great guy and an outstanding officer. We worked well together as a team.

Hired at East Los Angeles College
Part Time Instructor

My friend Rudy Deleon who was a Sergeant in Juvenile asked me if I would like an opportunity to teach in the Community College system. I told him that I would like the opportunity. Rudy (Sgt. Deleon) was already doing a lot of teaching. He told me that East Los Angeles College was looking for an instructor to teach "California Juvenile Procedures." He gave me the contact person and I made a phone call and talked to him. He was the Chairman of the Social Science Department. I was asked to come to his office at East Los Angeles College for an interview.

I made the appointment and went for the interview. The Chairman liked my police and education background. He said I was hired and was to begin teaching Juvenile Procedures out of Parker Center, which was an extension of East Los Angeles College. Teaching Out Parker Center, which is LAPD's administration building, meant that most if not all the students would be police officers working toward their degrees.

Working Off Duty Shop Lifting Details

Alicia and I were very happy about our circumstances, as everything was going better than we expected. I got a promotion and now teaching meant extra money coming in to help with our finances. Even before getting the promotion, I was taking in some side jobs to earn extra money. I worked part-time at DiCarlo's Bakery for a short time on my days off. I also worked shoplifting details at markets and department stores to earn extra money to help out at home. The pay working shoplifting was about five dollars an hour. Not a lot of money in those days (early 1960s). But it helped. Working shoplifting could be very dangerous at times, as a person getting caught shoplifting in many cases would become combative and would have to be restrained.

Here is one example of one of many shoplifting arrests. I was working at a Thrifty Drug Store in Wilmington, California. This store had a big shoplifting problem. One evening I observed this male suspect walk through the rear door of the store and started looking the place over. He walked straight through and out the front door of the store. I positioned myself by the magazine rack where I could watch him if he came back in. My immediate gut feeling was that he was casing the store to rob it. He did come back in via the rear door. He walked over to where I was and looked at me and asked me if I worked at the store. I told him no, that I was looking to buy a magazine.

He then walked over to the liquor counter and took a fifth of whiskey bottle and placed it inside his jacket. He then walked out the rear door of the store. As soon as he stepped out, I went after him and identified myself as a police officer and that he was under arrest for shoplifting. He immediately started running across the parking lot into the next street with me chasing him. Each time I got close he would swing the bottle of whiskey at me barely missing me several times. On one of his attempts to hit me, I struck him on his nose with my fist and knocked him to the ground. I gave him a knee drop to the stomach area, turned him over on his stomach and was in the process of putting my handcuffs on him. Somehow my handcuffs were double-locked. I had to get my handcuff key to unlock them in order to put them on him. As I was in the process of doing this, a young male adult ran up to me, and yelled at me to let his friend go or he would kill me. I took my two-inch revolver out of my holster and told the suspect that I was a police officer and that he as well as the suspect I had on the ground were under arrest. If he made any attempt to take my prisoner away from me, I would kill him. He didn't move. I was in a crazy predicament, at that moment.

A car full of gang members happened to drive by and asked what was going on. I told them that I was a police officer and these two men were under arrest and that I needed a hand. They got out of their car and asked me what they could do to help. I asked them to watch the one suspect while I handcuffed the other. They all circled the other suspect while I unlocked my handcuffs and placed them on the suspect. I thanked the gang members for their help and took both suspects back to the store.

When I hit the suspect with my fist, I broke his nose and he was bleeding. When I walked them back into the store, the manager looked at us and wanted to know what happened. I explained to him the circumstances and he was raving that I had injured the suspect and that the store was now going to get sued. I told him that he had a major shoplifting problem and that he needed two officers each shift to work this detail. He told me that the store could not afford to pay for two officers. I then responded that I would no longer be working the store's shoplifting detail.

I called the Harbor Division desk and they dispatched a patrol car that arrived and took the suspects into custody. The suspect who attempted to free his friend was a deserter from the Army and the Army Military Police took him into custody. The suspect who stole the bottle of whiskey was booked for felony burglary, as he entered the store with the intent to commit a theft.

That was the very last time I worked any shoplifting details. It was just not worth it, as some situations could become very dangerous and then there was a chance the police department would not cover you if you were injured working those details. It was a good experience, but I no longer needed that kind of work. My teaching position was safer, a challenge, and a lot more fun for me.

Alicia was grateful that I was not going to work those types of details any longer.

I was eager to start my teaching at East Los Angeles College. I took a Juvenile Procedure Class from Rudy Deleon that he had taught at Long Beach State. I always took good notes and I thought I would use the notes from his class to get started on my class. I remembered that I had loaned them to a Captain who was going to teach the class at another college. Rudy Deleon told this Captain to ask me for my notes, as he knew that I took excellent notes.

When I approached this Captain to give my notes back to me, he denied ever borrowing them. I was upset, as now I had to develop the class from scratch. I had taken courses on teacher training and part of the course was on how to develop a course. This was okay, as I had a good concept about how to develop the class and which textbook I would use. I put many long hours in developing this class with a lot of handout material.

Again, Alicia came to my rescue and typed up everything in duplicate for me. Remember, in the 1960s, there were no computers. Alicia used carbon paper to make the duplicate copies. I think Alicia worked harder than I did to help make this class a success. She typed up not only my course outline but also all my handout material and examinations. That was a lot of work. As usual she made me shine here too. The pay for teachers at this time was ten dollars an hour, which was fairly good wages during those years. Alicia and I earned every penny.

I taught two, three hours classes a week. One was during the day and one in the evening from 7:00 p.m. to 10:00 p.m. I enjoyed teaching. I was very nervous at the beginning, but after a few classes I settled down and it actually came natural to me. In those first classes, my students were only police officers. I would average at least thirty students per class. I received many compliments on my classes. Many of those early students were promoted in the department, including several who promoted to the rank of Captain and Commander, and upon retirement, some went on to become Chiefs of Police in other police departments. I was told on many occasions that I was the best instructor they ever had and thanked me for all the effort that I put into my classes. Nice compliments.

Since I started on my teaching career, I will sum this up and get back to the rest of the story. Teaching played a big role in my life, as I was a part-time instructor for thirty years in the Los Angeles Community College District retiring with a small pension. I taught at Los Angeles Harbor College for twenty-seven years and three years at East Los Angeles College. I ended up developing and teaching classes in Criminal Law, Criminal Procedures, Patrol Tactics, Traffic Control, Juvenile Law and Procedures as well some Police Administration courses.

Teaching was also a big asset to me on the police department, as I was selected to enhance the department's training programs.

Wrote Training Material on LSD (Lysergic Acid Diethylamide)

While working Juvenile Narcotics, I researched and wrote an article on LSD. This happened to be the very first article published on LSD by any law enforcement officer. The Captain of Juvenile Division asked me if the department could use the article for training purposes. Not only did our department use it but the article was also published in several noted police magazines throughout the country. Many were recognizing my narcotic background and expertise.

After the material was developed, the question came up as to who would teach and provide this material to the teachers and administrators.

Teachers Awareness Program for Drug Abuse on Campus

The Los Angeles Unified School District asked our Chief of Police if they would allow me to develop an education program to be presented to all the teachers in the district.

This turned out to be a carefully developed class. It became known as the "TEACHERS AWARENESS PROGRAM FOR DRUG ABUSE ON CAMPUS." I worked many long hours developing this class. After very close scrutiny by both our department and the LAUSD, the class was approved. I developed a whole series of color slides to be used with the material. It

encouraged me, as I was the one who developed the material and I was an experienced college instructor.

This was an interesting phase of my narcotic career. I did present this class to all senior and junior high school teachers and administrators in the LAUSD. Classes of several hundred teachers was set up and made mandatory for them to attend. The classes went very well. There were teachers present who believed that marijuana was okay, as it was as not as bad as alcohol. I could tell by many of the questions that many of the teachers were users.

My response to them was that they were not to voice their personal opinion as to the harmless effect of marijuana or any other drug to their students. It was obvious that there were some teachers that this class had no effect on. Is it a wonder that today in 2021, we have not only medical marijuana but also states that have passed the recreational use of marijuana?

While I was developing and presenting this class, I was also carrying a full caseload. It was a lot of work, but I enjoyed doing it.

New Station Wagon and Camping

There were several detectives working Juvenile Narcotics that were camping buffs. Sergeant Eugene Zappey would talk about Bass Lake, California. He would go there as often as he could. We had bought a new 1963 Impala station wagon and got a good deal. One of the detectives had an in, at the Hollywood Chevrolet dealership and he told me about this station wagon that they were going to sell and that it had been used in making commercials. He took me over to the dealership and I fell in love with this car. I told Alicia about it and she knew that we needed a bigger car and the asking price was what we could afford. So we bought it. A beautiful blue station wagon fully equipped.

Before the station wagon, we had my 1949 Oldsmobile that my brother Chuck wrecked in an accident when he borrowed it one day. The next car was a Renault Dauphine, which was a small, compact car. It was a good car, but it couldn't handle the stress of freeway driving. We had taken some trips in it. It was big enough for the four of us. I even fixed it up so that Elaine and Mark could lay down and sleep on the back seat. What I liked about the Dauphine was that it was small enough that if Mark was misbehaving I could reach him and scold him or give him a smack on his bottom. When we got the station wagon, I could not do that anymore. Mark would go way in the back of the station wagon where, of course, I could not reach him. Mark and I laugh about that when we think about it or talk about it.

Alicia and I also talked about buying a small camping trailer that we could tow behind the station wagon. We kept looking in the newspaper and saw one being advertised in Lomita, which was close to where we lived. Alicia and I went over to look at it. It was a fifteen-and-a-half-foot trailer. It could be hooked up to electricity and water, had an ice box, a butane gas stove, and could sleep four very comfortably. Perfect for us. It did not have a shower or toilet, but we understood that all camp grounds have those facilities. The trailer was being sold at a very reasonable price and the sellers took a liking to us and sold it to us for $200 less than what they were asking for it.

I put a trailer hitch on the station wagon and towed the trailer home. I had a perfect spot for it in the backyard, as I built the fence so that it angled, and put a big gate on the fence so that I could drive my car back there if I needed to. It was perfect for the trailer.

Mark and Elaine were two excited kids. They loved the station wagon and the trailer. In fact, we were all excited and couldn't wait to make our first camping trip in it. Sergeant Zappey talked so much about Bass Lake that we thought we would make that our first trip. Bass Lake was not that far away, located just north of Fresno, California. If I were to guess I would say about 300 miles away from San Pedro.

I had never pulled a trailer before so it was going to be an experience for me. My two-week vacation was coming up, but I also had accumulated many hours of overtime so I could take four weeks off.

We loaded the trailer with everything we would need and took off for Bass Lake. After pulling the trailer for about an hour, the motor started heating up. I would have to stop on the way many times and pour water on the radiator to cool it down. Having to stop so many times to do this ordeal, we did not get to Bass Lake until dark. Elaine and Mark had fallen asleep in the station wagon.

After we got a nice spot, I will never forget the excitement of Elaine and Mark when we woke them up to go into the trailer. The night was pitch black and when they got out of the car and looked up in the sky they saw the tall pine trees with millions of bright stars. They both got very excited and couldn't get over the beauty of the night's sky. They both were in awe and just wanted to stay outside for a while to enjoy this majestic night.

Bass Lake was a beautiful lake and with many camp grounds. This became a favorite place for our camping trips. The station wagon had a 327-cubic inch engine and it could not handle the towing of the trailer. After I cracked the engine block, I had to replace it with a 350-cubic inch block which was a larger motor. I also had a five-bladed fan installed, a transmission cooler, and a more accurate thermostat. No more problems pulling our trailer.

I have to mention this little fact also. A friend of mine gave me a five-gallon tubular water tank with a little electric water pump attached to it. He showed me how to install it in the storage space in the car and run a one-half inch rubber hose from the water tank to the front of the radiator. I placed a small spray nozzle on the end of it. I also placed a toggle switch under the dash, which hooked up to one of the positive wires to make an electrical connection.

When pulling the trailer if I noticed that the radiator would start getting hot, I would touch the toggle switch and water would spray over the radiator and immediately cool it down. That was a clever innovative idea and it worked. Pulling the trailer over the Grape Vine, which was a steep grade of highway-5 in California, you would see many cars pulled over to the side of the road to let their motors cool down before taking off again. I no longer had to do that, as I would only have to turn the toggle switch on and the radiator would not get hot.

One more comment about this issue and then I will leave it. On one hot summer day, the family and I were driving on highway 99 in California. I pulled in a gas station to fill the tank up with gas. The station attendant saw me filling up my five-gallon water tank in the storage area of the wagon. He asked me what was I doing. I proceeded to tell him that I was filling up my water tank. I also told him it was a new invention and that the water mixed with gas and doubled my millage on the tank of gas. He believed me. I had to tell him the truth. He laughed and told me that he did believe me and thanked me for telling him the truth. We had spent many wonderful vacations with this station wagon and camping trailer.

Many years later, I sold the trailer to my brother Nick for a dollar. He took it down to Mexico and put it on one of his friend's property, so that when he went there, he would have a place to stay.

I drove the station wagon for many years. I stored it in my garage and finally sold it in 2015. I was the original owner and kept it for fifty-two years. I hated to part with it, but I needed the space in the garage.

Watts Riots

While I was working Juvenile Narcotics, the Watts Riots erupted after a California Highway Patrolman stopped a traffic violator to cite him. This was in August of 1965. I happened to be on vacation and in the process of painting the outside of my home. I was contacted and told to stay close to home in case they needed me. I was called back and told that the California National Guard was activated. I was called back to work, but the major part of the riots was toned down. I got to work what they called the Minnie Riots. The south end of Los Angeles was engulfed in flames. Many people lost their lives. It would take many years to rebuild this part of the city.

I was in the Narcotic Unit now for a little over five years and I wanted to try to promote and make Lieutenant. I was going to have to do a lot of studying, as these promotional exams were pretty tough. I was even thinking of putting in for a transfer to a Patrol Division to get the supervisory experience that was so vital in promoting.

It was during this time that the Captain of Administrative Narcotic Division contacted me and told me that he wanted to talk to me. I went to his office located on the third floor of Parker Center and met with him. He wanted me to transfer to his division, as he was establishing a new unit, which he called the Public Appearance and Training Unit and wanted me to be in charge of it. He explained what he had in mind and that I would handle all the speeches and public appearances for the department and do all the narcotic training at the Police Academy.

He told me that he was losing too many man-hours having his case-carrying detectives do this and handle their caseloads. That would be my only responsibility. I would be the only person in the unit. I envisioned a very heavy workload if I took that assignment. I turned down the offer and explained to him that I wanted to promote and what he described to me would take up all of my spare time. He asked me to at least think about it. I told him that I would and left.

About two weeks later, this Captain called me and told me that he wanted to meet with me again. We discussed the new unit and said that he has reviewed all the officers working Narcotic Division and Juvenile Narcotics. He said he could not find anyone who possessed all the attributes that I had for this unit. He talked about my narcotic expertise, working Juvenile Narcotics, plus my writing ability, my lecturing, and teaching background. He felt that I was perfect for this new unit and that the department would benefit from me doing this. He also added that the developing of this unit would be a big plus for making Lieutenant and that if I took the assignment, he would see that I got a high enough interview grade to make Lieutenant. After a lengthy meeting and discussion, I accepted the assignment.

CHAPTER 11:

TRANSFER TO ADMINISTRATIVE NARCOTIC DIVISION

Official Narcotic Expert For LAPD

This was going to be a big challenge and a great responsibility. I was to represent the LAPD on any public appearances that had to do with narcotics. I would be making all speeches to civic organizations, schools, local, state, and federal organizations when they requested a narcotic expert from LAPD. I was responsible for all narcotic training at the Police Academy. This included all recruit classes, in service training and advance officer training for our department.

I was responsible for writing all position papers regarding anything to do with drugs or narcotics for LAPD. I was responsible only to the Captain and had no other immediate supervisor to report to. I would be required to maintain an ongoing record of all my activities, overtime hours, and expenses.

I was to review, change, write, and upgrade all materials the department had on narcotics. This included the Narcotic Display Boards kept in each division. All the display boards were antiquated and required upgrades.

Needless to say, my work was cut out for me. When I explained this new position and the work involved to Alicia, she supported me and told me that she would help me with anything that I asked of her. My wife was beautiful and understanding of everything that I was assigned to do for the department. I explained that I had no set hours, as I would have to go wherever there was a need to do the work that was required of me.

I have to emphasize that this was in the 1960s and narcotics were flourishing in our city and the country. The hippy movement was growing throughout the United States. There were advocates trying to decriminalize and make certain narcotics legal. As an example, possession of any amount of marijuana carried a penalty of at least year in prison. It was an irreducible felony. Anyone arrested with a small amount of marijuana and if convicted had to do one year in prison.

In my speeches, I would emphasize that when the laws were enacted, marijuana was the choice drug for anyone living in the ghettos or barrios. Back then, that was an okay penalty. However, when marijuana began to get popular in middle-class White America, the penalties all of a sudden were too harsh. I know of several Congressmen and legislators whose sons were arrested for possession of marijuana. Now, the penalties were too extreme and too harsh. We began to see a movement to reduce the penalties or to legalize marijuana.

One of the first position papers I wrote for the department was on this very subject. The position we took at this time (late-1960s) was that if "we decriminalize marijuana today we would never be able to harvest what we sow twenty-five years later." I look at this statement now (2021) and I see how rampant marijuana is in our society today. Our voters and lawmakers have not only approved medical marijuana use but many states have also voted to adopt recreational marijuana use. My personal opinion, as a narcotic expert of that era, is that this is a grave mistake and by legalizing this drug, our country will continue to see the moral fiber of our nation deteriorate.

The number of DUI drivers today is astronomical. We add to this those people driving under the influence of marijuana and it becomes mind-boggling. One of the lighted freeway signs now displays; "BUZZED DRIVING IS DRUNK DRIVING."

I did not realize how important the new assignment was until I really got wrapped up in it. I represented the department hundreds of times. Making speeches to our civic leaders, PTAs (Parent Teachers Associations), doctors' groups, and other meetings such as being invited as a panelist where drugs and narcotics were the topic of discussion.

I can remember once when I was the speaker before a medical doctor's conference and I was challenged by one of the doctors regarding something I had mentioned. Several other doctors in attendance stood up and told the challenging doctor to sit down and listen to what the Sergeant had to say. That he may learn something relating to the clandestine types of drugs that were being manufactured and abused. I was highly complimented by the group for my expertise and knowledge on the subject.

Federal Food and Drug Administration Conference, Las Vegas, Nevada

There were several other occasions where I represented the department worth mentioning here. The first being when the Chief of Police selected me to represent the LAPD at a Narcotic and Drug Conference being hosted by the Federal Food and Drug Administration and the *Las Vegas Sun* newspaper to be held at the Las Vegas Convention Center in April 1968. The Convention Center was filled to capacity with 18,000 people, mostly students from the surrounding areas of Las Vegas. The speakers were selected from universities, colleges, and other entities.

My time slot was for the afternoon. The first speaker was introduced and began his prepared remarks. He could not keep the audience's attention span focused on what he was talking about. He lost control of the crowd. The second speaker was introduced and the same thing happened to him. The noise factor was loud and getting louder, as people were talking and not paying any attention to what was being said. The convention was being deemed a disaster.

A Mr. Jack Wise, from the University of Las Vegas, approached me and asked me if I would go out of turn and be the next speaker. He thought maybe I would be able to control the audience. I told him I would try. I was then introduced as Sergeant Mike Markulis from the Los Angeles Police Department, Narcotic Division. I began my presentation, and as I was speaking, the noise factor started quieting down. I was getting their attention. After a few moments, you could not hear a pin drop. I was the nervous one now, and it was almost frightening that with 18,000 people in this Convention Center I was getting through to them. I spoke for a little over an hour. I thanked them for their attention and that I would be speaking again after the lunch break. I had developed a series of colored slides, which I was going to project on a 100-foot screen and discuss each narcotic and drug as it was being projected. After lunch, I again began my talk showing the slides. This was a big success, as I got a standing ovation when I finished.

The next day the *Las Vegas Sun* newspaper read, "LAPD SERGEANT SAVES NARCOTIC, DRUG CONFERENCE FROM BEING A DISASTER." The officials from the FDA thanked me. The *Las Vegas Sun* paid for all my expenses at the hotel even though the LAPD was paying the tab. The following day I was asked to appear on a TV drug panel at the University of Nevada. This had to be the highlight for me on this assignment. The Chief of Police received several letters from organizers of the conference and the *Las Vegas Sun*, commending me for "saving the Narcotic and Drug Symposium from being a disaster." I received the letters and will include them as an addendum in this book.

State of `Montana Attorney General's Conference

I will mention one other highlight of this assignment before I leave it. Also, in 1968, I was invited to go to Helena, Montana, and be a guest speaker for their Attorney General's Conference. I was to speak on the marijuana problem. It seemed that many hippies were moving to Montana around Missoula and that law enforcement was experiencing a big narcotic problem.

I knew I really had to do my homework for this presentation. I spent many hours researching and writing a comprehensive paper on this subject. The presentation was made before most of the law enforcement officials in the state of Montana. The speech went over very well and I was asked if I could leave my material with them so they could reproduce it and use it in their training.

I was treated like royalty during my stay in Helena. The Assistant Attorney General took me under his wing and gave me a tour of the state's Capitol and the surrounding area. Montana is truly a beautiful state.

While I worked this unit, the Lieutenants' Promotional Exam was given. I studied very little for this exam, as my assignment did not allow me the time I needed. My hours would be from early morning to late evenings most of the time. On many occasions, I would have to make three presentations a day. Breakfast meetings, lunch meetings, and dinner meetings. I also had to do all the narcotic training at the Police Academy. Well, all of this work prevented me from applying diligent study time for the exam.

I barely passed the written portion of the exam and now I had the interview scheduled. I went to see the Captain, who had asked me to do him a favor and to develop and work this special unit. He had been promoted to Inspector of Police and no longer had anything to do with the Narcotic Division. I asked him for some advice on taking the oral exam. He asked me what kind of score I would need to make Lieutenant. I told him at least a grade of 96. He laughed and stated, "I am not even worth a 96." He gave me a few pointers to remember. I thanked him and left his office feeling a little depressed. My interview date arrived and I prepared myself the best I could. I took my oral with two Inspectors of Police and one civilian sitting on the Board. It was an outstanding oral and I got a very good score of 93.33. It was not good enough due to my low written score. The list expired when I was sixteen away from making Lieutenant. If I could have gotten a 96, I would have made it. It just wasn't meant to be.

I felt that I had let Alicia down, as she knew how much I wanted this promotion. She stood by me and told me that there would be another opportunity in the near future and that I would make it if I really wanted it. She helped me through everything that I was doing or attempting to do. I was still teaching and she continued to type my course outlines, handout material, and examinations.

Cal State University of Long Beach Graduation 1962

Proud mom and dad at College Graduation 1962

My beautiful wife Alicia and me at College Graduation

Alicia and Elaine at College Graduation

Family Group picture at College Graduation

12,000 Jam Center For Biggest Event In Vegas' History

A powerhouse crowd of enthusiastic Las Vegans, adults, teenagers and subteens alike packed the Convention Center yesterday for an unprecedented seminar on drug abuse sponsored by the Las Vegas SUN and the U.S. Food and Drug Administration.

Overflowing the huge Convention Center rotunda and its several meeting rooms to standing room only capacity, an unexpected 12,000 youths and adults heard narcotics discussed in frank terms and responded with burning questions and dialogue sparked by keen interest and curiosity about one of the nation's most pressing social phenomena.

The rotunda normally seats 8,000 persons. Yesterday's seminar drew the largest crowd by far in the Convention Center's eight-year history.

Deputy sheriffs were forced to close the mammoth meeting hall's doors shortly after the 9:30 a.m. session started and turned away an estimated 6,000 persons from participating in the narcotics talk, the first ever held here, with guest speakers from as far away as Washington, D.C. and Boston.

Wide-eyed at the unexpected but gratifying turnout, lecturers from the U.S. Food and Drug Administration, police.

(See THOUSANDS, Page 4)

MISSILE PUTS ON COLORFUL SHOW OVER LV

A routine launch of a Minuteman I intercontinental ballistic missile from its underground silo at the Vandenberg Air Force Base, Calif. provided a "Fourth of July-like" show last night for residents of Southern Nevada as well as other parts of the western U.S.A.

The missile, launched about sunset, caused a spectacular fireworks show.

(See MISSILE, Page 4)

Sgt. Mike Markulis of the Los Angeles Police Department proved to be our anchor man because he moved in out of turn and did a tremendous job of getting and holding the attention of the younger people. He didn't try to do anything but tell it like it is. And the kids appreciated it.

FULL HOUSE — Elaine Roentgen, Federal Drug Administration consumer (at lectern), addresses more than 17,000 students packed into Convention Center for a SUN sponsored seminar yesterday. Other speakers on stage, are, from left, Dr. Ralph W. Weilerstein, Dr. Helen Nowlis and Theodore Cron, assistant FDA commissioner.
(SUNfoto)

"In Vegas — It's The Sun"

Las Vegas SUN

SOUTHERN NEVADA'S ONLY HOME-OWNED DAILY NEWSPAPER

H. M. "HANK" GREENSPUN, Publisher

P. O. Box 4275
LAS VEGAS, NEVADA 89106

900 SOUTH COMMERCE ● TELEPHONE 385-3111
121 SOUTH HIGHLAND ● TELEPHONE 382-2527

45

April 29, 1968

Mr. Thomas Reddin
Chief of Police
Los Angeles Police Department
150 N. Los Angeles Street
Los Angeles, Calif. 90012

RECEIVED
MAY 1 1968
CHIEF'S OFFICE

Dear Chief Reddin:

I must share with you the good feelings all of us in Las
Vegas experienced this past Tuesday when we were exposed to the
intelligence, knowledge, understanding and articulatness of a
police officer in your department.

Sgt. Mike Markulis was brought here as an expert on drug
use and abuse, along with others from around the country to
participate in the Las Vegas SUN drug seminar in conjunction
with the Food and Drug Administration. It was estimated that
it would draw from 500 to 1,000 people so when 20,000 adults
and teenagers attempted to crowd into the Convention Center
which could hold a maximum of 8,500 people, an exceedingly tense
situation developed.

It was difficult to contain order and the preliminary speaker
did little in holding the attention of the youngsters in the group.
Sgt. Markulis was slated for the afternoon session and he offered
to go out of turn after the first speaker appeared to be going
over the heads of the audience.

We were grateful for his kindness, especially after he
not only controlled the immense crowd but did an almost fantastic
job of keeping their interest with a remarkable ability and facility in communicating with young people.

Both kids and adults hung on every word and appreciated his
sincerity and genuiness in telling it exactly as it is without
lecturing or admonishing.

I cannot commend this officer too highly for he is an
invaluable asset to law enforcement and brings much credit to
the Los Angeles Police department.

MEMBER   AMERICAN NEWSPAPER PUBLISHERS ASSOCIATION   ●   AUDIT BUREAU OF CIRCULATIONS
UNITED PRESS INTERNATIONAL ● NEVADA STATE PRESS ASSOCIATION ● CALIFORNIA NEWSPAPER PUBLISHERS ASSOCIATION

CHAPTER 12:

TRANSFER TO TRAINING DIVISION

My work in Narcotic Division was noted by others on the department. The Captain of the Training Division, Police Academy, liked the work I had done in writing the lesson plans and handout material used in the different narcotic classes. He called me and wanted to talk to me. I went to the Academy and listened to what he had to offer. He wanted me to take over the General Instruction Unit of the Training Division. He was concerned that the recruit courses were outdated and needed to be updated. He also mentioned that working the Training Division would also be an asset to me in getting promoted. I told him that I would take the assignment.

When I got home, I explained to Alicia what I had done. I told her my hours would be 7:30 a.m. to 4:30 p.m. with very little work in the evenings. And, of course, I had weekends and holidays off. She was excited and felt that again we would be able to enjoy ourselves and our family much more.

Alicia was a perfect mother. She loved her family beyond measure. I loved her work ethic as a wife and as a mother. Her family, especially her children, was her world. I vividly remember and the kids do too, that when it rained, she would always bake cookies. Our favorites were peanut butter and oatmeal. Elaine and Mark could not wait to get home from school on a rainy day, as they knew their mom would have baked cookies for them. These thoughts bring tears to my eyes thinking of all the wonderful things she did for us. I miss her terribly even as I write this.

Officer-in-Charge of General Instruction Unit

As the Officer-in-Charge (OIC) of the General Instruction (GI) Unit, I had a total of ten officers, including myself, working this unit. We had the responsibility for teaching all the police courses except the specialized courses like Criminal Law and Report Writing. These specialties were under two other units.

The officers assigned to the unit held the rank of Sergeant and several officers were of the Police Officer rank. While assigned to the Training Division, the department implemented a new rank structure. It was referred to as the Jacobs Plan.

The rank structure changed, which included many sub-ranks with a pay differential within the ranks. We now had Police Officers 1, 2, and 3, Sergeants 1 and 2, Lieutenants 1 and 2, Captains 1, 2, and 3, Commander, then Deputy Chiefs, Assistant Chiefs, and the Chief of Police. The point I am trying to make is that I held the rank of Sergeant as the Officer-in-Charge of the GI Unit. Jacobs changed the OIC's position from Sergeant to Sergeant 2. That meant a pay raise of 5.5 per cent. Of course, that made me very happy as it did Alicia.

I asked all the officers assigned to the unit to review their lesson plans and submit them to me. I immediately noticed that many of the lesson plans were out of date and had to be updated. I worked with each officer and brought all their lesson plans up to current status. It was a lot of work, but the classes were now current to correspond with the laws and tactics. The Captain appreciated my effort and commended the unit for work well done.

To give an example as to why the upgrading of the lesson plans and handouts were so important is this. I received a phone call from one of our Administrative Commanders and he asked me if we taught our recruits anything about diabetic comas in our Drunk and Traffic Classes. I told him we did and he asked me to send him the lesson plans for those classes. He told me that the department was getting sued as a result of the arrest and booking of an individual for being drunk but he actually was incoherent because of the lack of insulin. These lesson plans were all updated and we made sure the subject of diabetes was included. I believe we all got the message to make sure our lesson plans were constantly updated and kept current.

My experience teaching part-time at the community college level was a great asset to me working this assignment.

I worked this unit for two years and I did have the time and opportunity to study for the next Lieutenant's Examination. I took the written examination and got a decent score. My background in the department impressed the Oral Board, and my overall score placed me high enough on the list to promote to Lieutenant.

Alicia, Elaine, and Mark were as excited as I was knowing that I was going to be promoted. Working the Academy, Mark asked me if he and his cousin Bobby could go with me one day and spend the day watching the training of new recruits. Mark was eleven years old at the time. I told him yes, as long as they did not get in the way of the training and behaved themselves. I took them and they got to view police training. They thoroughly enjoyed it and they had a good time. Mark has brought up that experience on numerous occasions when talking to his friends about police work. Although Mark never followed his dad's footsteps in becoming a police officer, he did take the exam for the Fire Department. He would have been accepted except for his eyesight, which kept him from becoming a police officer or a fireman. Mark ultimately chose to work for Puritan Bakery and has done very well for himself. Mark is the Sales Manager for Puritan Bakery located in the City of Carson. Alicia and I have always been extremely proud of him and Elaine in their accomplishments. Elaine is a retired court clerk with the Superior Court in Los Angeles. She retired after 40 years with the court.

Well, I got a little off-track. You just don't know where I will be taking you next on this journey of mine.

Altercation and Stabbed in Front of My House

On this one evening, I was going over the material I would cover in my class at Harbor College. Elaine came over to me and told me that there was a fight in front of our house. I got up, walked over to the front door, and looked out. There was a fight going on. There was a Black male sitting on top of a Hispanic male and hitting him with his fists. For a moment, I thought the Hispanic male was my nephew who lived next door. I went out saw that the Hispanic's face was bloody. I told the Black male to let the other man up as he had enough or I was going to call the police. He responded by telling me, "IF YOU CALL THE POLICE I WILL COME BACK AND BLOW UP YOUR M*****_F****** HOUSE." I will refer to this person now as a suspect. I then reached down and pulled him off the man on the ground. We exchanged punches, and I knocked him out. He received a laceration above his right eye. We were in the street in front of my house. I dragged him up on the lawn and as he was coming to, I gave him a good knee drop to the stomach.

My wife, daughter, and son were standing on the front porch watching this situation. I told my wife to go into the house and call 911 and tell the operator that an LAPD officer needs assistance. Well, she told the operator that her husband is an LAPD officer and he needs help. Every unit in the Harbor Division rolled on the call.

Oh! My wife was standing on the porch and saw that I was bleeding from my left arm and she told me. That was the first time I noticed that I had been stabbed in this altercation. The suspect was booked for Assault with a Deadly Weapon (ADW). I was taken to the San Pedro Community Hospital and stitched up. I recovered the knife the suspect used to stab me with at the location. The Hispanic male, after I pulled the suspect off of him, ran up the street, turned, and yelled "Gracias, Gracias," and kept going. He was never identified.

Later, I called the detective who was handling my case at Harbor to find out if he had filed the case. He told me the District Attorney would not file a felony ADW, but he had referred it to the City Attorney to be filed as a "Misdemeanor Battery." He went on to tell me that if the injury had put me in the hospital, he would have filed it as an ADW Felony. The difference between a felony and a misdemeanor in this case was putting me in the hospital or at the risk of dying—that would have been a felony. If I had told the suspect I was a police officer, the crime would have been a felony.

The next day, working at the Academy, I received a phone call from one of our administrative inspectors asking me what had happened and how I was feeling. He got mad on the phone, as he had felt that the case should have been filed as a felony. He then called the detective who handled the case and said he was going to talk to the District Attorney as well.

The irony of this incident was a few days after the incident, the suspect showed up at my house. He rang the doorbell and my son Mark went to the door and saw that it was the suspect. Mark came running up to me and told me who was at the door. I went to the door and the suspect told me he did not know that I was a police officer and apologized for stabbing me. I told him to get off my property and that if I ever saw him anywhere on my street that I would kill him. He left, saying that he will never walk on my street again. I have never seen him since. He pled guilty to the misdemeanor as I did not have to go to court on this incident.

The Training Division was another outstanding assignment, but it also had to come to a close. I saw many police recruits go through the training and become outstanding police officers. Many of them promoting up through the ranks, many of them getting seriously injured or killed in the line of duty.

I had one recruit who was having a hard time qualifying on the pistol range and was afraid that he would not graduate. I asked him to meet ne at the Harbor Division pistol range on a Saturday and that I would work with him. I told him I would also have the Range Sergeant work with him to help him develop his shooting skills. He did well and improved a lot. Regrettably, he had other mental issues that subsequently came to light. Several weeks later he committed suicide. I can't remember if he used his firearm or another method to take his life. A very sad situation.

CHAPTER 13:

TRANSFER TO HOLLENBECK DIVISION

One day, when I was on vacation, I received a phone call from my good friend and newly appointed Captain, Rudy Deleon. He was being assigned to the Hollenbeck Division. He asked me to come and work with him and be his Adjutant. This had to be around 1971. He told me that the assignment would help me promote to Lieutenant. I thanked him for the offer and told him that I had not worked Patrol in over thirteen years and that I was already on the Lieutenant's List. I also told him that position required someone with a good Patrol background. His response to me was, "Mike, it has been many years since I had anything to do with Patrol and between the two of us, we will shape up Hollenbeck Division." I told Captain Deleon that I was on vacation and for him to seriously look for someone else. He advised me to call him my first day back to work.

My first day back to work, my first phone call was Captain Deleon. He told me that he seriously considered me and for me to go to his office so that we may talk. I did, and the next thing I knew I was telling Captain Deleon I would take the assignment. It was an honor to be thought of so highly and to be offered an assignment as important as this. Captain Deleon was assigned a take-home car, as he was always on call. He lived in Lomita so I would drive my car to his house and ride to work with him.

Alicia was again very happy with this assignment, as I would work Monday through Friday, very little night work, if any at all, and I had weekends off.

I was on the next transfer list being assigned to the Hollenbeck Division. This was also a Sergeant 2 position, so I kept my stripes and pay schedule. The staff at the Training Division, including the officers working my unit, was happy for me and gave me a little sendoff party. The art staff at the Academy drew a caricature of the GI Unit staff and myself and presented it to me. It was a nice piece of art work and hangs in my hallway at home today.

The Hollenbeck Division is located in the East Los Angeles section of Los Angeles. This division also had a high crime rate and gang problem. Some of the oldest gangs in the city are located here.

Captain Deleon was an intelligent, hardworking captain. He worked very close with all his officers and the community. Community leaders would call him constantly, commending him on the excellent job he was doing.

Hollenbeck Youth Center

The city built a new Hollenbeck Police Station that we moved into. Captain Deleon got permission from the city to create a boys and girls youth center out of the old Hollenbeck Police Station. This was a well thought-out accomplishment. It was well received by the department and the community. It was referred to as the Hollenbeck Youth Center. He put an officer who was a professional boxer in charge of its operation. The center included arts and crafts as well as sporting activities. He also developed a youth boxing program, which was accepted by the community with a lot of enthusiasm. Several U.S. Olympic boxers received their training at that center. One boxer, Paul Gonzales, became a professional boxer after winning a gold medal in the Olympics.

This was an interesting and fascinating assignment. I was doing a lot of research and writing for Captain Deleon. I didn't realize how important the Adjutant's job was until I had to perform the duties of an Adjutant. This assignment was definitely a position which would help an officer get ready for promotion to Lieutenant. I was glad that I took the job.

Captain Deleon and I were good friends, and stayed good friends for many years. He retired from the LAPD and took a position with the State of California, Attorney General's Office. He was a Special Advisor to the Attorney General on all law enforcement issues. He also sat as a Hearing Officer for the California Parole Board. He was a well-educated individual, and was a professional instructor teaching in many colleges, including the University of Southern California.

I can say that Rudy was an inspiration to me, mentoring me not only on the police department but also with my teaching career. He was the one that got me interested in teaching. It was through his direction and counseling that I applied for a part-time instructor's positions at East Los Angeles Community College and Los Angeles Harbor Community College. I taught Police Science and Administration of Justice Courses for over thirty years. I loved teaching,

CHAPTER 14:

PROMOTION TO LIEUTENANT— ASSIGNED TO ACCIDENT INVESTIGATION DIVISION

My promotion to Lieutenant of Police finally came through. I was one happy camper as were Alicia, Elaine and Mark, as they knew how much I wanted this. I was transferred to the 77th Division but sent on loan to Internal Affairs Division for one deployment period. The Commander of Traffic Bureau wanted me to be assigned as a Watch Commander to the Accident Investigation Division. Needless to say, I was then transferred to the Accident Investigation Division, located in Parker Center.

Working for the Los Angeles Police Department was a wonderful choice for me. Always exciting, never boring. Thus far, in sixteen years on the LAPD, I had worked many different assignments.

Just to run down my assignments since graduating from the Police Academy, I have been assigned to Central Jail Division, 77th Street Division (Patrol), Harbor Division (Patrol), Harbor Vice Unit, Georgia Street Juvenile Division, 77th Street Division Juvenile Unit, Watts Juvenile Unit, Juvenile Narcotic Unit, Narcotic Division (Public Appearance and Training Officer), Training Division (Police Academy), and Hollenbeck Division (Adjutant).

Now my most recent assignment to date was the Accident Investigation Division, Traffic Bureau. There was no way one could get bored being a police officer on the LAPD.

The Accident Investigation Division (AID) handled all traffic accidents. This was indeed a specialty type investigation, especially if there were traffic fatalities or serious injuries. I was the Lieutenant Watch Commander on the P.M. watch and responsible for all the AID officers and their work-related assignments, including booking approvals on all traffic-related arrestees. I would roll on traffic accident fatalities and oversee the investigations. These AID officers worked very hard, from the time they cleared on the air to their end of watch (EOW).

AID was a choice assignment and those who were chosen had to have special investigation skills. Their reports and expertise were relied upon by many entities such as the courts, criminal and civil, attorneys, and insurance companies.

Elimination of the Traffic Bureau— Creation of South Traffic Division

After several months, we received notice that the Traffic Bureau was being eliminated and that all patrol officers were to take over, as part of their duties, the handling of all traffic accidents. This was a culture shock to all patrol officers as they wanted no part of handling traffic accidents. The Department Command staff worked diligently on this matter and came to the conclusion that this was the approach they wanted to take in this matter. However, as a safety net, they determined that one traffic division would be established in Operation South Bureau. This division was to be called South Traffic Division. The division would be housed at Harbor Area in San Pedro. Harbor Division was replaced with a new facility and under the new model, all geographic divisions in the City of Los Angeles would be called Areas.

The command staff wanted to keep this one specialized traffic division in the city and it was to be in South Bureau. The patrol officers in all the other bureaus would be responsible for handling their own traffic accidents. The South Traffic Division was to be a pilot program handling the traffic accidents in South Bureau.

The Accident Investigation Division would become South Traffic Division, move out of Parker Center, be housed in Harbor Area. Traffic Bureau would now no longer exist. The Police department budget was now saving a lot of money, as it did not have to fund those positions in the former Traffic Bureau. The South Traffic Division would now fall under the Command Staff of Operations South Bureau.

In addition to the Accident Investigation Division, there was the Traffic Enforcement Division (TED), consisting of Motor Officers within the Traffic Bureau who have now become part of South Traffic Division. This move also eliminated one Captain position, which happened to be the Captain of AID. The Captain of Traffic Enforcement Division now became the Commanding Officer of South Traffic Division (STD). Two separate traffic entities, AID and TED, became one.

Now came the logistics of AID and TED moving out of Parker Center and into their new space in Harbor Area. The Captain, myself, and the other AID Lieutenant met on numerous occasions planning for this move and making it happen.

The move was completed, all went well, and now a brand-new division was established. Being part of this was an exciting time for me as well as all the officers assigned to the STD.

I mentioned earlier that patrol officers in the other bureaus would now be responsible and held accountable for investigating all traffic accidents in their perspective Areas.

To determine how effective the new structure would be, the Department Command Staff wanted to compare the other bureaus without specialized traffic units to South Bureau where specialized traffic units continued to operate. If the patrol officers in the other bureaus proved to be efficient in handling their own traffic accidents, then STD would be eliminated and all traffic accidents in South Bureau would then become the responsibility of patrol officers.

I was still assigned as the Watch Commander on the P.M. Watch. It did not take long before Watch Commanders from the other bureaus were calling STD personnel for advice on how to handle certain type of accidents. On one occasion, I received a phone call from the Watch Commander of one of our Valley Divisions. They had an officer involved in a serious traffic accident outside the city limits and requested help in handling this accident.

When we had officers involved in a traffic accident in many situations, a longer and in-depth type of investigation was necessary as the department and the City can become civilly liable. I sent one of our units out to the San Fernando Valley to assist them on this investigation. A copy of this report went all the way up to the Chief of Police so he could see the importance of the specialized Accident Investigative Units.

At the year's end, South Traffic Division proved its superiority in this pilot program and the Department Command Staff decided to put specialized traffic divisions in each geographic bureau.

One side note to this equation was prior to STD being established, all motor officers at Traffic Enforcement Division had their own independent roll calls. Now, under one umbrella, motor officers and accident investigation officers held the same roll calls. Well, motor officers were known to be more rowdy than AID officers. Motor officers would like to pull pranks during roll calls and give the Lt. Watch Commander a hard time. On my watch, I had two motor officers who were more disruptive than the rest. I told them both to see me after roll call.

I counseled both about their behavior and told them that I was giving them a special assignment. They were to give roll-call training on a certain date that I gave them, which gave them ample time to prepare. Their subject was "The Los Angeles Police Department Code of Ethics." This subject is covered in the LAPD MANUAL.

The day came and I told all the officers that these two motor cops were going to give the roll-call training for the day. Both officers came to the front of the room and began their dissertation on the Code of Ethics. I was amazed as were all the officers as to their professional manner in which they made their presentation. They received a wonderful response from all the officers in attendance.

I thanked them for doing a wonderful job and wrote them a commendation for their presentation. I no longer had a problem or any disturbance during roll call after that.

STD Motor Officer Shot

One more side note before I leave STD. On one occasion, I sat in as the Commanding Officer of STD due to the Captain being on vacation. An STD sergeant came into my office and told me that one of our Motor Officers had been shot on Terminal Island by a robbery suspect.

I immediately rolled out, ordered a command post to be set up, and instructed that all traffic units should respond to the Command Post. First, I learned that our officer was shot in the shoulder during a traffic stop. Unknown to him, the suspect had just robbed the Navy Officers Club on Terminal Island. The officer was coherent and was going to be all right. The Operations South Bureau Chief rolled out to the hospital. A Sergeant was sent to the officer's home to transport his wife to the hospital.

From the command post, information came in regarding the possible whereabouts of the suspect. One location in west Long Beach was the site we focused on. The suspect was located and taken into custody. Working STD was a wonderful experience and holds many good memories.

CHAPTER 15:

TRANSFER TO HARBOR AREA DETECTIVE DIVISON

One day I was approached by the Captain and Commanding Officer of Harbor Area Detectives. He told me that he was going to be having an opening in his division for a Lieutenant and if I would be interested. After a long chat, I told him yes, and that it would be an honor to work for him. His name is Captain Marty Hairbedian, a well-known and respected officer on the police department.

When I got home, my wife and I sat down and I discussed the news about being transferred to Harbor Detective Division. She, as always, was very supportive as she always has been with me and my career on the police department. I would still be stationed close to home, as Harbor Station was less than a mile from our home. My detective assignment would put me back on the day shift with weekends off in most cases. This was great for our family life. My daughter, Elaine and son, Mark, were also very happy about my transfer to detectives.

Love of Family

Elaine and Mark were growing up too fast, as they were now young adults. Elaine was nineteen years old and Mark was sixteen. My God, where did the time go? We had thus far enjoyed our lives thoroughly. We had a wonderful family and home. Alicia and I were always very close, still in love with each other, and very blessed. Because of the comfort God provided, watching over us, and guiding us in this wonderful life of ours. Thank you, Dear Lord, for these blessings.

Elaine had graduated from high school and was going to Harbor College. She was also working at the College Book Store. Alicia and I had bought her first car, which was a VW Bug.

Mark was still in high school doing well in his studies. He was also playing varsity football. Mark was a big boy. As I am writing this, I remember what Doctor Korn told me when I first saw Mark after he was born. My first words were "Wow! Look at those shoulders, a football player for sure."

Mark was a good athlete when he was growing up. He played Flag Football and Little League Baseball. Mark could throw a baseball like no other kid his age. He played third base on his Little League teams. He had a great batting eye for his age, constantly hitting the ball, with many home runs. On one occasion, I took him to Wilmington where he had a game. He came up to bat and hit a home run over the fence. That was a great hit. The irony of that hit was the ball went over the left/center field fence, and hit the windshield of my car cracking it. I told Mark of all the cars he had to hit, it was mine. I tried to talk Mark into trying out for the San Pedro High School Baseball team. He chose to play football over baseball.

Alicia and I were very proud of Elaine and Mark. They were well behaved children growing up. A few worries now and then, but nothing compared to what I saw working on the police department.

I had also bought Mark a VW after he learned to drive. He and Elaine were both good drivers. Alicia and I, as parents, were very lucky and proud of our kids.

Back to my story about working on the police department. I was now assigned to Harbor Detectives, supervising detectives working the Burglary/ Theft Unit, Auto Theft Unit and Forgery Unit. There were two Lieutenants assigned to Harbor Detectives. The other Lieutenant was Lt. Schubach. He and I were already good friends, as he also taught part-time at Harbor College. Lt. Schubach supervised the Specialized Units such as homicide, all assault cases, robbery, and the Juvenile Unit. Detectives were always busy with heavy caseloads.

I tried to find crime trends so that I could get the information out to the Watch Commanders and our patrol officers so they could concentrate on where those crimes were being committed. On several occasions, I saw some crime patterns that were interesting. Our patrol units were hosting "Neighborhood Watch Meetings," advising citizens about crimes being committed in their neighborhoods. This was all part of Chief of Police Edward Davis' overall Basic Car Plan.

We did not have anything for our merchants who were being burglarized and having thefts committed out of their businesses.

Merchants Crime Prevention Seminars

Monitoring those targeted crimes, I put a plan together called "Merchant Crime Awareness Program." I talked with the Captains of Harbor Area about what this would entail. It meant that our detectives would be getting involved in Crime Prevention Meetings. With several of my detectives, we put together several Crime Prevention Meetings for the Merchants of the Harbor Area.

The first one was with the Ports-O-Call Merchants Association. We continued to get reports from various merchants regarding forged checks, shoplifting, and burglaries. I, with several of my detectives, attended one of their business meetings and discussed our thoughts on how to prevent many of these crimes. They thought that our ideas were very valid and they set up the logistics to get all the owners and employees to attend our first Ports-O-Call Merchants Association Crime Prevention Program. The meeting was held at a Ports-O-Call restaurant with several hundred merchant owners and employees in attendance. The merchants provided coffee and donuts/Danishes for this meeting. The Meeting was a total success as we (detectives) provided means and methods on how to prevent crimes in their businesses. We actually helped them set up a "Merchant Watch Program" similar to the Neighborhood Watch Program for home owners.

Several of these meetings were held and as a result we were able to see a big crime reduction at Ports-O-Call Village.

Looking more into the crime trends, I noticed that many of our car thefts were from the car dealerships in the Wilmington area. I took a close look at this problem and found that there was one car dealership that was not having any problems. I talked this problem over with the auto theft detectives and we decided to ask the owners of all the car dealerships in the Wilmington Area if they would meet with us and see if we could come up with an auto theft prevention program.

I contacted the owners or managers of each dealership, they liked the idea, and we went ahead and set up a breakfast meeting at one of the restaurants in Wilmington. Several of my auto theft detectives, the Harbor Detective Captain and myself met with them.

I explained the problem and they were eager to find a solution to this horrendous auto theft situation, as it was costing them a lot of money. I started off by asking the one dealership owner what they were doing because they had no auto thefts while all the other dealers had.

He went on to explain that all the car keys were locked up inside their main office when they were closed. He also explained that his car lot was fenced with a heavy steel chain so no one could drive a car off their lot. He also told us that at night when they closed down, the driveway entrances were blocked with a car so no one could drive a vehicle on or off the lot.

This owner stimulated the other dealers to start a dialogue that provided viable answers to their problems. The meeting proved to be effective and the owners and managers wanted to continue to get together.

Their auto thefts literally stopped as a result of this one meeting.

The Los Angeles Police Department under Chief Davis' Basic Car Plan was expanded and was then referred to Team Policing. Each Area was broken down to Team Districts with a Lieutenant in charge of a team.

CHAPTER 16:

PROMOTION TO LIEUTENANT II, COMMUNITY RELATIONS

Roger Mairs, my vice sergeant, had been promoted up the ladder and was now a Captain. He was selected as the Captain III, in charge of the Harbor Area. The Lieutenant II, of the Community Relations Office, Harbor Area, was promoted to Captain. This now left a Lt. II vacancy. Captain Mairs approached me and asked if I would like that position. I told him that I was happy working Detectives and would like to remain there. He told me that he needed me to work Community Relations, as it was a critical assignment working closely with the community. He liked what I was doing by getting detectives involved in meetings with the business community and he felt my living in the area would prove to be an asset to our community relations efforts in the Harbor Area.

I asked him if he would give me a job description of what my duties would entail as the Lt. II, Community Relations Officer. He went on to explain that I would be in charge of all community relations activities in the Harbor Area, which included all the youth programs such as the Explorer Scouts and Deputy Auxiliary Police. That included any community relations activity that had to do with Patrol and Detectives. I would have a staff of one sergeant and five officers.

I accepted his offer. When I went home that evening, I told Alicia about the change. That meant it was a promotion to Lt. II and with that came a 5.5 per cent pay raise. Again, Alicia was happy for me, as were Elaine and Mark.

Son Mark involved with Deputy Auxiliary (DAPS) and Police Explorer Scouts

I forgot to mention that Mark was one of the first DAP members. He attained the rank of Captain while he was in the DAPS.

Then he went on to be a Police Explorer Scout. He loved being involved in those programs, as it gave him insight as to the operations and functions of the police department.

Mark had to go through a rigorous Explorer Scout training program at the Police Academy.

When his Police Explorer class graduated from the Academy, Alicia, Elaine, and I along with several of his aunts, uncles, and cousins attended his graduation. We were all very proud of him as he looked very sharp in his uniform. He and his mom had the opportunity to meet and talk with Chief of Police Ed Davis.

Mark remained in the Explorer Scouts for several years, rising to the rank of Lieutenant. He was involved in many of the Explorer functions, assisting in various police functions around the city of Los Angeles with crowd control and security measures.

Alicia Asked to Attend a Hispanic Anti-Police Meeting

Before Captain Mairs, there was another Captain, Commanding Officer of the Harbor Division. Harbor was having problems with some community activists who were protesting police tactics, agitating and creating problems for the officers working the division. The Captain had heard that my wife, Alicia, was very active in the community and was President of the Barton Hill Elementary School Parent Teachers Association, helping out teachers and administrators by being a Spanish interpreter when there was a need for her interpreting skills. She was well liked, respected, and deeply admired for her volunteering Spanish skills.

This Captain talked with me and asked me if I thought my wife would consider attending a meeting with him with this group of Mexican activists. I told him that I would talk to Alicia and ask her if she would. I knew she would say yes. She had heard of this one individual who was the main agitator of the group, as his name was coming out in the local newspaper quite often.

The Captain and his Lieutenant picked Alicia up at the house and took her to the meeting with them. There was large group of Hispanic members in the group. Many in this meeting knew my wife and knew that she was married to a police officer. The one activist tried to downplay her Mexican heritage by saying that she was married to a LAPD police officer. Alicia was very proud of her Mexican heritage and challenged this individual by telling him so. She went on to say, "It is true I am married to Mike Markulis who is a member of the Los Angeles Police Department, and proud to be his wife, I am also very proud of my Mexican heritage. I may divorce my LAPD officer tomorrow and I will no longer be the wife of a police officer, but I will still be a Mexican."

All in attendance gave her a standing ovation and she won the group over by making the activists sorry they challenged her. This community group was no longer hostile towards the police and their tactics.

The Captain thanked Alicia and praised her for her honesty and integrity. He thanked her for doing such a wonderful job helping the officers of Harbor Division, making their jobs easier working with the community. Every time I ran into this Captain, he would ask about Alicia, and ask me to tell her "Thanks." I couldn't have been more proud of my wife. She was a remarkable woman, well liked, and highly thought of in the community, and loved deeply by her family. My love for her never ceases, but continues to grow each and every day of my life. I miss her terribly.

Variety of Police Citizen Groups Created

Being the Community Relations Officer of Harbor Area, I began thinking of things that I believed would help our officers and their police community skills. Discussing some of these visionary ideas with Captain Mairs, we went on to create and establish programs that made them a reality. One of them was a Police Clergy Council made up of members of the clergy from the Harbor Area.

They would meet once a month at the Harbor Area Roll Call room and discuss anything that was on their minds on how the police could work with them. Many of the clergy ran schools and they definitely saw a need for working with our officers and our officers with them. One member of the clergy became the Harbor Area Chaplain. They could also be called out in sensitive situations to help counsel a victim involved in a serious crime. The clergy became a viable part of our Community Relations Program. Captain Mairs personally took the clergy under his wings and gave them special attention.

Another viable organization we proposed and then became a reality was, "The Police Business-men Boosters Association." After running several articles in the local newspaper recruiting businessmen and making personal contacts regarding our thoughts on this program, we got the organization off the ground.

We had around thirty businessmen that thought the Boosters program was a wonderful idea. After several meetings to establish guidelines, we got this program rolling. They elected their officers and also met in the Roll Call room once every other month. The business-men learned that Harbor Area's police budget was very limited and they decided they would each contribute one hundred dollars a year into a fund to help buy those items and supplies that our detectives and officers needed, and did not get enough of through normal channels.

For example, Polaroid Film was needed to take pictures of injuries sustained by victims of domestic disputes, child abuse, and other critical evidence where pictures were needed. The detectives and patrol officers did not have the film available. The businessmen's organization now made this possible.

Special Nursery Room for Abused Children

Another example which proved worthwhile was turning one of our interview rooms into a Nursery Room to accommodate children who were brought to the station as victims of child abuse or when their parent or parents were arrested. The children had to be brought to the station and kept until they were released to a parent, relative, or proper children's agency.

Before this room was designed for the children, the detectives who were responsible for the case were also responsible for the care and maintenance of the child or children. The already traumatized child would be sitting at one of the detective's desks while the officers or detectives investigated and processed the involved case. This situation was intolerable.

I approached our women's support group to see if they would paint the room with pastel colors and put up pictures or decorations that children would like. The businessmen's boosters paid for the paint and decorations needed. They also purchased a television which was mounted along with children VCR tapes that could be played to keep children occupied while the detectives did their work.

I also requested that the businessmen's organization purchase stuffed toy dolls and animals that each child would receive and take with them when they left the station.

This was one of our best projects. I took pictures of the room and sent it along with one of my Activity Reports to the Chief of Police. The room was a huge success and the Chief made it mandatory for each station to have such a room to alleviate the stress of a child brought into the station.

The businessmen's boosters group felt good about their accomplishments. It was a wonderful group and they did not want anything in return. Discussing this group with my Community Relations staff trying to think of what we could do, in return, to show our appreciation. One of my officers was into golf and suggested we have a police/businessmen golf tournament.

Discussing this idea with Captain Mairs, who loved to play golf, he thought it was an excellent idea. My staff worked very hard on planning and organizing a tournament. The boosters bought into the idea because many of them were golfers.

We held the very first Police/Businessmen's Golf Tournament on the department. Two officers were paired with two businessmen to make up a foursome. The officers had to take a non-paid day off to play in the tournament. It was held at Palos Verdes Golf Course in Palos Verdes. Everyone enjoyed themselves and trophies were given out to the winners. We had high ranking officers from our bureau and other divisions that heard about the tournament and also wanted to play.

Needless to say, many of the other Areas heard about our success with the boosters/Police Golf Tournament and soon started their own. Harbor Area continued the tournament for several more years. In fact, the following year I bought a set of golf clubs, took six lessons, and played in the tournament. I came in second from the last. Actually, I thought I had come in last place. The last place participant got a trophy also. It was a cool-looking trophy that had a golfer breaking a club in two. That was the first and last time I ever played golf. I ended up giving the clubs to my son Mark, who took a liking to the sport and became pretty proficient.

I always seemed to have excellent people working with me. This Community Relations staff was no exception. One of the officers who ran our DAP program approached me and asked me about starting a youth boxing program in the Harbor. I told him that I thought it would be too expensive to get one off the ground. We talked about it for a while and he told me he had a friend who worked for Bush Gardens Brewery in San Fernando Valley who built professional boxing rings and donated them to youth centers. Officer Dave Goodwin told me that he would build one for us if we had a boxing program.

I discussed this idea with Captain Mairs. He suggested we give it a try. Officer Goodwin also had some connections with a boxing organization of retired professional boxers and wrestlers who would help us get this program off the ground. Dave contacted them and set up a meeting. The only one that I can remember as I write this is "Mike Mazurki," not only a retired boxer/wrestler but also a movie star. He was 6'5" and appeared in more than one hundred films. Officer Goodwin and I met with them at their office in Los Angeles. They were delighted to assist us in moving this program forward. After several meetings, we came up with some good ideas on promoting the boxing program.

The boxing ring became a reality and it was donated and set up at the rear parking lot of Harbor Station. The officers and detectives were impressed because it was a professional boxing ring. They were also impressed that Harbor Area was establishing a youth boxing program.

I met with the Director of the Wilmington Teen Post and discussed the possibility of some of their teens would be interested in boxing in the program. They loved the idea, as it would help them with some of their problem boys.

We got to the point that we not only got the program off the ground but with the help of the old retired boxers and wrestlers we set also up a boxing exhibition. We thought this would be a good way to raise some revenue for our youth programs. The Wilmington Teen Post wanted to get involved with this boxing exhibition.

We agreed on a date and the location would be the longshoreman Union Hall in Wilmington. We had tickets printed and distributed them with the Teen Post Director. We agreed on the program and that we would split the money down the middle–50 per cent to the Teen Post and 50 per cent for our Harbor Youth programs. The boxing program was a success, as it was a sell-out and we made a lot of money for both programs.

Officer Goodwin later resigned from LAPD to take a position with the Palm Springs Police Department. With Officer Goodwin gone, our boxing program went defunct. We donated the ring to one of the other stations that was interested in starting a boxing program.

Police Community Relations Festival

The last big Community Relations program I want to mention is the Police Community Relations Festival at Los Angeles Harbor College on a day when there were no classes held at the college. I was still teaching at the college and knew the president. I approached him and discussed the festival with him. I requested the use of the athletic field and the gymnasium for one day to put on this Community Relations program.

I stayed in touch with him, letting him know exactly how we planned to use the grounds. A quick rundown of some of the activities that would take place included: The LAPD Helicopter to land on the athletic field, which meant I had to get permission from the federal agency responsible for making that decision; the Bomb Squad showing their vehicle and to discuss explosives; Narcotic Officers with the dog, Ginger, to discuss narcotics and the use of the dog sniffing out dope; the Police Explorer Scouts and DAPS to discuss their youth programs and to work security for the festival. We also had several Black and White police vehicles, a Motor Officer and his motorcycle, and officers, to talk about driver safety and driving under the influence of alcohol and or drugs. We had our police community support groups present to discuss what they do to assist the police.

Nothing like this had ever taken place on this magnitude in the department before. We had several movie personalities from the TV series *The Rookies*, which aired in 1972 and 1973. We also had a child movie star who was from San Pedro, Michael Lookinland, who played in the TV series *The Brady Bunch*.

Many of the department's Area Commanding Officers came to the event to see what we were doing. The Operations South Bureau Chief who was also in attendance came over to me and referred to me as the "Ed Sullivan" of Harbor Area.

This was another huge Community Relations success story as several thousand people attended the festival. Many citizens that I talked to said this Community Relations Festival gave them a better insight into police operations and logistics.

The Chief of Police wanted to create a Community Relations Office where the Lieutenant would monitor all the Community Relations Offices in all the Areas. He selected me to do this. I would be assigned at the Police Academy. I was ready to do that assignment and then I got word from Captain Mairs that the position was not funded in the budget and was not going to happen. The local paper ran a big article on my departure for this new position. It then ran another article to explain why I was not leaving the Harbor.

Saying goodbye to his duties at Harbor Division is LAPD Lt. Mike Markulis (left), who helped pioneer the idea that policemen should do more than throw people in jail. Markulis, recently named to lead a citywide task force on team policing, is known in the Harbor Area for his involvement in community activities. With Markulis, above, is Lt. Warren Knowles.

Staff photo

Markulis to lead citywide task force

'Community' cop transferred

By John Davies
Staff writer

A San Pedro police lieutenant, who helped pioneer the idea that police should do more than throw people in jail, is leaving.

Mike Markulis, head of the Community Relations Office (CRO) at Harbor Divi-

machine operator. He was employed most of the time he wasn't attending Dana Junior High and San Pedro High schools.

In 1951, during the Korean conflict, he received his draft notice from the Army.

Markulis, at first, remained stateside due to an unexplained mixup. He eventually got into a supply company, however, and was stationed in Korean coastal cities,

during such a flashback, suddenly imagined his skin was on fire.

Detective work also played a part in narcotics job. One "natural" death turned out to be a complex pill slaying and Markulis unraveled the details.

In fact, Markulis later became LAPD's spokesman on narcotics, travelling around the country presenting

Police Academy Training Division

Mark with Dad, Mark's graduation Explorers Scouts Police Academy

CHAPTER 17:

BACK TO HARBOR DETECTIVES

Lieutenant Schubach was promoted to Captain and transferred to Rampart Area. I approached Captain Mairs and requested to go back to Detectives to take Schubach's vacancy. I had already put in a little over two years as the Community Relations Lieutenant.

I did want to get back into Detectives. He approved my request and I again was assigned to Harbor Detectives. I took a 5.5 per cent pay cut to do this and I was okay with it. Alicia was doing a fantastic job managing the household expenses. She said she didn't mind if that was what I wanted to do. My wife always supported me, as she knew how much I liked working on the department. I was a very lucky man to be married to this wonderful woman.

I was now back in Detectives, in charge of the specialized units, including Homicide, Assaults, Robbery and Juvenile. All the detectives working these assignments were seasoned detectives and good at what they did. My responsibility was to oversee and monitor their work. I would be their voice and discuss cases with the City or District Attorney, when necessary, regarding filing a case.

I would get called out on all homicide cases and oversee the investigations. My homicide detectives were outstanding investigators. I personally learned a lot from watching them work.

There were several cases worth mentioning here. On one evening I received a call at home that we had a homicide in San Pedro and I rolled on the case with one of the detectives. Patrol officers were at the scene and there was no suspect in custody. We walked into this house and there was blood splattered all over the interior of this house. On the kitchen floor laid a body.

I remarked to the detective that this had to be a brutal murder, as the body was all covered with blood. The detective whose name was Chuck Hart made no comment. He, like the good detective that he was, studied the crime scene very carefully as we walked from room to room. There were blood splatters everywhere. I thought that there must have been a bad struggle between the suspect and the victim.

Detective Hart pointed out several empty liquor bottles and a bottle of milk of magnesium located on the top of a nightstand. He then told me, "Lt., I think this is a death caused by natural means." He went on to explain that he believed our victim was an alcoholic and that his liver gave out on him and that he kept vomiting up blood as walked from room to room until he collapsed and died. If he had called 911 and asked for an ambulance, he might have survived.

We waited for the coroner to arrive and clean the body. The coroner found no trauma, that is, no gunshot, stab wound, or any kind of blunt force trauma. Detective Hart was correct in his analysis of this case.

I mention this only because it taught me not to jump to conclusions. I learned not to be judgmental until all the evidence and facts have been looked into.

Thousands of Aborted Fetuses in a Container Stored in The Port of Los Angeles

Another case worth mentioning was one where I received a phone call from a patrol officer who rolled on a call to one of the docks in the Port of Los Angeles. He wanted me to see this container full of little boxes with fetuses in every box. I, along with another detective, went to the location and observed fetuses that had been aborted and fell out of the little boxes. We were told that one of the dock workers detected a noxious odor coming from the container. He opened the large container door and out fell these boxes.

There was a noxious odor of formaldehyde coming from the container. I got nauseated from the smell. The detective and I believed these babies were aborted illegally. We estimated there were thousands that required investigation due to what I believed to be illegal abortions.

The fetuses that were on the ground were picked up and placed into the little cartons and put back into the container. I ordered the container be kept isolated until a decision could be made as to what would happen to them. I felt there were criminal violations due to what I believed to be illegal abortions.

This case was given to our Robbery/Homicide Division. They worked out of the Police Administration Building. They handled homicides that were of high-profile type cases. We learned the container was brought to the port from one of the abortion clinics and was slated to go to a perfume company that somehow made perfume from these remains.

I walked around for weeks smelling formaldehyde and thinking of those poor babies.

I later learned that all of the fetuses were cremated. No one was ever prosecuted.

CHAPTER 18:

TRANSFERRED TO DETECTIVE SUPPORT DIVISION

I was about a year into this position, when a Commander from the Detective Bureau in Los Angeles came down to talk to Captain Mairs, then came into my office and we discussed my work as a Detective Lieutenant. He asked me to go to work for him and take over the Gang Unit out of Detective Support Division. This was in July 1976. I now had completed twenty years with the Los Angeles Police Department. He said he liked my work ethic and that he could use me to be in charge of the Gang Unit. It would be a promotion to a Lieutenant II and I would be the Officer-In-Charge of twenty detectives.

I asked him what happened to the Lieutenant that was there. He told me that the lieutenant, Ted Cook, took the Chief of Police position with the Culver City Police Department. What a wonderful move that was for Ted. He was one of my Academy classmates. We had just completed our twenty years with the department and eligible for a pension at 40 per cent of our salary. Ted had to be one of the smartest officers in our class. A great officer and a wonderful human being. I went to his retirement luncheon and wished him well. He told me that all the detectives working the gang unit were excellent workers.

This unit had city-wide jurisdiction monitoring the city's gang problems and kept records of all the gangs in the city. I would also be responsible for keeping the official gang statistics for the city of Los Angeles. I would also have a take-home vehicle, as I would be subject to call-outs on gang murders. I asked the Commander if I could think about it and he told me, "No, you will be on the next transfer."

When I got home, Alicia and I talked about this next move. She was happy for me, but also a little sad because my office would now be out of Parker Center in Los Angeles. I would have a take-home car and that meant I would not be driving my personal car to work and back. She did like the idea that it was a promotion with a 5.5 per cent pay raise. I told her I thought it was a good move, and that it could help me get promoted to Captain. Alicia has been supportive of everything that I had done and accomplished on the department. She also was a wonderful wife and mother. I was fortunate to have a wife who was so supportive of what I did.

Divorce rates among police officers are one of the highest of all professions. The danger that comes with the job, long hours, and sensitive assignments can and does cause turmoil in many police households. Alicia understood that the wife's a police officer is compounded with many shortcomings as well as positive attributes. I married a beautiful lady who was by my side as long as I can remember. She has been on this journey with me from the very beginning and before.

On my first day at the Gang Unit, I met all the detectives and they were very sharp in appearance. We discussed their operations, work hours, overtime, and anything they wanted to know about me. I told them what I expected of them. They learned that I wanted the best work product they could give me. I later learned that they all had monikers working this unit. They gave me the moniker of "Flecha Derecha," meaning "Straight Arrow."

The unit would receive a copy of all the gang crime and arrest reports city-wide. Each detective was responsible for certain gangs. They would be available city-wide to answer any questions and to assist in investigations.

The department's criteria that defined a "gang crime" was disputed by some of the detectives. Some believed that when a gang member was involved in a crime with another gang member or it was a gang vs. gang confrontation, then it counted as a gang crime. I wanted to get a clarification on this. I met with the Detective Bureau Chief and Commander and we discussed this issue. They wanted to hear what I believed the definition of a gang crime was.

I told them that if the suspect is an "in-file gang member" and he commits any crime of violence, that it should be counted as a gang crime. They raised the question that if an in-file gang member is at home and gets in an argument and he assaults his mother or father, should that be counted as a gang crime? I told them yes, because of being a gang member and his propensity for violence. They agreed with me. I was now responsible for the new definition of a gang crime. I told my detectives that if they had a case where they thought it was questionable, we would talk about it and make a decision.

The detectives had their hands full, as we had over 25,000 gang members in our files that lived in the city of Los Angeles. The ethnicity of the gang members was Hispanic, Black, and Asian. We also had motorcycle and prison gang members that were predominantly White. All of our in-file gang members were violent or had the propensity of being violent.

We had two units work the evening hours to be available to units who may need their advice or assistance. Each deployment period we rotated the units from the P.M. watch to the day watch. This worked out well and the detectives liked this set-up. I had two Detective III supervisors assigned to our unit. One of the DIIIs would work the P.M. shift and be available for the P.M. watch officers.

I would get called out from home in the evening if the DIII supervisor felt that I was needed or if it was a homicide of great significance.

The Detective Support Division consisted of three main sections of which my Gang Activities Section was one. The other two were Criminal Conspiracy Section and the Special Surveillance (SS) Section. Each section had a Lieutenant II in charge. When the Captain of the Division was on vacation or took special time off, one of the Lieutenants would sit in for him as the Division Commanding Officer.

Special Surveillance Unit—
Bank Robbery and Shooting

On this one occasion, I was sitting in for him and the Special Surveillance Section had received information that several bank robbery suspects were going to rob a bank on this day. The SS Unit had staked out the suspects, and were going to tail them and if they committed the robbery, the unit would arrest them.

There were three suspects in one vehicle and the SS detectives followed the car to a bank in the city of El Segundo. The suspects got out of their vehicle, entered the bank and robbed it. As the suspects ran out of the bank, two of them were immediately arrested without incidence. One suspect ran south on the street and into a women's hair salon. One of the detectives went down the alley just west of the street and found the hair salon that the suspect had run into. As he was covering the rear door, the suspect was coming out and saw the detective. He fired a shot, missing him. The detective returned fire with his shotgun, struck the suspect, knocking him back into the salon and killing him. An ambulance immediately responded and pronounced the suspect dead on arrival.

When I arrived at the scene, I was immediately briefed as to the above scenario by the Lieutenant in charge of the unit.

This entire incident turned out to have some complicated issues surrounding it. First, it was an LAPD operation. The LAPD units followed the bank robbery suspects into the city of El Segundo where the robbery occurred. Therefore, the jurisdiction of the crime is the city of El Segundo. The El Segundo Police Department would only assist in the investigation of the crime. They claimed it was LAPD-initiated and an LAPD shooting so they would only assist the LAPD. The crime was a bank robbery and bank robberies fall under the jurisdiction of the Federal Bureau of Investigation. Because of the shooting of one of the suspects, the FBI investigators told me that LAPD would have to investigate the crime, clean it all up, and then they would take it over and file the case. I saw that we were not getting much cooperation from the other law enforcement agencies. I called in our bank robbery experts from the Robbery Homicide Division and our detectives from LAPD's Officer Involved Shooting Detail to assist in this investigation.

We only had one other problem: the women who were in the beauty salon refused to leave until their hair was done. It worked out okay, as that part of the salon was not in conflict with the investigation. Those women were not going to leave until they got their hair done, come hell or high water. The reader can see what police officers and detective have to go through at times to get their work done.

I worked the gang unit for three years and got called out on many occasions. One gang shooting was an interesting scenario. Gang members were armed and going to protect this one gang member. The gang members were waiting for this incident to take place. It was late at night when a vehicle containing three occupants pulled into the driveway of the gang member's house. The gang members from within the house started firing at the car and killed a sixteen-year-old girl. There were three occupants in the vehicle and only the girl was shot. They were not gang members but only pulled into that driveway to back out and leave the area. The driver turned into the wrong street by mistake. Our gang detectives assisted the detectives from the Hollenbeck Division with this case.

The gang problem continued to get worse in the city and the Areas with the biggest problems started forming gang units under the direction of the Chief of Police.

Establishing LAPD'S Specialized Gang Units (CRASH)

The first Area to form a specialized gang unit was Hollenbeck. The Lieutenant put in charge of that unit was a good friend of mine. We worked together when I worked Hollenbeck. We met on numerous occasions setting up his gang unit. They came up with the name of "TRASH," which stood for "Total Resources Against Street Hoodlums." The department started getting pressure from various community groups. The name was then changed to "CRASH," which now stood for "Community Resources Against Street Hoodlums." That was the term used for the new Area gang units.

Our gang unit worked very closely with the CRASH units. In fact, the District Attorney's Office contacted me and asked if I would help them set up their specialized unit to handle gang members and gang crimes. I met with D.A. James Bascue who would be setting it up. We also met several times with Lt. Bill Lynch of Hollenbeck and the D.A.'s unit was set up. Interesting to note that James Bascue was later appointed as a Judge of the Superior Court. I kept in touch with him over the years. James Bascue later became the Presiding Judge of the Superior Court System in Los Angeles County.

Attending the Delinquency Control Institute, USC

One day, I noticed a Department Directive stating that anyone interested in attending the Delinquency Control Institute (DCI) at the University of Southern California should apply. It was a six-week program with the applicant attending for the six weeks on department time. It was a scholarship and the applicant would get 12 unit credits towards their Bachelor or Master degrees. Well, I thought what a great opportunity to get back in school, especially if it would not cost me anything and get unit credits that could be applied towards a Master's degree.

With my background thus far in the department, I felt I was well qualified and may get selected. I submitted my application to the Commanding Officer of Juvenile Division who would make the selection, which had to be approved by the Chief of Police.

Several days later I received a call from the Captain of Juvenile Division and he congratulated me on my being selected to attend this DCI class. He told me that I was well qualified and that I would represent the LAPD well. I was excited and called Alicia to tell her the news. Of course, she was happy for me, and she told me, "I knew that you would get picked" and "That's my guy!"

When I got home from work that day, I discussed this opportunity with my family and what it meant to me. To think I would be attending the University of Southern California as a student. Attending this university on my own would be very expensive, and I know that we would not be able to afford it. What a wonderful opportunity, six weeks. DIII Suarez was a very capable supervisor to run the Gang Activities Section

I selected him to sit in for me while I was gone for those six weeks. Our Captain Tom Ferry was pleased about my being selected for DCI and also felt that DIII Suarez would do a good job sitting in for me during my absence.

I remember the first day I arrived at USC to start DCI. We had around thirty officers in the class. They were from different police departments from California and also from many other states. The Director of DCI introduced himself and his staff. He then asked us to introduce ourselves and talk about our departments and what we did. We had an interesting mix of officers. I was the only officer from LAPD in this class. The officers from other departments were housed in dorm-type apartments while they attended DCI. I chose to commute as I only lived half an hour away from USC.

After we got to know each other, the class elected their class officers. I was elected as vice president of the class. A nice honor. The president was an officer from Modesto, California. He held the rank of Deputy Chief on the Modesto Police Department.

The six-week class went by pretty fast. The courses were interesting and entailed a lot of work and studying. The whole class was bussed to Lake Arrowhead, California, for one weekend. The weekend was used for the class members to make their oral presentations on subject matters selected by the DCI staff.

The exams were difficult. My family was very supportive of me and knew that I would be doing a lot of studying. The final examinations were essay-type exams.

We got our grades on the last day of DCI. My hard work paid off as I got all As for the three courses. That was quite an accomplishment.

Our graduation was held at "The Town and Gown Center" at USC. Alicia attended the graduation and she was as excited as I was. We all received our Certificates of Completion. There was a program and we all had a very nice dinner.

Back to work at the gang unit, DIII Suarez briefed me on what had happened during my absence. Gang crimes were up. Our biggest gang problems were in the East Los Angeles Area and in South Central Areas of the city.

On one occasion, at one of our meetings, several of the detectives brought up their dress apparel. They believed they could do a better job if they wore soft clothes instead of suits or sport jackets and ties. My response to them was that I didn't feel it was a good idea. I did not want any of my detectives looking like gang members or being mistaken for gang members and getting shot at or getting into unnecessary altercations. They were professional police officers and were to continue looking like professional officers. Well, needless to say, after I left the unit, my replacement went along with the idea of wearing soft clothes.

Mayor's Gang Long Table Peace Table

The Mayor of the city of Los Angeles tried to get some semblance of peace with the Black gangs by starting what was called "The Long Table." He tried to get gang members to sit at this table and try to talk out their differences. The gang members were paid by the city to attend these meetings. They had to sign a roster each time they attended in order to get paid. Long story short, this program was short-lived, as one gang wanted more money than the other gangs to pay for the funeral of one of their gang members and they started fighting each other at one of the meetings.

There were all different types of intervention programs started by different agencies trying to curb the gang violence. In my opinion, I saw only one that seemed to have more of an effect on gang members than any of the others, and that was a Christian-based organization.

I had now been the Officer-In-Charge of the Gang Activities Section for three years. This experience became extremely important to my career, as now I was certified as a gang expert with knowledge about gang culture to add to my background.

Interesting to note, I now had worked the Central Jail, Harbor Patrol, Harbor Vice, Georgia Street Juvenile, 77th Juvenile, Watts Juvenile, Juvenile Narcotics, Adult Narcotics, Training Division, Hollenbeck Division / Adjutant, Accident Investigation, South Traffic Division, Harbor Detectives, Harbor Community Relations, and Detective Support Division Gang Unit.

CHAPTER 19:

TRANSFERRED TO HARBOR DETECTIVES, COMMANDING OFFICER POSITION

I received a call from Captain Roger Mairs from Harbor Area and he advised me that the department was restructuring the ranks again. They were getting rid of the captains in the Detective Divisions and replacing them with Lieutenant II positions. He wanted to talk to me about the Harbor Detective Commanding Officer position. There were several other Lieutenants seeking this position. I made an appointment for the interview.

My interview went well and Captain Mairs knew of my background and work ethics. He selected me to be his Detective Commanding Officer. I was thrilled that he selected me. I immediately called Alicia to inform her of the selection. Again, she was happy for me.

When I got home, Alicia, Elaine, and Mark wanted to hear about my new assignment. I explained to them that I would be coming back to the Harbor and would be in charge of the Detective Division. I would again be working from 8:30 a.m. to 5:00 p.m. with weekends off, subject to overtime and call-outs. Again, they were happy for me. The year had to be around 1978.

All the detectives in the Gang Activities Section were also happy for me. They knew that I lived in the Harbor and that it was a good move for me. They also had a farewell party for me and held it at the Saint Sophia Greek Orthodox Church Reception Hall. They presented me with a nice scroll laminated with humorous comments—a very official looking scroll with comments made up by the detectives. One of my favorites was the moniker they gave me, "Flecha Derecha," meaning "Straight Arrow". A nice send-off by a group of professional detectives of whom LAPD can be proud of.

I moved into my new office at Harbor Station. I held a short meeting with all the detectives and civilian staff. I knew most of the personnel that worked there. One thing about working the Harbor Area was that there was very little movement unless it was for promotion, transfer to a specialized division, or retirement. There were many questions asked of me as to what I expected from them. My comments were directed towards their work ethics, loyalty and honesty to themselves to their partners, and the goals of the Los Angeles Police Department. I stressed loyalty and honesty. I stressed that if any of them ever got criminally involved in any of their cases, I would not hesitate to send them to prison. It felt like a good meeting, as I got positive feedback from many of the personnel. I had an outstanding secretary who, on occasion, would guide me on the right path as to timeliness of reports and meetings.

The detectives loved what they were doing and enjoyed coming to work. It was a pleasure to work with them. We would get together and discuss cases, especially sensitive ones such as homicides, gang crimes, child abuse cases, and assaults with serious or life-threating injuries.

Lieutenant Mitchel Maricich

There was a Lieutenant I who was assigned to Harbor Detectives with me. He was an outstanding, dedicated human being. His name was Mitchel Maricich. I had known him for many years, as we both grew up in San Pedro. When I was the Student Body President at Dana Junior High School, Mitch was Student Body President at San Pedro High School. We met on several occasions. Mitch played the drums and was quite good. I also played the drums, but was not very good but I tried.

Just another little side note regarding Mitch: When my daughter, Elaine, was born on April 23, 1956, I was at San Pedro Community Hospital to visit my wife and my new baby. I saw Mitch looking through the glass partition where all the new babies were. I walked up to him and he pointed at his new baby boy born a day before my daughter was born. I congratulated him and then pointed out my new baby girl. He congratulated me and we were two proud parents. Mitch was already on the police department with four years of experience and I was in the Police Academy ready to graduate.

Mitch and I remained good friends for many years. His son Danny and my daughter Elaine had many of the same classes together sitting next to each other as their last names started with "Mar" throughout their high school years. They also remained friends.

Now Mitch and I were working together as a team, running the Harbor Detective Division. Some years later, Mitch retired when he had thirty years in the department and took a position as Field Deputy for Los Angeles County Board of Supervisor Dean Dana.

Mitch's role as a Field Deputy included not only working with the community but also working with law enforcement agencies in the Fourth District. Dean Dana wanted to investigate and find out what the Harbor Area's biggest crime problems were. He selected Mrs. Angie Papadakis to chair this committee through a "Round Table" on Crime with community members. Mitch represented Dean Dana's office. I was the one representing the Police Department. After many meetings, the Round Table found that the gang problem was one of the more severe problems.

We were asked to try to find a way to solve or eliminate the gang problem. The Round Table came up with a recommendation to form a program to try to eliminate gangs.

Established the Gang Alternative Program (GAP)

A core group of members was selected to develop the program. I represented the Police Department. There were fifteen that were to be on this Board, including one person representing the Los Angeles City Council and a member from the Los Angeles Unified School District (LAUSD). The rest were representatives from the businesses, industry, and the community. The program was to be called "The Gang Alternative Program" (GAP).

Through Dean Dana's office, we were able to acquire grant funding through United Way for the first year. The grant was for one hundred thousand dollars. The mission was to try to eliminate gang membership. This program was not an "Intervention Program," as there were many of these types of programs. Our mission was to eliminate gangs by keeping kids from joining gangs.

Working with LAUSD, we believed we had to start the program at the fourth-grade level. LAUSD, after approving the curriculum and looking into the areas where gangs existed, identified schools that were selected to put the program into effect. Twenty-five elementary schools were selected. The GAP Board then advertised for a director and three class room advisers who would be paid staff to run the program.

GAP got off the ground and was implemented in twenty-five selected schools. The program became a huge success and very popular with the children. The motto that the children came up with was "NEVER HAVE, NEVER WILL."

The GAP Board continued to oversee the program. I was elected President of the Board for the first three years. I, as well as every Board Member, believed that if we could continue this program year after year that eventually gang membership would vanish.

Today as I write this, we are in our thirty-fifth year of GAP. I am retired and still a Board member. We now have a budget of over two million dollars a year with numerous employees. The GAP program has been expanded to a program specifically to remove graffiti. Every year thousands of square feet of graffiti are painted out. GAP now includes after-school programs called "After the Bell" tutoring and keeping the kids active. GAP is also now recognized nationally and in the last few years internationally. A true success story.

This happened because a search for an Executive Director led us to Doug Seibert who had a PhD in this field. Dr. Seibert was the one instrumental for making the GAP program a true recognized success. He, with his knowledge about gangs, not only made GAP nationally famous for its gang prevention methods, but has also made GAP famous on an international level.

Dr. Seibert is now retired but makes himself available as Director Emeritus and teaches classes on the philosophy of gang prevention.

Another side note to this success story is that the present Executive Director of GAP, Juan Torres, was at one time a GAP student. He frequently mentions that it was the GAP program that helped him to persevere in life and to continue his education. He was hired as a GAP adviser and he continued his education graduating with a Bachelor's and then a Master's degree. He now has been selected as the Executive Director of the Gang Alternative Program. A true success story for this young man and the GAP program.

As a result of Mitch's dedication, involvement, and belief in the program, each year at an annual fundraiser, a Board Member is selected to receive the prestigious Mitch Maricich Award. Even though he is no longer with us, he is still remembered for his dedication to the program. I was honored to be the recipient of the Mitch Maricich Award in 2003.

I had one of the best assignments on the Police Department as the Commanding Officer of Harbor Detective Division. A position which many Lieutenants would love to have held. In fact, the Detective Commanding Officer's position at Harbor Detectives was always in high demand.

Writing this story of mine, there are times when I get somewhat confused as to the dates or time periods that I am in. GAP started in 1985. This was an interesting period but also a sad one in that it was in 1985 that I lost my father, George John Markulis.

**My Father, George John Markulis, Passes Away, 100 Years Old*

My father was to turn a hundred years old on January 7, 1986. My brothers and our wives were putting together a centennial birthday party. We were well on our way in the planning stages for his big party. The invitations were printed and we had rented the location where the party was to be held.

I remember several times when my father told me, "I don't think I will make it to a hundred." I would tell him that he was a healthy man for his age and that he would live well beyond a hundred. Well, he was right and I was wrong. Wishful thinking on my part.

My mother was in the San Pedro Community Hospital as a patient and had been there for several days. I would go and visit her and then go by the house to make sure my father was all right. My father was okay by himself for being almost 100 years old. He never had any caretakers and could do everything for himself. He got along very well and only had to use a cane. My mother was supposed to be released on December 1 and I was going to the hospital to check her out and take her home to my father. When I got to the hospital and talked to the doctor, he advised me that he was going to keep her in the hospital for one more day.

After visiting my mother, I stopped by their home to tell my dad that mom was not coming home today, and that the doctor wanted her to stay one more day in the hospital. My dad was very disappointed, as he was looking forward to her coming home. He cooked one of her favorite meals. He asked me to stay and have dinner with him. I told my dad that I had a few errands to run and that he probably would get some visitors and that he could serve them that delicious meal. I also told him that I would call him and if he had no visitors, I would come back to the house and have dinner with him.

Shortly after I left him, I ran the errands and went home. Alicia was next door at her mother's house. I went over there to let her know that the doctor kept my mom in the hospital for another day. Alicia and I went back in to our home and the telephone was ringing. Alicia answered the phone and it was my sister-in-law Carmela telling Alicia that my mother tried calling my dad on the phone and there was no answer. She tried calling me and there was no answer at our house because Alicia was next door visiting her mother. Carmela said she did get a hold of her husband Jim and told him to go by the house and check on dad.

Alicia and I immediately went to my dad's home and I went in and found my brother Jim holding my father in his arms while sitting on the floor. Jim said that our dad was not breathing. I immediately tried giving my dad CPR to revive him. Alicia called 911 for an ambulance. Jim and I picked up my dad and put him on his bed. My giving him CPR did not revive him and when the paramedics arrived, they pronounced him dead. He passed away on December 1, 1985. Thirty-eight days before his 100th birthday.

I can't explain the guilt that I felt for leaving him when I did several hours earlier. I keep telling myself that if I had stayed with him instead of leaving when I did and having dinner with him, he would not have died. I still believe that my father died of a broken heart, as he wanted his wife to come home from the hospital on that day. I should have stayed....

Needless to say, we did not enjoy a celebration of my father's 100th birthday party. The family celebrated his birthday with tears, memories, and great sadness, grateful for his presence in our lives.

Since I am on the subject of my father, let me give you a little insight into his life. He was an individual who was admired as a youth growing up in Greece and as an adult in the United States. He was born in 1886, in a little village on the island of Crete, Greece.

He was the only boy of a family with two sisters. His father owned many acres of olive groves. He was a hard worker. He only went to school up to the third grade. My father was mostly self-taught. He always had an inquisitive mind. It always amazed me to think that this man was born during the horse and buggy days, lived to see the advent of the radio, television, automobile, and airplane and then saw a man being sent to the moon and back to Earth. I remember him often asking questions about many of the things that fascinated him. An example would be the television. He would ask about the workings of it. Why is it that you can turn a knob and change a channel to another channel? He always read the newspapers, both American and Greek newspapers.

Dad was a very handsome, 6' Greek. He was also very strong, working the coal mines in Carbon County Utah from 1912 to 1943. One injury caused him to mangle from his right leg, breaking it in several places and causing that leg to be almost two inches shorter than his left leg. Dad walked with a noticeable limb after that injury. Dad was a very strong man. He was noted for holding the record for bringing out more coal in one day than any miner in Carbon County.

He worked a little over thirty years in the coal mines, during some very hard and difficult years, the Depression years. We would find our family moving from one coal mining shanty town to another. Dad even moved us to Pennsylvania for several years where he worked the coal mines there.

Missing many of their Greek friends in Utah, dad and mom moved their family back to Helper, Utah.

Many coal miners were coming down with Black Lung Disease. My father received a letter from the State of Utah to go to Queen of Angels Hospital in Los Angeles and have some chest x-rays taken to see if he had any signs of Black Lung. I took my father and after the doctor examined him and checked his x-rays, he told my dad that after working in the coal mines for thirty years, his lungs were clear. There was no sign of Black Lung Disease. The doctor was amazed as to how healthy he was. My dad told the doctor it was because of his Greek blood, eating well and using olive oil in his diet. The state of Utah gave him a small Black Lung Pension because of his tenure in the coal mining industry.

Markulis Family at GAP Function

GAP Board of Directors

Paul Dofton (President of the Board) myself with
certificate and Juan Torres Director of GAP

Original Board of Directors of the Gang Alternative Program (GAP)

Dr. Douglas Seibert PHD, Past Director. Made GAP
Nationally and Internationally recognized.

CHAPTER 20:

MOVING TO CALIFORNIA AND EYE SURGERY

A few years later, dad had to have eye surgery due to glaucoma destroying his left eye. He had to go to Los Angeles to have the eye operation. He and my brother John left for California where they stayed with a Greek family in San Pedro.

Dad's eye operation went well but he lost his left eye. The Greek family, Tony and Evangelina Louros, with whom they stayed, owned a restaurant down on the water front in San Pedro. They offered him a job as the night cook and told him that it would be too dangerous for him to go back working the coal mines with only one eye. My dad accepted his offer and moved our family out to California.

This was in September 1943. My dad purchased his first home. This was a two-bedroom, one-bath, kitchen and living room with an ornate fireplace. This Spanish house also came with a detached garage. Our family fell in love with this house. The one bedroom was shared by the four brothers and the other bedroom was mom and dad's.

One more item regarding our home, which was located at 671 W. Oliver Street. The Harbor Freeway was being constructed from Los Angeles to San Pedro. When it reached San Pedro, the state had to buy up some properties and that included our home. Mom and dad found an apartment to live in after the state purchased their home.

My mother was a very beautiful lady. I want to add some comments here regarding her. Although she was devastated with her move from Greece to Utah, she supported her husband with everything that he did. A coal miner's wife was a difficult role, knowing that her husband would work under ground where there could be a mine disaster causing serious injury or even death.

My mother's story is in the first book I wrote, *Terpsihori*. It talked about her life and what she endured moving from Greece to America and raising five sons during the Depression years.

My mother was a remarkable lady. Knowing that we were now moving to California, she had to find a way to move our belongings from Helper, Utah, to San Pedro, California. What she could not pack and ship, she gave away to friends and neighbors in Helper. My mother then bought Greyhound bus tickets for the three of us from Helper to Salt Lake City. She wanted to meet with several relatives and friends before continuing her journey to California. A first cousin, George Galanis, met us at the bus terminal and took us to the hotel he was living in.

As we were walking to the hotel, we noticed that the streets were empty of pedestrians. George told us that there was a polio epidemic in Salt Lake City and that everyone was staying at home in fear of getting polio. We stayed at the hotel with our cousin. The next morning, we went to visit another cousin at her home. We received a warm welcome. On entering her home, we saw a huge iron lung containing a boy about twelve or thirteen who had contracted polio. The iron lung helped the boy breath and kept him alive. Our visit was a short one.

Our Cousin George had gone to the railroad station and purchased train tickets for us from Salt Lake to Los Angeles, California. We left the next day, in the afternoon. The train ride gave us the opportunity to see some beautiful sights. My mother was extremely happy that she was moving and would soon see her husband. She regaled us with stories about growing up in Greece, both in Crete and in Piraeus. After talking about it and remembering her family, it brought tears to her eyes.

When the opportunity to move to California came up, she supported the idea with a lot of enthusiasm. The year was 1943, the war was still going on, and my mother, for the first time in many years, saw the Pacific Ocean. It surely was not the Aegean or Mediterranean Sea, but to her the Pacific Ocean was beautiful. No more coal mines or Rocky Mountains.

My Mother, Terpsihori Michael Markulis Passes Away On April 22, 1995

My dad worked as a night cook for the Greek family with whom he stayed with during his surgery. My mother loved living in California. She lived until April 22, 1995. She lived ten years after the passing of my dad. They were not a financially well-off family. My mother did not want to burden her sons with any funeral expenses. She skimped and saved enough money to pay for her own funeral. She was a very proud woman.

Living in San Pedro, which is also the Port of Los Angeles, merchant marine ships from all over the world would at one time or other come to this port. Our local newspaper contained a ships log, which gave the names of ships and countries where they were from.

My mother would look for the ships log every day and when she would see a ship from Greece coming to the port, she would find a way to contact the captain of the ship. She would call and invite the captain and some of the crew members to our home for a delicious Greek dinner. They appreciated the invite.

This venture paid off for her as she got an invite to travel back to Greece on one of the merchant ships at no cost to her. This was in 1952 when I was stationed in Korea. She took the captain's invite and went back to Greece for the first time since she had left in 1929.

I already mentioned that when I was in Korea, I gave some Greek soldiers who were rotating back to Greece a ride into Pusan. When they learned that my mother was at that time in Piraeus, they wanted all the information on her family so that when they got back to Piraeus, they would look her up. Piraeus was their home port.

Love My Family, Our Traditions, and Customs

Spending thirty-seven years on the police department gave me an opportunity to learn about different cultures of people that I came in contact with. However, I will say that I have always been proud of my Greek heritage. In those thirty-seven years, I can honestly say that I never came across any Greek criminals. I strongly believe that it is the Greek family structure that maintains a strong love of family that is passed down from one generation to another. My brothers and I would never do anything to embarrass our parents or tarnish the Markulis name. The pride of family ties and love of family is deep-rooted and passed from one generation to the next. I do believe other cultures maintain these same feelings regarding family.

Special holidays such as Easter, Greek Easter, Thanksgiving, and Christmas Eve/Day are celebrated with a love of family atmosphere. Two of our Markulis favorite holidays are Greek Easter and Christmas Eve.

A new tradition was started by our then present generation in 1981 to keep our family ties close. It was a Christmas Eve Best Present contest. Names of family members were drawn when we shared our Thanksgiving Day. The family member would have to make the gift or buy a gift from a second-hand or antique store for the person whose name was drawn. A cost limit for the gift was set. On Christmas Eve, the person presenting the gift would have to say something about the person whose name he or she chose. We always had several guests that would judge the gifts, select the winner, and make the presentation to the winner. The winner's name would then be engraved on a perpetual plaque and the winner would keep the plaque for the year and bring it back the next Christmas Eve. I happened to be the winner of the last Christmas Eve Contest in 2019.

I will give you a short explanation of what I am talking about. I drew my son's name. When my son was five or six years old, I made him a lamp out of a large cap-pistol. I kept the lamp after he got married and moved out of the house. For Christmas Eve 2019, I refurbished it and added a small frame with a picture of him when he was five or six years old. These were my comments that I made regarding him and the gift.

"A great opportunity to talk about my son. I am very proud of my son. He has always been a good son. I remember when he was born. He gave his mother such a hard time when she was in labor that the doctor decided to take him by cesarean. He was a big baby, over nine lbs. The doctor remembered my first words, 'Wow, look at those shoulders. A football player for sure.' Growing up, Mark was always very neat, meticulous, and organized. His room was always spotless. He would know if someone was in his room, and if anything was touched.

My brother John saw the good qualities in Mark and brought him into management. Puritan Bakery got a wonderful employee, as he does his job well. I have talked to many Puritan customers who have praised Mark for his loyalty to them customers and to the Bakery.

"Mark has been a wonderful husband and father. His wife Evie and his children have always come first in his life. He provided the best education for his children through parochial schools, Saint Barnabas, Saint John Bosco and Saint Joseph High Schools. I don't know how he managed that, but he and his wife did. They even provided a USC Graduate Program for Madeline who always managed to graduate at the top of her classes. I only wish I could have been the kind of father that Mark was. This Christmas Eve Gift Contest has been going on since 1981. In fact, Mark and his wife Evie were the first winners. I forgot to mention that I was the winner for the 2019 Christmas Eve contest with my son's Mark gift.

Moving forward, I was still working Harbor Area Detectives up until 1988 when the Deputy Chief of South Bureau called me and advised me that he wanted me to create a new Homicide Division within South Bureau. I advised the Chief that I had thirty-four years on the Police Department and that I was happy at my present assignment and would like to stay as the Harbor Detective Division Commanding Officer. South Bureau encompassed four Areas and most of the homicides in the city of Los Angeles were committed in those four Areas. I told the Chief that I could not see myself being called out on all of those homicides at all hours of the night and weekends.

The Chief agreed with me and let me stay in the Harbor. Another lieutenant, much younger and eager than I was, took the assignment. I lost three of my detectives to South Bureau Homicide Division, as I no longer had the responsibility to investigate the homicides in the Harbor Area.

South Bureau averaged between 200 and 300 homicides a year. After the first year of operation, the lieutenant that took that position got burned out and retired. He was much younger than I was. He made a lot of money working overtime, but did not want to do that anymore.

Working with Long Beach Probation- San Pedro Pilot Program

In the interim, as the Commanding Officer of Harbor Detectives, I was working with Long Beach Probation Director Barry Nidorff on a program where we would assist Probation in monitoring probationers that lived in the Harbor Area. The theory behind this program was that the Probation Department would give us a bimonthly printout with the names of the probationers and their conditions of probation. I, in turn, would pass out the booklet to all of our police units including patrol, vice, narcotics, gang, and traffic units in South Traffic Division. While in the midst of the planning of this new crime prevention program, Barry Nidorff was promoted to Chief Probation Officer of Los Angeles County Probation Department.

The new Director of Long Beach Probation was now Jane Martin. We worked together finalizing this program. The program was a big success. For example, if an LAPD unit stopped to investigate a situation of a person or a group of individuals, possibly gang members, they would check their names with the probation list. If his/her name popped up as a gang member, and one of the conditions would be "not to hang around or associate with other gang members," he/she would be arrested on the charge of Violation of Probation. He would be booked for the violation and there would be no bail. A teletype message would be sent to Probation, alerting them of the person taken into custody and they would handle the case from that moment on. This was a wonderful program and hailed by both departments as a success, not only in monitoring probationers but also as a crime deterrent program.

CHAPTER 21:

TRANSFER TO SOUTH BUREAU HOMICIDE

The Chief of South Bureau called me and told me that I had no choice in this matter and that he needed me to run South Bureau Homicide (SBH). He told me that he was transferring me to SBH. One of things he wanted me to do was an analysis of centralized vs. decentralized investigations of homicides.

Criminal and Juvenile Justice Delegation to USSR

Prior to taking this assignment, I received a phone call from now retired Captain Rudy Deleon who was then working for the California Attorney General's Office. He told me about a Criminal Justice Delegation that was being formed to go to the Soviet Union to study their criminal justice system. I would be representing the Los Angeles Police Department. I discussed the possibility of going on this delegation with Alicia and she believed it would be a wonderful venture for me to do this and that I had her blessings if I really wanted to do this. I accepted the invitation and made the proper notifications and filled out the necessary paperwork. The department approved my request and that I could go on city time. We are talking now in 1988. All the arrangements were made.

Rudy and I flew from Los Angeles International Airport (LAX) to New York. We met all the other delegates at the hotel and got acquainted with them. There were approximately twenty-five members from many different law enforcement agencies across the country. I was the only representative from a police agency. There were several others from sheriff departments, but mostly they were from federal departments such as State and Federal Bureau of Corrections. We met our team leader who was a retired warden from a federal prison. We were all briefed on what we were going to do and given our specific assignments. My assignment was to write a brief on the judicial system under the USSR system and try to do a comparative analysis between their system and ours.

Our plane flew out the next day from New York and flew in to Frankfurt, Germany, for a few hours' layover. Our connecting flight was on a Russian-built plane that was not as up-to-date as our American Air plane. We flew from Frankfurt into Moscow. What I remember was landing in Moscow, and getting an eerie feeling seeing armed soldiers standing guard over each aircraft. They took us through customs. As I recall, I was the only one that customs personnel pulled out of our delegation. They shook me down and went through my luggage. This happened to me each time we flew into another city, for example, Kiev and Leningrad.

Before I left the States, I went to the Police Academy and bought many LAPD badge pins to take with me. I passed them out to different people I met during the trip. Every person that got one appreciated and liked them. We were told not to approach any police officers (militia men in USSR) and talk to them. In Kiev, I saw this lone militia man standing on a corner. I approached him and tried to explain to him that I too was a militia man in America. He looked at me in a puzzling manner not understanding a word I am telling him. I then took out one of my LAPD Badge pins and showed it to him. He then broke into a big smile as I told him to keep it. He grabbed my hand and kept shaking it. He was a human being just as I was. I could tell he appreciated the gesture. Before I left him, he reached up and took his badge off his uniform and gave it to me. I did not want to see him get in any trouble and tried to resist taking it, but he insisted. So I left the USSR with this officer's uniform badge.

This story gets better. When we were leaving Leningrad to fly home to the USA, we were going through customs and while the agent was going through my luggage, he came across this militia man's uniform badge. He immediately stopped and asked me where I got the badge. I tried to explain to him that I traded it with a militia man. He did not quite understand, until I showed him one of the LAPD badge pins. He then got the drift of what I was trying to explain to him. He kept starring at the pin. I asked him if he would like one. He gave me a big smile and nodded yes. I gave him the pin. He immediately closed my luggage and passed me through customs. I have told this story many times when I got back home. I take those LAPD badge pins whenever I travel abroad.

Toured Moscow, Kiev, and Leningrad

We toured three major cities in the USSR—Moscow, Kiev, and Leningrad. Not only did we have the opportunity to study their criminal justice system but we also had the opportunity to do some sightseeing. We visited their court systems, their jails, a prison, and an orphanage. It was interesting to note that most of the judges were women. Those arrested were guilty and the burden was upon the arrestee to prove his innocence. We sat in a trial where three individuals were charged with robbery. Each defendant had the opportunity to explain to the court what transpired. After their testimony, the three-judge panel found each individual guilty. They were to return on another date for sentencing. The whole trial lasted about an hour.

We got to meet with prosecutors and judges where they discussed how their system works. We also learned that drugs and narcotics were becoming a big problem in the Soviet Union.

The orphanage that we visited was very well maintained, including a one-to-one staff-to-child ratio. We were really impressed on the operation of the orphanage. Our delegation even took up a collection that we gave them upon our departure.

We also visited a juvenile detention center where juvenile inmates were learning a trade. They were assembling telephones that were to be sold or used for government purposes.

This is only a brief synopsis of what we studied and saw in the USSR. It was an experience of a lifetime.

Returning to the States and Work

I was told by the chairman that they were in the planning stages for another Criminal/Juvenile Delegation for the following year of the Eastern European Bloc countries that were under control of the USSR. He asked if I would be interested in joining them. I told the chairman that if my department approved of it, I would love to go on that one also.

It was nice returning home to my family. They were all excited about my trip and also the souvenirs I brought back for them.

I went back to work and completed the necessary paperwork for that trip to the USSR. I also gave a presentation to the Department Command Staff about my experience and the trip.

The local newspaper, *San Pedro News Pilot*, ran a feature of the trip to the USSR on their front page. A very nice article describing the trip.

I was briefed by Lieutenant Rich Moloney who sat in for me in my absence on the homicides that had been handled while I was gone. Nothing seemed to be different as the homicides in South Bureau continued. South Bureau Homicide detectives were constantly busy, if not overworked, because the number of homicides they were handling never slowed down. We were averaging 300 homicides a year. Our SBH were responsible for handling all the homicides in South Bureau, which included Southwest, 77th Street, Southeast, and Harbor Divisions. This is the area covered from the Santa Monica Freeway south to the ocean in San Pedro.

Homicide detectives are a special breed of cops. They were the very best of investigators. They worked long hours and knew that when they concluded with a case they had not only solved it but that justice had also been served.

I do want to mention a very special incident that happened while working SBH. My detectives, I believe, had one of the most sensitive jobs on the department. Investigating murders and working with and talking to the survivors takes its toll on the detectives. As I said, I believe that homicide detectives are a special breed of cops. This unusual incident is one of the best things that came out of a murder investigation. This investigation involved the murder victim's sister, who had also been shot but survived. Detective Simmons was responsible for the investigation of this murder.

Detective Simmons came into my office because he wanted to talk to me about a personal matter. He went on to ask me for my permission to get married. He then told me that he wanted to marry the murder victim's sister who was on the mend from a gunshot wound. Because it was an active case, he thought that he would have to get my permission to marry the young lady. My response to him was, "Do you love her?" He said that he had fallen in love with her and wants to marry her. I told him, "Marry her!" They had a Catholic Church wedding. I was invited as were many homicide detectives. We have remained good friends.

Civilian Staff Assigned to SBH

The civilian staff that worked this division was the best on the department. I had one Personnel Service Representative (PSR) civilian that was loaned to SBH from the Communication Division. When we would get a call that we had a gang homicide, she would get on the computer with the information she had and come up with clues that the detectives could immediately begin to work with. Because of her computer knowledge, especially of our personal computer program monitoring gangs, she was an invaluable employee. The Chief put out an order that all PSRs had to return to Communication Division. I immediately went to my Chief in South Bureau and tried to make an exception as to our PSR. It just happened that it was our Chief from South Bureau who was responsible for the decision on sending all PSRs back to Communication Division. He refused my request.

Losing and Getting Back a Vital PSR to SBH

I was determined to try anything to keep her. She was an important part of SBH because of her knowledge not only of the computer but also of other aspects of gang homicides in the South Bureau. I wrote a report and sent it directly to Chief Daryl Gates, bypassing my Bureau Chief. I then called Chief Gates' Adjutant and explained my situation to him. I asked him to make sure that Chief Gates got my report. He stated that he would make sure that he saw it.

Chief Gates did receive the report, sent it on to Assistant Chief Vernon with the following comments on the report. "Bob, what do you think? Should we consider this?" Chief Vernon's comment on the report was, "Yes, we should approve it." The report was then forwarded to the other Assistant Chief and he thought it should be denied. I believed that it was a lost cause until several weeks later I bumped into Chief Gates coming out of a meeting and he approached me and asked me how was the PSR working out. I told him that I never did get her back. He asked me why not, as he had approved it. I looked at the Chief and told him, "Because you did not follow through on the request." The Chief got this mad look on his face and did not say another word, but walked away.

The next day I was in a briefing meeting with my Chief of South Bureau. His phone rang and he answered it. It was one of the Commanders that worked directly for Chief Gates. He told Chief Hunt that he had some good news for Lt. Markulis. Chief Hunt responded by telling the Commander that he just happens to be in my office right now. The Commander told Chief Hunt that Lt. Markulis' request was approved and that he was getting back the PSR that he requested. Chief Hunt thanked the Commander for the information and hung up the phone. He looked at me and angrily said, "You went over my head and sent a report directly to Chief Gates." I told him I did and I felt that strongly about getting her back because she was so valuable to SBH. Chief Hunt told me never to do that again. I told him that I would not. All the SBH detectives were happy that my persistence worked out.

SBH had a motto that was humorous in a way, "RIP, REST IN PEACE, OUR DAY BEGINS WHEN YOUR DAY ENDS." A little morbid humor. Homicide detectives had to maintain their sanity while they handled their murder investigations.

Eastern Bloc Countries that were Under the Control of the USSR

The following year, 1990, I did get selected to go to the Eastern Bloc countries that were under the control of the USSR. This was with the same delegation that had gone in 1989 to the USSR and studied their criminal/juvenile systems. This trip was also for two weeks. This delegation consisted of fifteen members of different branches of law enforcement in the United States. There were members from the Department of Corrections Administrators in the delegation, and representatives of various sheriff departments. I was the only member that represented a police department. Our mission was to study their criminal/juvenile systems, offer suggestions on how they might improve their systems, and bring back with us any ideas, methods, or means to improve our systems. Needless to say, we had much more to offer them, than they us. I talked about LAPD Chief Daryl Gates' LAPD'S Dare Program (drug prevention programs), and presented them with the relevant material. This went over big with the different police administrators we encountered.

Ride-along with Vienna Police Department

We started our tour in Berlin, Dresden, Germany, then on to Prague in the Czech Republic and several cities in Austria, including Vienna. In Vienna I had the opportunity to go on a ride-along with the Vienna Police Department. The first call we rolled on was a traffic accident on one of their freeways. We got on the freeway going in the opposite way the traffic was moving. We were traveling Code 3 [red light and siren] into traffic. Vehicles traveling in our direction just moved to the side as we proceeded to the accident. Interesting approach on driving Code 3 on freeways. We arrived safely at the scene. No ambulance needed, as there were no injuries.

A matter of interest on this traffic accident was that one of the vehicles was driven by an American tourist. When I found out who he was, I went over and talked with the gentleman. We both found this incident sort of humorous in that he, a driver involved in a traffic accident in Vienna, meets an LAPD officer riding with the Vienna Police investigating his traffic accident.

Another interesting matter on this accident was that the Vienna officers had cleared the cars off the freeway in a matter of minutes so that traffic could resume. They used special equipment brought in by their Fire Department. This was an easy investigation since there were no injuries.

I enjoyed my ride-along and gave the officers LAPD pins that I brought with me. I also left them Dare material, which was appreciated as they were now having a drug problem.

Toured a German Concentration Camp in Czechoslovakia

We also toured Hungary and several other Eastern Bloc countries. In Czechoslovakia, we had the opportunity to tour one of the German concentration camps, Terezin where they imprisoned thousands of Jews. Terezin executed many Jewish citizens. However, most of the Jews who were executed from this camp were first deported to Auschwitz or Treblinka in Poland.

Touring this Camp left not only me but also many members of our delegation emotionally upset because of what these Jewish people must have gone through. We got to see the barracks where they were jammed in and we could feel the anguish that they must have suffered. The shower room where the poison gas was released along with the crematory where the bodies were cremated. There was a huge cemetery also on the property where bodies were buried. Also, a place where Jews who tried to escape were either hung or shot.

This was an experience that will stay with me for a lifetime. For those who do not believe that the Holocaust occurred, they should tour one of these camps. An experience that I will never forget.

I found the people of these Eastern Bloc countries to be very courteous and welcoming to our delegation.

Chipped on the Berlin Wall

When we were back in Berlin, we went to a section where they were demolishing the Berlin Wall. I rented a hammer and chisel and chipped on the wall. I brought back with me chiseled pieces of the wall.

This trip to the European Eastern Bloc countries was as interesting as the trip to the USSR in 1989. I brought back many souvenirs for the family.

Returned to the States and Back to Work

My experiences to the USSR and the Eastern Bloc countries will always remain a historical memory of my tenure with the Los Angeles Police Department. An interesting facet of both trips was that I was the only police officer from the United States that was selected by the committee to take part in these delegations.

I was still a part-time instructor teaching at Los Angeles Harbor College. In fact, besides my teaching, I was selected to be the chairman of the of the Administration of Justice (AJ) Department, and as such responsible for the AJ classes being offered each semester.

There was a lot of responsibility that went along with being chairman, but at the same time there was no extra pay that went with this position. I didn't mind that as I enjoyed doing it. I was told that sometime in the future, a salary increase would come with the position. Being chairman of the department was a factor taken into consideration when I applied for the Director's position at the University of Southern California after I retired from LAPD.

I was also a long-time member of the California Administration of Justice Educators Association (CAJE) and attended most of their conferences each year. This year, in April 1992, CAJE had scheduled a conference in Sacramento. I submitted all my paperwork for the conference. I asked Alicia if she would like to go. We had some dear friends that lived in Hollister and Saratoga. Alicia thought this would be a great opportunity to take her sister Lucia and visit our friends while I attended the conference. All the arrangements were made. I would drop Lucia off in Hollister, take Alicia to Saratoga and they would stay with our friends, and then I would pick them up after the conference was over.

Me chipping on the Berlin wall in 1989, took pieces home.

Civilian Secretarial and Clerk Staff at South Bureau Homicide, taking me to lunch for my retirement. Sheila Hailey, Zella Baker, Netta Burnaugh, Sabrina Williams, Lena Johnson and Debra Avery. Also, with us Detective III Roosevelt Joseph.

CHAPTER 22:

RODNEY KING RIOTS IN LOS ANGELES

The date was April 29, 1992, and we were well on our way to Sacramento. I had dropped Lucia off in Hollister where she was to stay with Nash and Ruth Bravo. Alicia and I continued towards Saratoga when we heard on the radio that riots had broken out in Los Angeles. The riots resulted from the acquittal of four LAPD officers for assaulting Rodney King. The riots were causing problems of great magnitude as fires of businesses and killings were taking place.

When Alicia and I arrived in Saratoga to our friends Jim and Helen Leininger's home, I immediately used their phone and called my boss, Deputy Chief Matthew Hunt. I told him where I was and asked him if I should return to Los Angeles or continue to Sacramento to the conference. He told me that I was to return immediately as most of the rioting was in South Bureau and that we were already experiencing homicides. Alicia called her sister Lucia and told her that we were going back to San Pedro.

The next morning after having a nice breakfast, Alicia and I left the Leininger's. The Leininger family and we go back many years. Jim's wife Helen was daughter to Ruth and Ignacio Bravo who lived in the San Pedro Area for many years before moving to Hollister, California. Their family, Alicia's family, and I were very close friends. I was on the Los Angeles Police Department and also teaching Administration of Justice classes in the community colleges in East Los Angeles and Harbor. Jim had started Law School in San Jose. I gave Jim many of my handout materials and examinations for some of the Criminal Procedures and Criminal Law classes that I was teaching. He appreciated them very much. We remained very good friends. Jim and Helen have both since passed away. They are in my thoughts always. I still remain in contact with their children.

Alicia and I were on our way back to San Pedro. We stopped in Hollister to pick up Lucia. We knew that it was going to take us anywhere from six to eight hours to get home, depending on the traffic. The traffic moved fairly well until we reached Los Angeles County. The traffic on the freeway was stop-and-go, but mostly stop. Traffic in all lanes was not moving. We had gotten in the car pool lane and it was not moving. In fact, the driver of the vehicle behind me kept honking his horn and at the same time flashing his LAPD badge at me motioning me to get out of the lane. I flashed my badge back at him and we then both laughed. I wondered how many more cops were in the same situation we were in. We listened to the news reports on the radio and, of course, the news was not good at all. Burning, looting, assaults, and murders were occurring.

We finally got home late evening. I immediately got on the phone and called SBH. I talked to Lt. Molony and told him that I was coming in as soon as I freshen up. He told me that all of our detectives were really busy handling back-to-back homicides.

Alicia wasn't too happy that I was going to work. She knew that a big part of the riot was where SBH was located and that I would be driving through the riot area to get to my office. I told Alicia that I knew of another route, which was a little longer, but that I would not have to drive where the main riots were occurring.

I finally arrived at my office and began talking to the detectives and Lt. Molony. They were telling me of some of the problems they were encountering due to the riots, burning, and looting.

South Bureau Homicide is located inside the Baldwin Hills Mall along with South Traffic Division. These two police divisions were responsible for saving the mall from destruction. When looters started breaking into the mall, little did they know that there was a contingent of officers already inside. The officers immediately deployed inside the mall, stopping the vandals and the looters. The owners of the mall were extremely happy that in their planning of the mall, they had allowed these two police divisions to be housed inside.

There were all kinds of stories that the detectives were telling me. One story which was indicative of so many others was when the detectives rolled on a homicide where the victim was shot and killed in his vehicle. The detectives could not get any assistance to go and retrieve the body from the vehicle. Ambulances would not go because they were too busy rolling on assault cases, and the coroner would not go to the crime scene as it was too dangerous. Finally, one of the SBH detectives saw a tow truck driving down the street. He stopped the driver and ordered him to tow the vehicle to the field morgue that had been set up.

The officers and detectives working the field morgue could not believe that a tow truck towed a vehicle with a dead body in it. Everyone was trying to do the best they could under very difficult circumstances.

I got in one of the detectives' vehicles and drove through the riot area and to one of the homicide scenes. Businesses were on fire. Uniform officers and detectives had their hands full trying to investigate a murder and keep some semblance of control over their crime scene. Many of the murders were going to be followed up on in order to locate witnesses.

More than sixty people lost their lives amid the looting and fires that ravaged the city over the five-day period, starting April 29, 1992. Ten were shot to death by law enforcement officials. An additional forty-four people died in other homicides or incidents tied to the rioting. By year's end, Los Angeles had 1,096 homicides, 1992 remains L.A.'s deadliest year.

As a result of the several days of rioting, besides the sixty people that were killed, 2,300 were injured, and hundreds arrested. About 1,100 buildings were damaged, and total property damage was about $1 billion, which made the riots one of the most devastating civil disruptions in American history.

Chief of Police Daryl Gates and Assistant Chief Bob Vernon Retire

The Mayor of the city of Los Angeles, Tom Bradley, had an ongoing conflict relationship with the Chief of Police, Daryl Gates, and tried to get rid of him ever since he became Mayor. Mayor Bradley was on the Los Angeles Police Department and rose to the rank of Lieutenant. He had gotten his law degree while in the department, practiced law for a short time, ran for City Council and was elected as a councilman for his district. He then ran for Mayor and was elected and reelected several times. He wanted to get rid of Chief Gates, but because all the ranks on the police department were covered under Civil Service, he was unable to fire the Chief.

The Mayor did have a five-member Police Commission, which was actually the head of the department. The five members were political appointments by the Mayor. The Chief of Police was responsible to the Police Commission. The five members, appointed by the Mayor, could not find any reason to recommend the Chief be removed.

The riots created many problems within the Police Department and the Chief Gates decided to retire. The second-in-command, my friend and former partner, Assistant Chief Bob Vernon also decided to retire. It seemed that the command staff of the department was also at odds with each other. I formed the opinion that our great department was crumbling from within. I had now almost thirty-seven years in the department and it was time for me to retire.

I talked my situation over with Alicia and she agreed with me that I should retire from the department. I would continue to teach at Harbor College part-time to keep somewhat active.

CHAPTER 23:

MY RETIREMENT FROM LAPD

I had to go to the Personnel Division, located in Parker Center, to sign my retirement papers. I had made an appointment with the Retirement Counselor, Thornton Henderson. When I got to Parker Center, I got in the elevator to go the sixth floor where the Personnel Division was located. I rode the elevator for about 20 minutes, trying to get up enough nerve to get off on the sixth floor. I think that was one of the hardest things I had to do. Once I signed those papers, I ceased being a Los Angeles Police Officer. Thirty-seven years of my life were dedicated to the LAPD, the greatest police agency, not only in the United States but also in the world. Sgt. Henderson took my Active LAPD Identification Card and gave me a Retired LAPD ID Card. He also took my badge, and told me if I wanted to keep it I would have to encase it in plastic. That it would cost me, I think, $185. I wanted to keep my badge so I had him encase it. Even encased, it looks nice. I also received a RETIRED LAPD badge. If I wanted to keep my four- inch 38-caliber hand gun, I would have to buy it from the city, which I did. Well, I was now retired. When I got back to SBH, Deputy Chief Matt Hunt, Commander Ron Banks, and all the homicide detectives were there to give me, Lieutenant Molony and Det. III Roberts a nice send-off. I forgot to mention that Molony and Roberts also retired. I was escorted to my car by several of my detectives.

Retirement Party

I retired on June 29, 1992. I had a retirement party that was held at the Princes Louise Restaurant Annex in San Pedro on August 14, 1992. It was organized and planned by my dear friend, SBH detective Dickie Simmons. There were over 400 people in attendance. The guests were from the police department and friends and colleagues from the community. It was a great honor to be recognized by so many people.

I was awarded with many plaques and certificates for my service. Most of them are in my office at home.

During my thirty-seven-year tenure with the police department I was recognized several times for acts of bravery. In 1959, my partner and I received a Class A commendation, which was the highest award presented at the time. Later it was replaced with the Medal of Valor. My partner and I were responsible for stopping a shooting incident and a mini riot outside a high school in Wilmington. My partner ended up in the hospital after being dragged by the suspect's vehicle. I received minor injuries.

I also received the Police Star for Bravery in what was a shooting incident. I approached and took the suspect into custody who was under the influence of PCP, armed and barricaded in his home. The suspect would not surrender to any other officer that was at the scene. His father and I grew up together and were friends.

I was also acknowledged for and received several highly recognized administrative achievement awards issued only to Commanding Officers on the department. One was for "The Battle on Crime," issued for innovative ideas on reducing crime in the Harbor Area. The other administrative recognition was for the Methods Used to Administratively Command South Bureau Homicide.

I was fortunate to have received hundreds of certificates, letters of appreciation, and acknowledgements for outstanding dedication and service from the community as well as other organizations and jurisdictions during my tenure on the Los Angeles Police Department. I also received from Harbor College "The Amicus Collegi Award." A wonderful career. I was also selected as the man of the year for the Harbor City-Lomita Chamber of Commerce. I loved my work with the Los Angeles Police Department and loved going to work every day.

My Wife Alicia Also Retired

I remember the day that I officially retired from the department, went home, and told Alicia that I am now retired. I remember as I held her close in my arms and I told her, "You know, not only did I retire but you did also." Alicia deserved that retirement more than I did, as it was her love, devotion, and hard work that made me the success that I was. From that moment on I shared her role in everything we did. We did it together.

We bought a new motor home and wanted to do a little traveling. We heard of this campground called Silent Valley up in the San Bernardino Mountains. Alicia and I drove to Silent Valley and found that it was close to Idyllwild. We liked it and we bought into it. It was a great RV campground and we also knew our grandkids would also like it.

When we bought the RV, we had taken our two grandsons Michael and Matthew with us and we saw how excited they were looking at the RVs. They convinced us to buy one. It was a 34-foot Bounder made by Fleetwood. It had everything in it—kitchen, bedroom, bathroom, two TVs, a little living room, and a basement for storage.

We bought it before I retired from the police department. The very first time we took it out for a test run was with Michael and Matthew. We took it to the Newport Dunes RV resort campground for a weekend camping trip. They thoroughly enjoyed it as did Alicia and I.

I had to look for a place to store the motor home. I had room for my 16-foot trailer in my backyard, but not for a 34-foot RV. I found a place in Harbor City where I could store it, but the storage fee was $200 a month. I had no choice because I could not park it on the street.

Silent Valley RV Campground

Alicia and I had some friends that told us about an RV campground called Silent Valley located above the city of Banning in California. We took a ride to see exactly where it was and what it had to offer. The campground was about nine miles from the city of Idyllwild. We got to tour the campground and found it to be several thousand acres with beautiful trees, hiking trails, streams, and a lake stocked with fish. The campground also had a nice restaurant and several small snack bars. The campground was equipped with full hook-ups which were included in the cost. We liked it and believed that our grandkids would also like it. We bought a share into the campground.

We found ourselves going to Silent Valley at least once a month. We would take Michael and Matthew quite often, as they really enjoyed it. The campground offered special classes in the arts, music and country western dances. Michael and Matthew, especially Michael, liked the country western line dances. Alicia and I thoroughly enjoyed watching him dance. He got to be pretty good. We would barbecue a lot or go out to the restaurant for dinner quite often,

Both Michael and Matthew, especially Matthew, would make friends easily. There were times when Matthew would disappear for a while and we would have to go out looking for him. One time he was gone for several hours, and Alicia panicked, thinking the worst about Mathew wandering off, getting lost, or someone kidnapping him. After making some inquiries, we found him by the lake with several friends fishing. Alicia was very frightened, thinking of the worst. She lectured about him how important it was for him to let us know if he was going to go somewhere.

Alicia and I enjoyed watching Michael and Matthew having a good time. On one occasion, the weather was cool, with lots of dark clouds overhead. Michael was in the RV with Alicia and me. Matthew was outside standing on a big boulder with a tree branch in his hand talking to himself or to Mother Nature. He had a tree branch in one hand, raised up to the sky, and he was saying, "RAIN, RAIN, RAIN," and it started to rain. About ten to fifteen minutes went by and he again raised his hands saying in a loud voice, "RAIN STOP, RAIN STOP," and it stopped raining. Alicia and I couldn't believe what we just witnessed. That was a moment we will never forget. It was as if our grandson had special powers. We teased him many times about that incident.

We spent many happy times with our grandkids in Silent Valley. When they got older and into their teens, their interests changed and they no longer went with us. Alicia and I took several long trips in the RV and enjoyed our time together. The RV was the only way Alicia enjoyed traveling. If you remember, when Alicia and I were married we flew to Mexico City on our honeymoon. There was a lot of turbulence both going to Mexico City and flying back. Alicia told me she would never fly in an airplane again. Sometime later I took her to the theater to see two movies, *The Poseidon Adventure* and *Airport*. In one film, the ship capsizes and there are only a few survivors. In the other film, a large airliner crashes into the ocean and sinks. Alicia told me that she would never go on a cruise or fly again. The RV she enjoyed. It was like she was in her own home, with all the privacy she wanted and was still able to see beautiful scenery that this country had to offer. We traveled to California, Nevada, Arizona, New Mexico, and Oregon. Alicia and I both thoroughly enjoyed our RV.

We also bought a 1987 Subaru Hatchback that we towed behind the RV. When we went to our destination campsite, we would use the Subaru to sightsee. We saw magnificent sights such as the Grand Canyon, both the South Rim and the North Rim. We visited national parks and forests. We visited my home birth state, Utah, and the town where I was born and raised. We had planned to go to the Four Corners, this was the only place in our country where four states— Colorado, Utah, Arizona and New Mexico— touched each other. But the day we were planning to go there, they had an outbreak of some contagious virus and people were dying. The advisories on the news were saying to stay out of the area until this was over. So, this is one place we never got to visit.

I was so grateful that we had bought this RV, as it was the only way we would get to travel and see some of the fascinating places in our country. Alicia and I were what people would call plain folk, as we thoroughly enjoyed our home, our children, and our families. When our children were little, we always took them wherever we would go. The one time when we got a babysitter to take care of Elaine so that we could go to a movie, Alicia started crying in the theater and I asked her if she was all right, and she said no. She didn't like leaving Elaine with a baby sitter. I told Alicia it was all right and we left the theater and went home. From that moment on, we took Elaine and Mark everywhere with us or we did not go.

Of course, as the grandkids got older and did not want to go with us anymore, Alicia and I found ourselves not using the RV as much. We were storing the RV and paying $200 a month storage fees.

Some Tales About My Brother John

One day I was visiting my brother John at Puritan Bakery and he asked me if I still had the RV. I told him yes. He asked me where I was storing it and how much I was paying. I told him and he suggested that I store it on the Puritan Bakery parking lot. I told John that was not a good idea because every employee who owns a recreational vehicle would want to store their RVs on the lot also. John's response to that was "F____T____! That's my parking lot and I can say who can park there and who can't, and you can!" So, as a result of John's decision I parked the RV on his lot. The only use it was getting was when Mark took his family to Pismo Beach several times a year. It got to the point where it was not being used that often and I often mentioned to Mark that if he could find a buyer for it, to go ahead and sell it. Well, in 2020 Mark found a buyer for it and we sold it. I had that motor home for twenty-nine years and it was in good condition with low mileage. I kept the RV on the Puritan parking lot for at least five years. John saved me some $15,000 by allowing me to store the RV on the Puritan lot. He was a good brother and I miss him terribly. John passed away in February 2013.

My brother John and I were very close when we were growing up. We got into a lot of mischief and did get a lot of scolding and whippings from our parents, mostly by my mother. John was very energetic and always found a way to earn money, even running away from home in Helper, Utah, when he was nine or ten years old. My father borrowed a pickup truck and he and I went out looking for him in the farm lands around Helper. We found him in this one camp where he was working on commission as to how much crop he harvested. After that incident, our mother got him a job in a Greek-owned candy store. John did not get paid in currency but candy. We liked that because John shared the candy with us.

When we moved to California in 1943, John was then a teenager and worked several places and made friends each place he worked. He worked at a gas station, a dress shop, a market and a shipyard. In the shipyard, he did such an excellent job that he was promoted to a supervisory position. He was only sixteen years old. He lied about his age on the application for employment, saying he was eighteen years old.

He impressed his supervisor when on one assignment he was to take inventory of nuts, bolts, and washers. John said there were thousands of them. He was to separate them and after counting them, he was to put them in glass containers. John said that it would take weeks for him to do that. He thought out the situation and came up with a solution where he could do the work in a few hours. John took one of the containers and counted the item and filled up one container. He then weighed the container and got an exact weight. He then stored the container. From that moment on, he would not count out the item. He would put the container on a scale and then pour the item into the container until he got the exact weight he was looking for, seal the container, and then store it. His supervisor went to check on John and asked him how he was doing. John told him he was through and gave his supervisor all the paperwork showing inventory sheets. He was so impressed with John's work that he promoted him to a supervisor.

John had to quit that job because he had to go back to school. That is when he got the part-time job working at DiCarlo's Bakery. A book can be written on my brother's life as a result of his direct and perceptive lifestyle in wanting to earn money. John did help our parents out a lot financially. He would tackle anything if he believed it would earn money for his home and his family.

Before John passed away, he was a self-made millionaire. He partnered in the Puritan Bakery business and made that company a multimillion-dollar operation. He was one of the most popular Greeks in the baking business to the point where he earned the name "O Jannis O Psomas," John the Breadman.

Meeting President Ronald Reagan

I thought in my retirement years I would slow down. It was just the opposite. I found myself to be very busy. Shortly after I retired from the LAPD, I had an opportunity to meet the recently retired President of the United States, Ronald Reagan. My nephew Raul Dominguez's wife, Vickie, worked for an agency that rented vehicles out to President Reagan's Secret Service staff. The person she worked with could arrange a meeting with the President. She knew how much I admired President Reagan and asked me if I would like to have her make those arrangements. I told her I would like that very much. She talked with this individual and he made arrangements for me to have an audience with President Reagan.

I took Vickie with me and we went to Century City where President Reagan had his office. We told the Secret Service Agent who we were and that we had an appointment with the President. It was an extreme honor to meet and shake the hand of one of the greatest presidents this country ever had. He wanted to know something about me, and how I liked being in law enforcement for thirty-seven years. He thanked me for my service. He talked about his life and he pointed at a picture hanging on his wall when he worked as a lifeguard in his youth. He talked about what a privilege it was to serve as President of this great country.

I mentioned to him my visit with a Criminal Justice Delegation to the USSR and how much the Russian people admired him for standing up to Gorbachev with regards to the Cold War. I told him, "I was told that Gorbachev was spending all their money on their missile and space program while their people were starving." I told him, "I saw people standing in line to get bread and food." President Reagan's comments regarding building "Star Wars," a system designed to stop any missile from reaching the United States. Gorbachev learned from his scientists that such a system could be built. The people in the USSR believed that discussion ended the Cold War.

My visit with the President lasted for about an hour. I had my picture taken with the President. He signed it, "To Michael Markulis, With Best Wishes, Ronald Reagan." A treasure indeed. A moment in time to be remembered for a life time.

Last Day of work, Lionel Roberts, me and Rich Malony

My son Mark at my Retirement Dinner August 14, 1992

Pictures of Retirement Dinner. Alicia crying after our
son Mark's comments and presentations.

CHAPTER 24:

1996 OLYMPIC GAMES, ATLANTA, GEORGIA

I received a phone call from one of my good friends, Dallas Binger and was asked if I would be interested in working the Olympic Games in Atlanta, Georgia. I told him that I was interested, but that I would have to discuss it with my wife.

Alicia and I talked about it and her response was if I wanted to do that to go ahead. I called Dallas back and told him yes. The general manager for the security was my old boss, now retired Chief William Rathburn. I called him and told him I was interested in working during the Olympics. We discussed all the options. I would have to pay for everything except for my uniform and room and board. I would have to pay for all my travel expenses.

I flew into Atlanta and checked in with the Olympic staff. I was to stay in one of the dorms at the University of Georgia which was located in Athens, Georgia. The venue that I was assigned was the soccer venue located at the university. This venue drew over 80,000 people during the soccer games. I got to watch the men and women soccer tournaments. The USA women's team took the gold medal. China's women took the silver and Norway's women team took the bronze.

I also got to see some of the other events and the closing ceremony, which Chief Rathburn arranged for me to attend. I took many pictures, which I shared with my family when I got home. I don't recall if I mentioned that when the Olympics were in Los Angeles in 1984 Alicia and I attended the closing ceremonies there.

United States Olympics Atlanta Georgia 1996

CHAPTER 25:

EMPLOYMENT AT THE UNIVERSITY OF SOUTHERN CALIFORNIA

I was still teaching as an instructor at Harbor College, keeping myself somewhat active. I was also attending the USC Delinquency Control Institute (DCI) Alumni Association meetings. The director retired and the assistant director moved up to the director's position. Knowing all about DCI, I submitted my application and resume for the assistant director's vacancy. My application was accepted and I was scheduled for an interview with the dean and assistant dean of the School of Public Administration.

I had discussed this opportunity with Alicia and she told me if I wanted to go back to work full-time to go for it.

When I went for the interview, I was told by the dean that I was not being interviewed for the assistant director's position but they were interviewing me for the director's position. Of course, I was surprised and I asked what happened to Director Clyde Chronkhite. I was told that he left USC for a position with a University in Illinois. I was pleased to think that I was qualified for the director's position. Those positions require at least a Master's degree. I have a Bachelor's with many units towards my Master's. I never finished. I did have in my favor the knowledge of DCI and that I had gone through the program as a student getting all As in the three courses that DCI offered, which were applied towards my Master's degree.

My interview went well and I was told by the dean that she would let me know. A week went by and I received a telephone call that they wanted to re-interview me. We made the appointment.

I went for this interview and again, met with the dean and the assistant dean. They interviewed me again and then told me that I was hired as the new director of DCI. I was to start immediately. I filled out all the necessary paperwork. I was now on the staff of the University of Southern California as the Director of the Delinquency Control Institute, Center for The Administration of Justice under the School of Public Administration.

I went home and told Alicia that I was hired. She hugged me and I could tell she was a little sad for she liked the idea of retirement. I did tell her that I told the dean I would take the job for a year because I already put in thirty-seven years with LAPD and my wife and I were looking towards retirement. That comment helped a little. I could tell that there was a little sadness in her demeanor.

Alicia has been very supportive of me in everything that I have done or attempted to do. DCI was going to be a challenge for me in that being the Director was not only running the DCI program but also raising funds for scholarships. I would also be responsible for conducting audits and studies of certain government programs. There was a handsome fee involved, which was then applied toward the DCI scholarship fund.

DCI was also putting on, for a fee, child abuse classes for law enforcement and social workers. DCI would offer these classes three or four times a year in different parts of the state. These classes went over big and were always in high demand. I would obtain highly qualified instructors for these specialized classes.

One class that I took a special interest involved social workers working in the Los Angeles County Dependency Court. The judge I worked with was Judge Emily Stevens who was a good friend of my daughter, Elaine, in that she clerked for her when she was working the Municipal Court. As a result of that relationship, we got off to a good start and developed an outstanding class. Working with Judge Stevens and some of the other judges, the class took shape in a very positive, sensitive way with a lot of empathy for dependent and neglected children.

As you can see, my duties at DCI kept me quite busy. My main focus was the DCI program. The program was world-renowned, as we would get officers not only from the United States but also from different countries like the United Kingdom, Russia, Mexico, and Australia. There were three main courses, all concentrating on Juvenile Behavior and Juvenile Justice. With each course, the student earned four units, a total of twelve units towards a Bachelor's or Master's degree. The student attended the six-week, all-day program. The instructors were highly educated and experienced in their field.

I put through four classes, two classes per year. They were classes 97, 98, 99, and 100. I should mention that the first year snuck up on me pretty fast. I submitted my letter of resignation to the dean, as I planned to stay only for one year. The dean told me that she was very satisfied with my work ethic and asked me to stay and continue to run the DCI program. I told her I would stay for one more year. She was grateful. I told Alicia that I was asked to stay and continue my work at DCI.

My Son Mark Enrolls at USC

One nice side note of working at DCI was that I was able to get my son Mark to attend USC with tuition remission for a year and a half. Because of my position as a director, my children could attend tuition free. They would only have to pay for their books. This came about when my son Mark approached me and told me he was thinking of going back to college and take some classes. He had graduated from Los Angeles Harbor College with his Associated Arts degree and had taken classes at University of Dominguez Hills before he dropped out to get married. He was going to go back to Dominguez, but after some discussion he took me up on the idea of going to USC. He had no problem being accepted at USC, as all of his transcripts were excellent. So, my son Mark was enrolled as a student at USC and attended for a year and a half. When I retired as director, his tuition remission stopped.

Obtaining Movie Actor Robert Stack as the Guest Speaker for the 100th Centennial Class at DCI

Each of the four DCI classes that I put through were outstanding classes and they all graduated with a beautiful certificate from USC. Each graduating class has a main speaker, generally from the university. But I wanted the 100th class to be a special graduation. I knew that Robert Stack, the movie actor, had graduated from USC and in many of his movie roles he portrayed a law enforcement officers. One of his longstanding series was *The Untouchables*, playing the part of Elliot Ness, an FBI agent fighting organized crime. When I suggested his name as the guest speaker, I was told that he had been approached several times before and he turned down the request.

I thought I would try again. Having Robert Stack as the Keynote speaker would put the icing on the cake for this prestigious centennial graduating class.

I obtained his private phone number and called him. After talking to him for several minutes, he told me that he would think about it and for me to call him back in a few days. I did wait for several days and called him back. He told me that he had a busy schedule and that he couldn't fit it in. I went on to tell him how important it was for him to attend this prestigious graduation consisting of police officers from all over the United States and several countries. I finally convinced him and he accepted the invite. That had to be one of the highlights of all the graduations of DCI classes at USC. For the first time, many of the top USC administrators attended the DCI graduation. Robert Stack was greeted with a standing ovation. He made an outstanding speech commending the officers for their work and how important their work was in our society.

DCI kept me busy. Scholarship funds came from private people and agencies. One of DCI's largest contributors was an individual who retired from one of the major insurance companies. When he died, he put a clause in his estate, that when his wife passed away, there would be one million dollars to be used for scholarships. I called the dean to inform her. She immediately told me that the one million dollars would be going to the University of Southern California and DCI would only be able to use the interest earned on that money for scholarships. I understood, but was somewhat surprised it that it meant only two scholarships per class would be awarded from this estate.

Another incident regarding scholarships was when USC put a ban on smoking on campus and I received a call from a major tobacco company representative who told me that because of the ban, the university just lost a large endowment that was to be used for scholarships. That hurt the program and it meant that I would have to try to find a way to raise funds for those lost. Some of the government contracts that we were able to obtain helped pay for some scholarships.

Bringing in Probation and Parole Officers to DCI

I was able to put through four DCI classes—97, 98, 99, and 100. All the students were police officers. I decided that we should have probation and youth authority and parole officers in these classes as well.

I called Jane Martin from the Los Angeles County Probation Department whom I worked with when I was Commanding Officer of LAPD's Harbor Detective Division and she was the Director of the Long Beach Probation Office. We worked on the San Pedro Pilot Program, monitoring all probationers in the Harbor Area. She was now a Bureau Chief on the Executive Leadership Team. I told her what I had in mind for DCI and that I felt that Probation and Parole Officers should be part of the DCI program. I explained to her that DCI would provide one free scholarship if the LA County Probation Department would pay for one scholarship for two of their officers to attend. I explained to her that the student would earn 12 units towards their Master's degree. She stated that she would have to take it up with their Executive Board and that she would get back to me. She called me back and told me they liked the idea and said they would accept the offer. This was the first time that Probation Officers would be attending DCI.

The next day I called the Director of the California Youth Authority and offered him the same thought. Even though they would lose their officers for six weeks, both departments believed it would be an excellent incentive for their officers.

Los Angeles County Probation and the California Youth Authority selected outstanding people to attend. This was a first for DCI.

My Letter of Resignation to the Dean

I submitted my letter of resignation to the dean when my two years came to a close. She accepted it and then we discussed who I thought would be an excellent director for the program. The director who was in charge when I went through DCI was still at USC. He was now in charge of the Foreign Student Program. He had lost a big percentage of his workload, as the Foreign Student Program had slowed down. I suggested to bring him back to DCI and have him be in charge of both programs. That way they would save one director's salary.

I later learned that the dean took my suggestion and made him director of both programs. I also learned that later on he quit USC and took a position with an American university in a European country.

The years were passing by pretty fast now. Alicia and I were enjoying our family in our retirement. We were using the RV quite often, mostly going to Silent Valley. We were very happy. Our family was very important to us. We spent all the holidays together. Alicia and I enjoyed watching Elaine and Mark grow up. Then, of course, our three grandkids growing up so fast.

Miracle Baby and Now a Miracle Lady

Our youngest granddaughter was a miracle baby. I say this because when she was born, she was born with a cancerous brain tumor at the base of her skull. She had to have surgery when she was seven months old. My son and daughter-in- law were on pins and needles worrying about her as was the rest of the family. She was operated on at Kaiser Hospital in Hollywood. She had the finest doctors that Kaiser had for this type of surgery. The doctor was able to remove 95 per cent of the tumor. There was still 5 per cent of the cancerous tumor in her brain. The doctor said he did not want to be any more aggressive as taking all the tumor out could leave her somewhat handicapped. He did say that she may have a problem with her coordination such as bouncing a ball or picking up a pencil. Mark and Evie went to great lengths to get her all the therapy they could for her as she was growing up. She had to be monitored every six months. The MRIs eventually showed no sign of the cancer. The power of prayers and her own immune system took over and showed no sign of the cancerous tumor. She was cancer-free.

Madeline accomplished so much because she would not stop until she completed the task at hand. Mark and Evie had her participate in all kinds of sports activities and even signed her up for Club Volleyball. She made the team and excelled as an outstanding volleyball player.

When she was at Saint Joseph's High School, she made the Varsity Volleyball team. Not only did she make the team but she also excelled in the sport. She graduated with honors at St. Joseph's.

She went on to California State University Dominguez Hills and completed all her studies, graduating at the top of her class, summa cum laude, receiving her Bachelors of Arts degree.

Madeline continued with her studies and was accepted at the University of Southern California. After working very hard in the field that she wanted to go into, Occupational Therapy, she graduated receiving her Master's degree.

She told us many times that she wanted to go into this field of study because she wanted to help those who were struggling with some sort of handicap like she did. Madeline, as I have said over and over, "was a Miracle Baby and now a Miracle Lady." Madeline is applying her trade now at Little Company of Mary Hospital in Torrance, California. She also works at the Lomita Care Center in Lomita, California. She has made us extremely proud, despite all the difficulties she had, and through stubbornness and determination on her part, she achieved her goal. Our Miracle Baby is definitely a Miracle Lady.

CHAPTER 26:

AUTOMOBILE ACCIDENT, INJURIES, AND RECOVERY

The year is now 2006, and I had been retired for fourteen years from the Los Angeles Police Department. Alicia and I were very happy. Elaine and Mark had purchased their own homes—Mark in Carson, California, and Elaine in Norwalk, California. Mark had three children. They were not that far away from us so we still maintained a close relationship. Elaine has worked hard throughout her career, serves her church with dedication, and is a great aunt to her nephews and nieces. She proved that over and over with her nephews and nieces. Elaine and Mark always maintained a close relationship with their cousins on the Markulis and Sanchez sides.

My brother Jimmy was getting married on his birthday, September 17, and Alicia and I were excited about him getting married again. His second marriage. We were looking forward to going to his wedding. The night before, September 16, Mark's wife was celebrating her birthday. Alicia and I went to a small party that Mark was having for her. We enjoyed ourselves, as again our family was together again for this celebration.

We left the house and were driving home on Sepulveda Blvd. in Carson. We must have been on the road around five minutes when we were rear-ended. The other vehicle was going at a high rate of speed as our car went airborne and landed on the opposite side of Sepulveda facing eastbound traffic. We were driving west bound. After we came to a full stop, I asked Alicia if she was all right. She replied, "I don't know." I temporarily lost my cell phone. I was getting out of our car to see what kind of condition the other party was in. I knew Alicia was hurt and as I got out of our car a lady came out of her house and asked if we needed an ambulance. I told her yes.

The vehicle that hit us was parked on the curb on the opposite side of the street. There were two young male Hispanics standing by their car. I asked them if they were hurt. The one male told me the other man was shot. I looked at this person and saw that he was shot in the back. I told him that an ambulance was on its way.

I went back to my car and I could see that Alicia was hurt and could not move. Along with the ambulance, a fire engine company rolled to the scene. The car was so badly damaged from the impact that the firemen had to use the Jaws of Life to cut the door so they could get her out. A Deputy Sheriff rolled up on the scene and I told him that I was the driver of the one car and that the driver of the other car was across the street by his car and that he had been shot. We looked across the street and saw their vehicle, but the occupants were gone.

Hospitalization and Investigation

The Deputy Sheriff did not seem to care (in my opinion), as he handled the accident like it was a minor fender bender. Alicia was taken in one ambulance and I in another ambulance. We were transported to Harbor UCLA Hospital. Alicia was hurt pretty bad as her whole upper body, including her face, was black and blue. I had a minor abrasion injury to my left shin bone. There was no further response from the Sheriff's Department. I was livid because this traffic accident, if handled by LAPD, would have been classified as a Class A Major Injury accident. There were no pictures taken and no statements from the doctors at the hospital or from Alicia and me that should have been in the police report. I did meet with the Captain of the Carson Sheriff's Office and he also showed only a little interest in the investigation. The report had not been completed as the deputy took it home to complete and he was on several days off. I had taken pictures of my car and pictures of my wife. Alicia was all black and blue as she hemorrhaged internally. My pristine 1982 Mercedes 300 was totaled. No pictures, period.

Alicia was transferred from Harbor UCLA Hospital to San Pedro Community Hospital. She was in the hospital a little over a month. While Alicia was in the hospital, my brother John went out and bought us a brand new Chrysler 300. I did not want to take it, but John and his family insisted that it was a done deal. I took the car, thanking John and his family. I kept the car for two years and then sold it. It was too difficult for Alicia to get in and out of. I bought a 2010 Subaru Legacy. It was the perfect car. Alicia would have loved it.

Alicia Was Getting Weaker

I got a little ahead of myself. The accident occurred in 2006, and God gave Alicia back to me for three more years. Alicia never fully recovered from the automobile accident and she had some medical problems with her liver. Her platelets were out of control. With my son Mark and my daughter Elaine, we were with Alicia constantly, taking her to all her doctor's appointments. You could tell she was getting weaker. I monitored her condition every day. Alicia was also a diabetic and I had to inject her with insulin twice a day—once in the morning and once in the evening. I went by the doctor's scale on how much insulin to give her. One day, her diabetic reading was low in the evening. I gave her the amount of insulin prescribed and she went to bed. I woke up late at night and Alicia was not in bed. I saw the bathroom light was on and called out to her. She did not respond, I got up and went to the bathroom, and Alicia was on the floor. She was not responsive. I couldn't pick her up because of the position she was in. I called 911 and the ambulance crew and I picked her up and put her on the gurney. Alicia was in a coma. They transported her to Harbor UCLA Hospital where she was admitted overnight. The fall she took caused her to turn black and blue again. My poor Alicia was in the hospital overnight. I stayed with her all night and took her home the next day. My beautiful, wonderful wife was having a hard time and was getting weaker all the time.

On one doctor's appointment, I took her to her doctor in Torrance. She was scheduled for lab work. Mark and Elaine met me at the doctor's office.

The doctor wanted Alicia to be admitted to the hospital, as she was very sick. Her liver was giving out on her. The doctor told us she wouldn't survive but a few more days. We took her home and had hospice care for her. We put a hospital bed in the living room and had a nurse with her twenty-four hours. My wife was dying right before our eyes. Alicia knew she was dying and all I wanted to do was hold her in my arms and never let her go. Elaine and Mark stayed with her also. We were one very close family and our love of family was beyond measure.

Alicia told me that she wanted me to do one thing for her and to promise her that I would do it. I told her I would. She told me above anything else, she wanted me to take care of her sisters, Lucia and Julia. I promised her I would. She also wanted me to promise her that I would never marry again. She told me, "There isn't anything you can't do for yourself. You can cook, clean house, do laundry, there isn't anything that you can't do." She also told me to not to be by myself all the time, that I should go out. That I still had a life to live. She thanked me for all the wonderful years we had together. Fifty-five years of a wonderful marriage we shared. We actually knew each other for sixty-six years. I didn't want her to leave me but our Dear God had other plans for her.

The night before she passed away, I told my neighbor Chuy Ruelas that Alicia was dying. They knew that she was very sick. Chuy and his youngest daughter Mariela sang professionally and had wonderful voices. Alicia and I would always go to their performances and sometimes to their parties to hear them sing. I asked Chuy if he and Mariela would come over in the evening and sing a couple of Alicia's favorite Mexican songs. He told me they would. The next night, Chuy and Mariela and many of their family members came to the house and sang a half dozen of songs, including Alicia's favorite, *Jurame*. Alicia was surprised and she shed a few tears. I couldn't thank Chuy and Mariela enough. They performed the best that I have ever seen them perform. Alicia was very happy and thanked them for doing that. Alicia passed away the next morning, October 23, 2009.

Funeral Arrangements

Alicia had already paid for her services through a funeral plan at Green Hills Memorial Park. I took Elaine and Mark with me to make the funeral arrangements. Alicia had also written out instructions as to what she wanted done when she passed. I took the sealed envelope with me to the mortuary. I had Mark open the letter and read it to Elaine and me. Her instructions were concise and to the point, and wanted them followed exactly as she instructed. They were: 1. Her body was to be cremated. 2. Her ashes were to be scattered over the ocean from an airplane. There were some other personal remarks in the instructions for Elaine, Mark, and myself.

Alicia was so cute. In life, she would never take another trip in an airplane and would never go on a cruise due to her fear of the ocean. I guess she felt that she would overcome those fears by going to the Lord in this manner.

Alicia's memorial service was held on October 31, 2009, at Green Hills Memorial Park with a reception at Ports-O-call Restaurant. There were hundreds of people that attended both the services and the reception. It was a beautiful send-off for my beautiful wife. She was admired by so many people. She had many friends.

Several weeks later, Elaine, Michael my grandson, and I went on this small airplane with Alicia's ashes. We flew midway to Catalina and at precise 33 degrees 35 minutes N. latitude 118 degrees by 16 minutes W. longitude at altitude of 2,000 feet at 3:15 p.m. on November 14, Alicia's ashes were released above the ocean. Michael and I said a prayer for her when the ashes were released. Alicia's last wishes were granted.

My Visits with Alicia at Royal Palms Beach

Royal Palm Beach in San Pedro has got to be one of the most beautiful beaches in the world. Alicia and I both loved this beach. We would periodically go down there just to enjoy the beach and the surf. Not too many people are aware of Royal Palms. We would just sit in the car and enjoy the scenery.

On clear days, you can see Catalina Island only twenty-five miles away. It would appear as if it is sitting right on top of the water.

This was the perfect place to visit my beautiful wife. I would always take one or two roses in a bottle and place it on the rocks where she could see it. I visited her often. I still do.

On one occasion I was visiting her and I walked out a little too far. As I was placing the roses in the rocks, I slipped and fell down on the rocks and into a puddle of water. I was on my stomach and no matter how hard I tried I couldn't get up. I was frustrated, considering the fact that I was seventy-eight years old but still in fairly good shape. After about ten minutes of trying to stand up and getting extremely tired, I took my cell phone out of my pocket and called 911. The operator answered and I explained my situation to her. Like a dummy I told her I was on the west end of Royal Palms when in fact I and I was on the east end. I could see the ambulance driving to the west side of the beach. I was now rested enough and figured I would try and get up on my own again. This time, after a struggle, I managed to get myself up. A young couple happened to walk by, saw me struggling, and came over and assisted me to the path. I thanked them and told them that I was fine.

The ambulance crew and some police officers who rolled on the call came over to me. I was embarrassed, as I knew several of the officers. They walked to my car with me. I thanked them, then left Royal Palms for home. That was the last time I walked that far out on the rocks. I still go down to Royal Palms and visit my beautiful wife and today I am eighty-nine years old.

Grieving Her Loss Was So Hard And Is Still Hard

It was a struggle, living in our beautiful home, with Alicia not with me anymore. She is always with me in spirit. I find myself talking to her quite often. There were several times when I lost an item and I asked her where it was. One time it was my passport and I asked her if she could tell me where it was. I could clearly hear her voice telling me to look in the mail drawer. Well, it was there. Another time, I couldn't find one of my hearing aids and I asked her if she could help me find it. I clearly heard her voice telling me to look under the bed. I did and it was there. I had looked under the bed before I asked her and I did not see it.

Alicia is always with me in spirit. Our home is exactly the same as when she passed away. I worry about all the lovely things she collected. What will happen to all these things that she cared for and loved so much?

My love for that wonderful lady had no limit or ending. There were times when I had to leave her early in the morning. I would prepare her breakfast for her and leave it on the table with a cup of coffee or tea in the microwave. I would leave her a love note that I would put on the table. Little did I know that she was saving those notes and tucked them away in one of the kitchen cabinets. One day as I was straightening out this one cabinet, I found all the notes that I had written to her. She saved every one of them. Believe me, I shed a lot of tears knowing how much those notes meant to her. I showed them to Mark and Elaine, and Mark asked me if he could keep them. I told him he could.

Well, my son made a book out of them and gave me the book, which he titled, *Love Letters*. Inside the book, Mark wrote,

"These pages contain the LOVE STORY of Alicia and Mike Markulis. Written on the simplest of papers. They were written with the ink of gold that is the love that pours from the soul of Mike. Though written on a mere paper towel, they were cherished by Alicia as if they were written on the finest of parchment. She saved each piece and hid them away as they were for her and her alone. However, a love this grand should be shared. It gives us all hope that one day we too should be blessed as to have a love that grows stronger with the passing of each new moon, with each revolution of our sun. Day in and day out, this love will grow stronger and wiser. This love will nurture us all. This love will teach us to appreciate, to be patient, to be sorry, to be joyful, to laugh, to cry, to respect, to love, to sing it from the depth of our being that it is all right to love. That it is right to love. That it is right to say I LOVE YOU, JURAME. I LOVE YOU."

I cannot tell you how much I, and I know my beautiful wife, appreciate what Mark had done with those notes of love that I would set out for Alicia when I had to leave her. His book, *Love Letters*, is to be cherished forever.

There are no stronger words than what my son Mark has written that can describe the love of a family.

I also want to share that for the twelve years Alicia has been gone, I have written love letters and notes to her on special occasions such as her birthday and our wedding anniversary. I had them published in the *Torrance Daily Breeze* newspaper, in their Celebration Section. I want her to know that we keep her present in our minds and souls and will continue to do so until we meet again.

I also want to add here what my granddaughter wrote about Alicia in a journal she gave me on February 12, 2010, four months after Alicia had passed. She wanted me to record my thoughts of Alicia when I was thinking of her.

"Dear Papou, I just want to let you know how much I love you, and that I feel so blessed to love you as my Papou. You are the role model of the family in so many aspects. You are one of the best examples of love that I know of. The love you give as a father, husband, and Papou is absolutely amazing. You and grandma ma have a very special marriage. You two have had a lifetime of love and happiness that will last forever. I can only hope to someday to have a marriage filled with everlasting love like you and grandma may have had. You love her and take care of her without fault. Grandma ma was always taken care of by the best. The love that you two shared have been poured out over our entire family. I know that I would not be the person I am today without having you and Grandma ma in my life. I know that this has been a very difficult time for our family and not one of us can even imagine what you are feeling but we all are hurting and grieving together. There has been a huge void left by grandma ma's loss, but we must hold on to the love and happy memories we have of her. She will never be forgotten. The love she had for us is absolutely beautiful."

Madeline continued for another three pages of how her grandma ma's passing has affected her and the entire family. I sometimes think that my family and I are the only ones who feel this love of family. I pray to God every day that He intercedes in all of our lives and bring love and happiness to us all.

CHAPTER 27:

OUR FAMILY TRIP TO GREECE

In May of 2012, I took my whole family, seven of us to Greece. I had never been there and I wanted to see where my parents were from and for my kids to know where their roots were. We flew from LAX to London and then to Athens and then to Crete. We spent two weeks in Crete and visited Vamos, my mother's village, and found a cousin, Olga Galanis. We had a nice visit with her. We thoroughly enjoyed our visit to Crete.

We met with Chris Louros, his wife, and several of his children. His mother Kay Alex Louros are dear friends of the Markulis family. It was at Kay's home that my father and John stayed with when they came to California for my dad's eye surgery. Chris and his family lived in Crete. He worked for a company that fueled airplanes in Crete. Chris had dual citizenship and he and his family traveled constantly back and forth from the United States to Crete. Chris has a wonderful family and I believe, at the last count, he has nine children. Chris's wife Cathy was an all-American tennis player when she was attending University California at Los Angeles (UCLA). A very interesting family. We thoroughly enjoyed our visit with them.

We stayed at a very nice beachfront hotel. Michael, Matthew, Madeleine, and Elaine were constantly in the water. We had a beautiful view of the sea and the islands not too far away. We spent a lot of time visiting museums and ancient landmarks.

One place we visited several times was Chania with a noteworthy harbor inlet with many tourist shops and restaurants. We did a lot of shopping there. The harbor was enclosed with a breakwater and a lighthouse. The water was crystal clear and you could see the bottom thirty feet below. It is one of Crete's noted tourist attractions.

There is a history of Ancient Crete of which Greeks are so very proud of. One historical incident was during WWII when Italy asked Greece to peaceably surrender or face war. Greece's response was, "OXI [NO] Let it be war!"

After bitter fighting, Italy could not take over Greece. Hitler had to send his elite paratroopers to invade Greece and Crete. After bitter fighting, the Germans took over Greece. They won that battle but Greek guerilla fighters took to the mountains and continued to fight the Germans. They never surrendered.

Hitler even made a statement that the toughest fighters they faced were the Greek guerilla fighters. Winston Churchill's remarks were "not that Greeks fought like heroes" but that "heroes fought like Greeks." As you can tell, I am very proud of my Greek heritage. My children are also very proud of their Greek heritage. And they are equally proud of their Mexican heritage. I have a wonderful family. I don't think I have ever seen a "Love of Family" like mine. Alicia did a wonderful job raising Elaine and Mark. They loved Crete and talked about going back again and revisiting.

The years are passing by. Both of our grandsons are now married. Michael married Leah on October 5, 2015. Matthew married his partner Patrick on August 19, 2018. Madeline is working as an Occupational Therapist at Little Company of Mary Hospital. Her father, upon her graduation from USC, got her a beautiful golden retriever that she named Mando.

On the Island of Crete Greece. Greek Moto Officers, exchange dialogue about police work in each of our countries. Gave them LAPD badge pins, nice meet.

My Family on the Island of Crete Greece

Michael and Mark at Monument at Crete Greece

CHAPTER 28:

A NEW RELATIONSHIP

About a year after Alicia passed away, I bumped into an old friend, Jane Martin, at Costco, Signal Hill. I mentioned earlier that she was the Director of the Long Beach Probation Office when we worked on a successful, joint project, monitoring probationers living in the Harbor area. Later, after I retired and was Director of the DCI program at USC, she paved the way for the first Probation Officers to be part of the program.

It was nice to meet her and she asked me how I liked being retired. I told her about losing my wife and that I missed her terribly. She could tell that I really missed her as I got teary-eyed just talking about her. She gave me her phone number and told me if I ever felt like talking to give her a call. I had been seeing a grief counselor, but I was still struggling. One day, I was feeling down and decided to give Jane a call. We met for coffee and ice cream. I felt comfortable talking to her and we met more often, including a pleasant dinner. It was nice being with her and we started going to the theater and movies. We enjoyed each other's company.

Jane was a world traveler and I had traveled also to Mexico, USSR, the Eastern Bloc countries, Japan, and South Korea. We started going on cruises together. Our first cruise was Alaska. I fell in love with cruising and seeing all the wonderful places in different parts of the world. Together we took cruises to the Mediterranean, British Isles, Scandinavian countries, down the St. Lawrence River in Canada, including visiting two of Jane's cousins in New York City, and then a very busy five-day tour of the city. I love that city. We have also taken several road trips to Spokane, Washington, and visited an army buddy; Missoula, Montana, to visit a retired LAPD classmate, and also a friend of Jane's; Yellowstone National Park; Idaho; Nevada; and Utah.

Mediterranean Cruise/ Layover in Crete

On the Mediterranean cruise, we had a planned layover in Crete. I took Jane to my mother's village, Vamos, and met with Olga Galanis, my cousin. I gave Olga several copies of my book *Terpsihori* to share with friends in Vamos. This was the second time I had met Olga. I asked her where Agio Pablo (Saint Paul) was. She told me that Agio Pablo's was only ten minutes from Vamos. Agio Pablo's was my father's village. When I took my family to Crete in 2012, we found Vamos with no problem but went to the wrong Agio Pablo. I was told that everywhere that Agio Pablo (Saint Paul) went and gave a sermon, they named the village Agio Pablo. There were many different villages named Agio Pablo. The one we went to in 2012 was a beach-resort town and I knew from the way my father described his village that this was not it.

We saw this old gentleman walking in the street and our guide asked him if he knew the Marcoulakis family. He said he did and that we were in the middle of the Marcoulakis property. I took pictures of Agio Pablo and found this ancient arch where I think my mom and dad had a picture taken with a donkey when they were on their honeymoon. I used this picture for the cover of my book I wrote about Terpsihori, my mother.

I even knocked on a door and talked to a lady about the Marcoulakis family. You could tell that she was not comfortable talking to me and so we left and walked around the area. It was quite emotional to walk on the streets that my mother and father had walked on when they were growing up. We finally left Agio Pablo and our guide took us to several historic places on the island of Crete. We had a wonderful visit to Crete before we went back to our ship.

We were in Crete only for about nine hours. Our time was limited. I really felt thankful that I was able to visit my parents' birth location for a second time. I only wish that we could have found the right Agio Pablo when I brought my family to Crete in 2012.

It seems this journey that I am taking you on has many curves and side-roads.

CHAPTER 29:

DIAGNOSED WITH CANCER

I will jump to 2019, when a huge medical issue developed. I started having a problem swallowing my food. At times, I would even throw up. I went to my doctor and she referred me to a gastroenterologist. Both doctors believed that the sphincter valve on the base of my esophagus had to be dilated. When the gastroenterologist went in to look at the base of the esophagus, he spotted a tumor mass. He took a biopsy and found it to be stage three cancer. Very serious.

I was now under the care of an oncologist, who became the lead doctor for my treatment. Between the two doctors, the oncologist and the gastroenterologist, I was advised of my options. I was told I was too old, eighty-eight years, for this surgery and that I would not survive it. The surgery would entail the removal of my esophagus and pulling up my stomach to perform the function of the esophagus and stomach. My other option would be chemotherapy and radiation treatment. I opted for the chemo and radiation treatment. If they could reduce the size of the tumor through this treatment, then there was a possibility that the d could operate and remove the tumor.

I was two weeks into the chemo and radiation treatment. I felt myself getting weak and even a little dizzy from the treatment. On July 11, I was scheduled for a doctor's appointment. I woke up in the morning and walked over to the closet to get my clothes to get dressed. I didn't realize how weak I was and fell down, hitting my left side against the closet door. I could not get myself up and my daughter who had spent the night called the paramedics.

I was transported by ambulance to Little Company of Mary San Pedro Community Hospital. I was taken to the ER, they took x-rays, and found that

I had broken my left shoulder. The break was clean and that there was no need for me to be admitted. My daughter Elaine tried to explain to the ER doctor about my circumstances, regarding the cancer and the chemo and radiation treatment that I was going through. The ER doctor gave me a sling for my left arm and told me to go home. I had no one living with me and there was no way that I could care for myself.

Elaine called my oncologist and she was able to admit me into Torrance Memorial Hospital. While there, I picked up several more doctors to monitor my condition. The medical staff, doctors, nurses, and occupational and physical therapists were all terrific. I continued my chemo and radiation therapy. What was nice was that all the doctors, my radiation treatment, and the therapists were at Torrance Memorial Hospital.

I was there from July 11, 2019 to October 1, 2019. I was visited every day while I was in the hospital by Mark and Elaine. Their daily visits made me feel comfortable, as they monitored my condition and asked many questions of the medical staff.

During my stay at the hospital, the LAPD swat team was running an exercise at the hospital. My daughter talked to the Lieutenant-in-charge and mentioned to him that her dad, a retired Lieutenant, was in the hospital undergoing cancer treatment. The Lieutenant and members of the swat team wanted to meet me. I had the pleasure of meeting these fine officers who risk their lives every time they are called out on a crisis situation. I had been retired now for twenty-eight years and several of the officers still remembered me. What a wonderful moment that was.

A miracle of miracles happened to me. This is why I believe so strongly in the power of prayer. There were a lot of people praying for my recovery. My family, many friends and my priest, Father Mike, from St. Katherine's Greek Orthodox Church were praying for my recovery. Elaine's pastor from Montebello Cavalry and their congregation prayed for my recovery often. There were times while in the hospital that I felt that I was not going to survive this ordeal. I really felt like I was going to die. I also prayed on a daily basis that My Precious Lord would heal me or make me comfortable as I continued on this journey of my life. Well, the miracle I am talking about was that the cancerous tumor was gone. There was no sign of the tumor and the biopsies revealed that I was cancer-free. I am being monitored every three months. All of my doctors told me I was cancer-free and the fact that the tumor was completely gone was a MIRACLE.

Today is January 4, 2021, and the world is suffering of the Corona Virus Covid-19 pandemic. Millions of people worldwide have come down with this virus and millions have died from it. Vaccines have finally been developed and being administered. I was given this prayer several days ago by my daughter. This is a good place to put it in my autobiography.

Dear God
I end this year with
this simple prayer
well the sick. Restore
happiness to those in
in despair.
Bring love to the lonely,
Please heal the
broken people.
food to the
hungry and peace
to our world.
Amen

Well, my journey of my life for my autobiography has comes to an end. My son Mark was right when he encouraged me to write my story. The more I got into it, the more I realized, I did have a story to tell. I hope you have enjoyed reading what my life as a cop, an educator, and most important of all, a family man was all about. I took you on a journey of what my life has been like over these last eighty-nine years. There were many occasions on this journey that I moved forward to a different time period because of something I felt should be included at that moment in my story. I found this method of recalling incidents was important and should be placed in my story as I recalled them.

My journey continues! I believe God still has a plan for me. My father lived to be a 100 years old. I pray! God will keep me around, let me enjoy my family and friends, and to see that hundredth birthday.

Los Angeles Police Swat Team running an exercise at Torrance Memorial Hospital. I was undergoing cancer treatment at the time, nice visit.

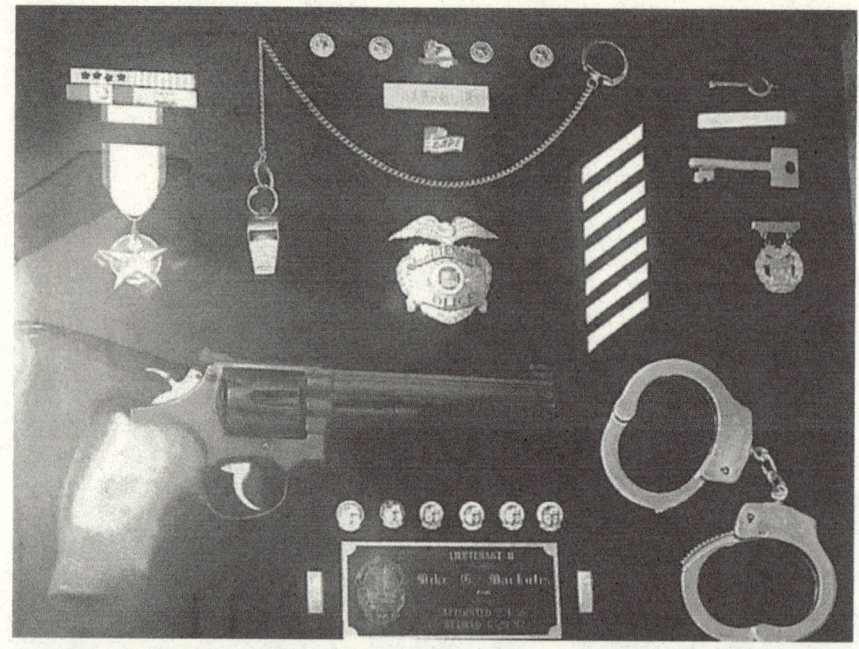

Two Shadow Boxes presented to me at my retirement party August 14, 1992

ADDENDUM

Recipient of Battle on Crime Awards Ceremony

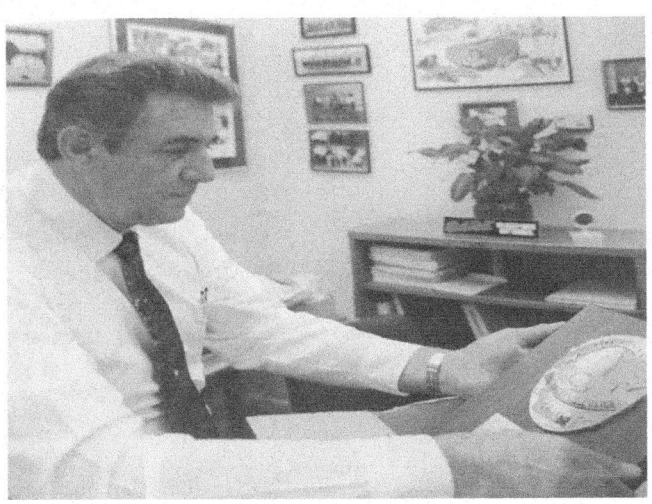

Plaque received at Ceremony Dinner

Chief of Police Gates, presenting me award certificate

Robert Stack at Centenial Graduation in DCI

Leslie Nielson, guest at South Bureau Homiside

Congressional Record

United States of America — *Proceedings and Debates of the 102nd Congress, First Session*

Vol. 137   WASHINGTON, TUESDAY, JANUARY 29, 1991   No. 19

HOUSE OF REPRESENTATIVES

A CONGRESSIONAL SALUTE TO
LT. MICHAEL G. MARKULIS

HON. GLENN M. ANDERSON
OF CALIFORNIA

MR. ANDERSON. Mr. Speaker, today I rise to pay tribute to a man who has served his community with great distinction. On January 30th, Lieutenant Michael G. Markulis of San Pedro, California will be honored by the Harbor City-Lomita Lions Club as its "Citizen of the Year" for his outstanding contribution to both its members and the community at large.

Not only a veteran of thirty-four years of dedicated service with the Los Angeles Police Department (LAPD), Lt. Markulis loyally served two years with the U.S. Army during the Korean Conflict. He received his Honorable Discharge after attaining a rank of Corporal with a spotless service record.

His distinguished law enforcement career has included a great variety of positions and responsibilities, but if one were to draw a common thread through it all, it would be his tireless service to his community. Currently, the Commanding Officer of the Harbor Detective Division, Lt. Markulis' commitment to his men on the job and his fellow citizens during his time off makes it no surprise that there is a long waiting list to join his nearly forty-member elite investigating team. In addition to his duties with the LAPD, Lt. Markulis is very active with the Harbor City Chamber of Commerce and as the Cochairman of the Harbor Area Gang Alternatives Program.

A graduate of San Pedro High School and the University of California at Long Beach, Lt. Markulis furthered his education by taking numerous additional courses including earning his teaching accreditation. Focusing on Police Science and Education courses, Mike Markulis not only excelled at his police work, he also educated his fellow officers and the members of his community so that they might all live in a more peaceful and harmonious social environment. Not surprisingly, he is a sought after public speaker and frequent representative of the LAPD because of his consummate professionalism and obvious leadership qualities.

The Harbor City-Lomita Lions Club is grateful for the contributions Lieutenant Michael G. Markulis has made to the life of his community both as a distinguished law enforcement officer and a civic leader. My wife, Lee, joins me in extending a Congressional salute to Lt. Markulis today. We wish him, his wife, Alicia, and their children, Eliane and Mark, all the best in the years to come.

roving reporter

Janet Barker

6-4-82

It seems like it takes a tragedy to get our attention sometimes.

The murders of two Riverside policemen delivering a warrant helped remind us of the tough job police officers have.

The only time most of us encounter policemen is when we are presented parking or speeding citations. At those times, an officer's presence is not welcome.

The following is not a pro-police testimony nor an anti-police outburst.

In view of recent publicity, it is, rather, a story about how one police officer views his job.

———

As he stood up from the desk in his spacious office, it was clear this guy was tough.

From his neatly groomed hair to his John Wayne gait, Lt. Mike Markulis is 100 percent policeman.

Markulis looks like a police officer, even without the uniform and badge. Confined to three-piece suits and executive decisions these days, his demeanor is one of absolute authority.

After 26 years with the Los Angeles Police Department, Markulis takes that as a compliment. He is committed to police work, despite recent public scrutiny.

Police tragedies seem to be in the headlines almost daily.

The Hollywood officer who was a part-time burglar . . . police Chief Daryl Gates' comment on blacks and the chokehold . . . Ron Settles' jail cell death and the two Riverside officers who were slain — all have served as a catalyst for public review of police procedures.

When offered the chance to shed light on the role of police work from an officer's perspective, Markulis jumped at the opportunity.

Born in Utah and a resident of San Pedro "practically my whole life," Markulis said that over the years he has seen a lot of changes in society and in the courts.

The lack of public support for the police isn't law enforcement's biggest problem, Markulis said. It is, however, the leniency of the courts. "It's so frustrating to have to tell a citizen, 'We can't do anything for you,' because there are laws dictating our limits.

"Guilt or innocence (when a case finally gets to court) is no longer an issue. What counts now is whether we followed procedure correctly. . . . Everything is so tech-

nical. It's procedure, not substance that counts. . . . You can't help but take these frustrations home with you."

As a young patrol officer, Markulis said, he used to take his job home. He said usually it is difficult for new officers not to be looking for corruption 24 hours a day.

He said police work is tough on family life and divorce statistics among policemen prove it.

Married for 24 years and the father of two children, Markulis has beaten the odds. He considers himself a family man first, policeman second.

"If it wasn't for my wife, I couldn't have made it. She's the one who did it for me. . . . I think she is proud of me and what I do," he said, while recalling an early career struggle.

Police work isn't anything like TV shows such as "McLain's Law" and "Hill Street Blues" make it out to be, he said. "I wish it could be my law. It's too bad we can't do things like McLain does on his show."

Despite the restraints and constant flak, Markulis, the commanding officer of Harbor Division detectives, says he's proud to be a policeman.

"Law enforcement work is like a service organization," Markulis said. "We must be responsive to the community."

He illustrated his point by outlining a typical police officer's day.

An officer may begin his day by responding to a traffic accident. He sees an injured person and administers aid while waiting for emergency care.

Markulis said, the person in this circumstance views the officer as a "professional person," someone to rely upon.

From there the officer may get a family dispute call. A 22-year-old officer must suddenly change roles and turn into a marriage counselor, he said.

His next job may be to pursue a wreckless driver. In this case, Markulis said, the patrol officer becomes an expert car racer.

The officer must be able to change hats many more times during his shift, Markulis said.

"My God, I don't know how these guys survive today," Markulis said, noting a sometimes hostile public reaction toward police.

"I get defensive when people start complaining about police. I don't like to hear the bad-mouthing about police.

"There are times when a citizen m not like the way a police officer has h dled a situation, but there are ways correct it."

Markulis suggests complaints be r istered with the police station. "We ha a good checks-and-balance syste . . . .These guys (police officers) hate c ruption of any kind. If they see a crook cop, there is no hesitation at all abc turning him in.

"We police our own. . . . It's sad becau a bad cop discredits the entire depai ment."

Markulis had jotted down some maj points he wanted to make during his inte view. Preparedness is a trait many office pick up as rookies.

The outline included an abbreviated ve sion of the Police Officers' Standard Conduct, a code of ethics Markulis doesr take lightly.

Markulis has worked practically a phases of law enforcement, from polic work inside the county jail to narcotic investigation.

When an officer is killed in the lin of duty, Markulis said, it hits the whol department like a death in the family.

"We all realize that it can happen t any of us at any minute on any day. . . . I is something we have to learn to liv with and accept," Markulis said.

"People just don't realize what officer go through."

The joke, "If you need a cop, call Win chel's," is an inaccurate portrayal of law enforcement work, Markulis said.

———

It is easy to pick on the police.

Sometimes the police need glaring headlines and public complaints before they will, indeed, push for a change. Police officers, like so many groups of professionals with similar interests, are a brethren.

Society has elements in it that need to be controlled. Faced with danger, we ask the police officer to put his or her life on the line in order to control crime.

We place a significant burden upon these men and women.

Maybe it's time to reassess our views of law enforcement — before the next headline announcing the death of a police officer.

Maybe it's time to say "thanks."

June 27, 1992 last arrest and search warrant operation results

Mark Markulis is with **Madeline Markulis** and **2 others.** ...

October 18, 2017 at 6:09 AM ·

I want to wish my Father a very Happy and Healthy 86th Birthday! He's a great Father and Papou, always there for all of us. He is a role model that I always look to for guidance. We are so Proud of all of his achievements. He has served his Country and Community with Pride and Respect. I wanna be like him when I grow up. Happy Birthday Dad, I Love You, God Bless You.

ON THE AFTERNOON OF MARCH 11, 1979, LT. MIKE MARKULIS WAS INFORMED BY TELEPHONE THAT THE SON OF AN ACQUAINTANCE WAS BRANDISHING A WEAPON AND WAS UNCONTROLLABLE. THE LIEUTENANT WAS ABLE TO TALK TO THE BARRICADED YOUTH BY TELEPHONE AND CALM HIM SOMEWHAT BEFORE RUSHING TO THE SCENE.

WHEN HE ARRIVED AT THE RESIDENCE, HE CONFIRMED THAT THE FAMILY HAD LEFT THE HOUSE. LT. MARKULIS THAN TALKED TO THE SUSPECT, INSTRUCTING HIM TO COME TO THE WINDOW AND PUT DOWN HIS WEAPON. WHEN THE YOUTH FAILED TO COMPLY, LT. MARKULIS ENTERED BY A REAR DOOR AND ENCOUNTERED THE ARMED, DISORIENTED SUSPECT. FROM A POSITION OF COVER, THE LIEUTENANT WAS ABLE TO CONVINCE THE YOUTH TO PUT DOWN HIS WEAPON. HE THEN WAS TAKEN INTO CUSTODY.

THIS DISPLAY OF _____ ANGEROUS
SITUATION UPHELD _____ POLICE DEPART-
MENT AND IS RECO

DURING THE AFTER _____ CAPEE FROM
THE PSYCHIATRIC _____ LICE THAT HER
ON WAS AT HER HO _____ GARY BEAN,
THOMAS OWENS, TI _____ , WHO HAD
REVIOUSLY ATTEMP _____ E INFLUENCE
F PCP, WAS LYING _____ . WHEN HE SAW
E OFFICERS, HE ASSUMED A MARTIAL ARTS STANCE, SHOUTED OBSCENITIES AT
E OFFICERS, AND ARMED HIMSELF WITH A LARGE KITCHEN KNIFE.

Charactures of General Instruction Unit, Training Division.
Leaving Training Division, transfer to Hollenbeck Division.

New York Police Department Officers, I met in the city of New York.
I had the honor to be escorted by them in the new 911 Towers.

Celebrations

IN LOVING MEMORY

June 20, 2019

My Beautiful Darling Alicia,

Happy Anniversary!!!

Today we would have celebrated our 65th wedding anniversary. The Lord took you HOME 10 years ago. A lifetime of beautiful memories and believe me, I live on those memories each and every day. I reminisce on those memories almost everyday that you have been away. You remember when we first met. I do! And I will never forget that day. You were thirteen and I was twelve. It was early morning and I was walking on the path adjacent to your little home and you were sitting on your front stairs brushing your long beautiful black hair. The sun was bright and I remember you looked very pretty with the sun sparkling on your hair as you brushed it. I remember thinking what a beautiful girl. Our eyes caught each other and you smiled. I smiled back, and little did we know that eleven years later we were to be wed. You had a wonderful family and I became best friends with your brother Robert. Our houses were back to back to each other except yours was on O'Farrell Street and mine on Oliver Street. Because Robert and I were good friends, I visited your home a lot. You can say that we grew up together. You were ahead of me throughout our school years. You worked at J J Newberys and I at Dicarlo's Bakery. We both graduated from San Pedro High School, The Korean War had just broken out and I was drafted into the army. Two years in the army and in Korea. We wrote to each other almost every day. Yes, we were in love and we missed each other tremendously. I came home from Korea and I asked you to marry me. What a joyous feeling that was when you said yes. We married on June 20, 1954 in that quaint Greek Orthodox Church in Long Beach. Greek weddings are long, but the ritual is very beautiful and meaningful. You were exhausted but knew that you and I were now married. We flew to Mexico City on our honeymoon. We had a fabulous time. The high lite of our honeymoon was you meeting your grandmother for the first time. We toured Mexico City, met several of your Uncles, Aunts and Cousins. We climbed the Pyramid of the Sun, got rained on coming down. But, we loved it. We took a boat ride on a small boat that was named "ALICIA" at the Floating Gardens. Our honeymoon came to an end and we moved into that small apartment on 3rd street in San Pedro. As small as it was, it was a castle to us. We saved and two years later, we bought a lot and built our home on it. The home was next door to your mother's home on O'Farrell Street. We raised our two children, a daughter, Elaine and son, Mark there. Our home was simple, but full of Love of Family. We were very happy. I had applied for a police officer's job on the Los Angeles Police Department and was accepted. I was sworn in on February 1, 1956. Through your help in doing all the hard work, i.e. clean and neatly pressed uniform each day, shining my shoes, leather and shining my brass gave me all the time to study. You were responsible for me graduating number one of my class. You did the same all the way through college. I did well because of your love and help. You continued to do this when I began teaching part time at Harbor Community College. You typed all my lesson plans, examinations and handout material. We did this for 30 years. You helped me when I studied for the Sergeant and Lieutenants exams. I retired from the LAPD after 37 years. We bought a trailer and traveled with our children then later a large motor home and traveled with our grand children. Yes, we had three grandchildren and enjoyed them immensely. My Darling, we still have our home and it is the same as when you left it. Nothing has changed in our beautiful home. All of your precious collections are still in the China Cabinet. The paintings of our children and grandchildren are still hanging in the living room. The ONLY thing missing is you, although I feel your presence every day. I know you are watching over us because we all feel your love and presence. God Bless You My Love and know we all love you "To Infinity and Beyond".

Your Loving Husband

MIke

Celebrations
CELEBRATE LIFE'S SPECIAL MOMENTS

Alicia Sanchez Markulis

Today, October 23, 2010, we are celebrating the life of a beautiful, special lady, Alicia Sanchez Markulis. She touched many lives in her eighty years that she spent on this earth. It was one year ago today that she said her good byes, and peacefully left us to be with the Lord. On that morning, her saddened expression changed to a beautiful, peaceful, angelic look. It was then we knew that she was a special angel sent to us by God to lead the way for us with tender loving care. She did that with everyone she came in contact with. Her angelic beautiful eyes and smile greeted all with love and admiration and wonderful pleasant thoughts. All immediately felt her special warmth, as two hearts speaking to one another, with a language of counsel, love and direction. No matter whom she touched, they loved her dearly. She was a wonderful gift from God to her family whom she loved, and they in turn loved her from "Infinity and Beyond." She changed our lives forever, as only God knows. The Love that we feel for her will never go away. It is time for memories that cannot be erased. A time of reflection that bring smiles and laughter to each one that knew her. Those that never had the privilege of meeting Alicia in person, but are meeting her here and now for the first time, know that she would make you feel special, needed and loved. She would fill you with warmth and love. She is our guardian angel, watching over us all. Thank you for all your prayers and thoughts, Mike G. Markulis and Family.

Celebrations

IN LOVING MEMORY

OUR HOME

My Darling Alicia, the castle that we call our home is the same and as simple as it always has been. Yet, it is fortified with love that soothes and comforts me of the memories we shared.

Our treasures are not made of gold or of exotic tapestries, but of memories contained within our hearts. These are treasured memories of which I will never part.

GOD made you an angel, with heavenly eternal love. You fill our home and my life with sunshine each and every day, a daughter, Elaine and a son Mark, three grandchildren, no richer man there could not be.

For you and I are the lucky ones. This castle that we call our home is simple as can be, yet we are richer than any kingdom could ever be.

God gave us, our home, and all the treasured memories within it which brings comfort and peace to me and I thank you God for all these wonderful BLESSINGS.

Mike

Celebrations

IN LOVING MEMORY

Happy Anniversary Alicia

As I sit, alone, in our home, I feel your presence, your touch and your whisper as:

You know my heart
You know my mind
You know my words before I speak them.

Although, it has been eight years since you left to be with our Lord, My everlasting Love for you has never waivered. And, because my Lord God has forgiven me of my sins, I'm assured that we will be together again as you always said, "To Infinity and Beyond."

Our Anniversary date is near, June 20th, sixty-three years ago we were married in that quaint little church in Long Beach. A beautiful bride you were, and yes, a lovely couple we made. A wedding made in Heaven, a simple Greek Orthodox Wedding which everyone raved about then and still do now. My Darling Alicia, I miss you so and Love You with all my heart....HAPPY ANNIVERSARY MY LOVE: Your Mike

Celebrations

IN LOVING MEMORY

My Dearest Alicia,

I have been wanting to write something special for you and the only thing that comes to mind is how much I miss you and love you. I pray each night for your comfort in Heaven knowing that you are with our Precious Lord and that gives me peace of mind. I know that someday if the Son of God has forgiven me for all my worldly sins that I will be with you. Heaven must be glorious where there is no sickness, pain or suffering and a place of LOVE. I came across this scripture from I Corinthians 13; 4-8 that describes LOVE:

Love is patient,
Love is kind
It is not jealous;
Love does not brag
And is not arrogant,
Love does not act
Unbecomingly;
It does not seek its own,
Is not provoked,
Love does not take into account

A wrong suffered,
Love does not rejoice
In unrighteousness,
But rejoices with the truth
Love bears all things,
Believes all things,
Hopes all things,
Endures all things.
LOVE NEVER FAILS;

Mike

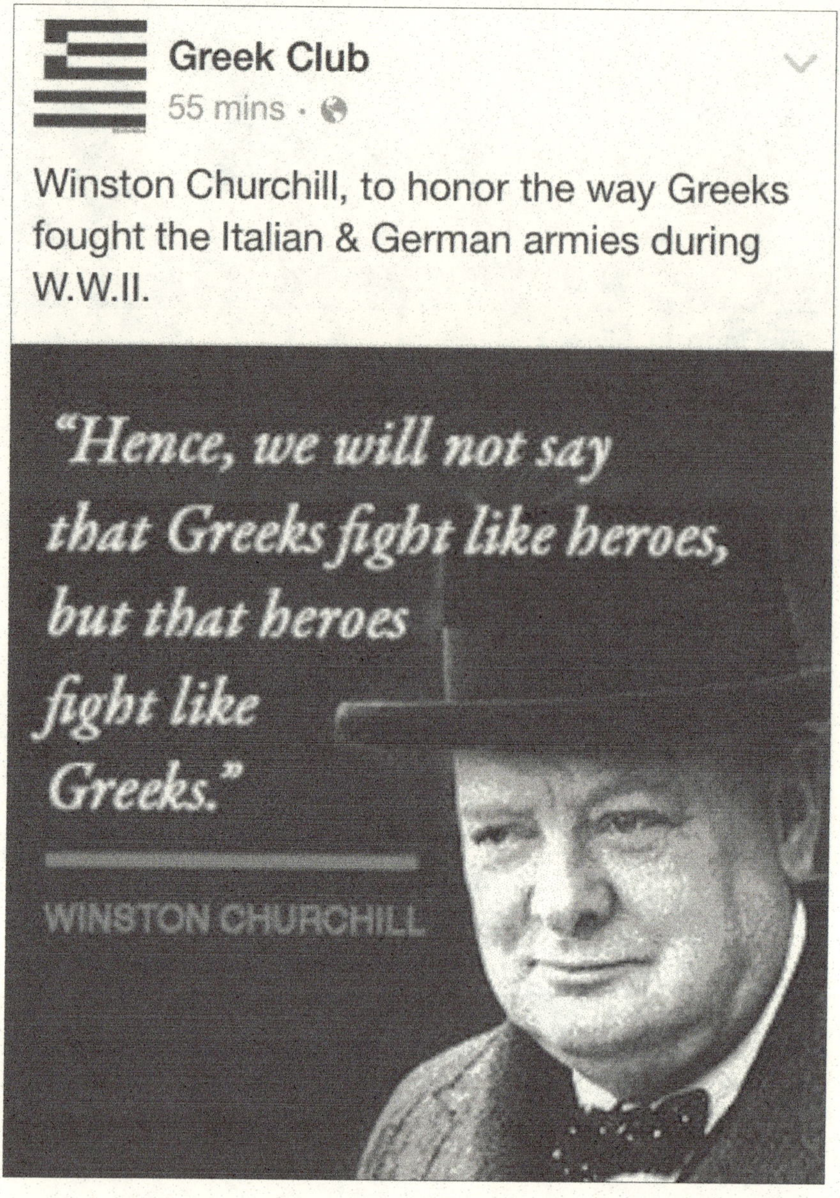

Greek Club

55 mins · 🌐

Winston Churchill, to honor the way Greeks fought the Italian & German armies during W.W.II.

"Hence, we will not say that Greeks fight like heroes, but that heroes fight like Greeks."

WINSTON CHURCHILL

Markulis Family 2021

THANK YOU MY WIFE ALICIA
FOR ALL THE GREAT MEMORIES!